THE
ENEMIES OF THE
POOR

THE
ENEMIES

 RANDOM HOUSE · NEW YORK

OF THE
POOR

JAMES J. GRAHAM

CONTENTS

PREFACE

The views expressed here derive in large part from a variety of personal experiences, most of them as an attorney, which may explain some of the emphases and biases expressed in the book. During the years 1963 to 1966 I represented poor clients, both white and black, in the North and South on behalf of a CIO union, the Amalgamated Clothing Workers of America.

More recently, I have researched, litigated and taught anomalies in the law of public assistance at Columbia University's Center on Social Welfare Policy and Law, the New York University Project on Social Welfare Law and the University of Arizona College of Law; finally, I helped organize and since December, 1965, when it came into existence, I have been a sometime participant in the sundry activities of Christians and Jews United for Social Action (CUSA), a community-action organization based in a racial slum in Brooklyn, New York, known as Brownsville.

For the sake of accuracy and reader interest I have included portions of a CUSA welfare rights meeting and taped interviews with activists and other individuals, among them numerous welfare recipients, who are in the best position to describe the Welfare System.

The comments of the black and Puerto Rican recipients, to the disappointment of some readers, may sound surprisingly nonprofane. When expressing their indignation at the inadequacy of the welfare budgets and the rise in prices on check-day in the Brownsville bodegas and supermarkets, these AFDC mothers sound remarkably like a group of conservative housewives. I am most grateful to these welfare mothers who could not be identified here by their proper names, who graciously consented to yet another study of their way of life with no assurance that this critique of the present system of income maintenance will better their circumstances. My thanks also to those community activists, lawyers, caseworkers, social workers and others whose names and comments appear in these pages, and to my wife for her patience during the writing of this book and for many sound observations gained as an employee of the New York City Social Services Department.

Finally, I am grateful to my editor at Random House, Alice Mayhew, and to the following who read and commented upon portions of the manuscript: John and Laura Scanlon, Jack and Betty Sheinkman, Harry Frumerman, Leonard Mayhew, John Leo, Arthur Moore, Roger Dunwell, Rick Miller, James J. McFadden, Carol Katz, Dean Charles E. Ares of the University of Arizona College of Law, Dean Alex Rosen of the New York University School of Social Work, Dr. Charles Grosser of Columbia University School of Social Work and Professors Daniel G. Collins, Homer Kripke and Jack Kroner of the NYU School of Law.

JAMES J. GRAHAM
TUCSON, ARIZONA

January, 1970

INTRODUCTION

SINCE IT IS quite respectable now, and probably always has been, to help alleviate the plight of the poor for grander purposes—the glory of God, the prevention of summer riots in the ghettoes, the revolt against upper-middle-class parents living in the suburbs—this book focuses on the welfare poor for the combined purpose of publicizing their sorry situation and commenting on the health of certain major institutions in American society that by their very nature have a special responsibility to citizens on relief.

The churches, the legal profession, welfare administrators, organized labor and the poor themselves play intertwining roles that have hardly been altered during the past few hundred years. I have included extensive historical materials to show that the relative condition of those on public assistance, on both sides of the Atlantic, in every generation, in respect to the rest of the population has not greatly changed since the time of Elizabeth I.

The emphasis is on the *welfare* poor, because they are easily defined statistically, although their identity is more blurred than generally realized. A fair number of solid citizens were raised in homes supported by welfare payments, or find themselves on relief with the onset of old age or the death or disablement of a working spouse.

Accordingly, the focus of the book also shifts on occasion to the poor generally, and in particular to those 2 million

Americans whose full-time employment earnings keep them off relief but below the poverty line. It is also impossible to comment intelligently about the welfare system without discussing, for example, factory wage scales in marginal industries or racial discrimination in craft employment, factors which have helped to swell the relief rolls in our large cities, and especially in New York City, where a politically liberal climate camouflages widespread economic oppression of black and Puerto Rican workers.

Moreover, the irrational tendency of this and every preceding generation to view the welfare sector as a social aberration to be segregated physically and spiritually from the rest of the population has operated to the detriment of both recipients and marginal workers. During the Middle Ages, prior to the assumption of relief responsibilities by the State, "God's Poor" occupied a special status as one of His instruments for the salvation of the affluent. Today, of course, America, but perhaps not England, where universal assistance prevails, regards the welfare poor as a public nuisance to be regulated by quasi-police measures which include the distribution of bare survival rations. "Welfare colonialism" has become an epithet among modern reformers, and not too long ago spokesmen for the Students for a Democratic Society accused the Johnson Administration of treating the ghetto poor as a separate nation. At the same time we find a related kind of paternalism among some naïve idealists of the New Left who romanticize the black mother on Aid to Families of Dependent Children (the largest and most controversial relief category) as a Noble Savage type.

It is my impression that the truth is singularly undramatic. AFDC mothers, for the most part, are middle-class people who for reasons beyond their control do not have any money. These recipients have the same aspirations and failings as everybody else, and what they want most right now are relief measures that will permit them and their children to blend easily into the social landscape.

The common humanity beneath the welfare statistics should be most apparent to the administrators and their subordinates, the caseworkers; but there is often a love-hate relationship between worker and client that probably more than any of them realize reflects community attitudes toward the welfare poor. In addition, both suffer the same type of mutual alienation from the rest of society as the policeman and his prisoner; but whereas the officer is permitted to take professional pride in his work, no prestige attaches to public assistance employment. In order, therefore, to fully appreciate the degrading character of the present welfare system, it is necessary to understand the roles of those who administer the provisions.

I have also included two chapters on the activities of the militant poor because for centuries, apathy and fear of reprisals have silenced the protests of our most helpless citizens and squelched their ambitions. Whatever one thinks of the merits of their cause, in the long run the newly discovered eagerness of AFDC women to walk a picket line demanding their rights as human beings may be a more significant factor in reducing the welfare rolls than the sweeping reforms being proposed by the Nixon Administration. The doings of Brooklyn's CUSA organization illustrate, on a small scale, the potential of the poor to achieve self-rehabilitation while rattling the status quo.

To line up the lawyers, the clergy and labor leaders in a chain of opposition to what the poor and their champions consider to be their best interests may be incomplete and perhaps unfair. The groups selected are not the whole of society, and poverty is that rare social problem for which we are all to blame. America has not adopted the humane innovations in public assistance administration to be found in more class-conscious Western nations because noblesse oblige cannot flourish without aristocrats. This country is still ruled by a coalition of frontiersmen building stockades to keep out the Indians and urban entrepreneurs who do not want to admit that poverty has ever touched their lives. For most Americans, the poor are too close to home. We balk at greater use of tax monies to aid them because such expenditures are a threat to our own security. It is important to Americans to believe that only immoral people are on relief and that most of these are black or Spanish-speaking.

It is a mistake, however, to overemphasize the racial equation in the welfare problem. Though a highly disproportionate number of blacks across the nation do receive public assistance, it is still a fact that close to 50 percent of the AFDC children are white. It is true that in the big cities the failure to empathize is encouraged by racial prejudice, but at the same time recipients of aid to the aged (60 percent of whom in New York City are white) suffer almost as many humiliations as blacks on AFDC. Conversely, middle-class blacks, as a group, with no more justification and for the same reasons, at best are as studiously indifferent to reliefers of their own race as Irish Catholics are to the blind, the disabled and the aged who live off the public dole.

The philosophy that sustains public assistance as we know it today began to evolve about 1834 in England, when intellectual disciples of Reverend Thomas Malthus managed to persuade politicians concerned about rising welfare costs that it was a holy thing to keep the lame, blind, decrepit and impotent poor on bare survival rations in order to discourage them from breeding. One of the "abuses" corrected by the reform legislation of 1834 was the widespread practice among administrators of furnishing relief away from the workhouse to able-bodied paupers.

Malthusians crossed the Atlantic, of course, along with laissez-faire, Social Darwinism and Herbert Spencer, to be greeted at the boat by William Graham Sumner of Yale.

Since the middle of the last century, therefore, Americans have insisted on regarding those who were forced to live off the community as pathologicals. An able-bodied man who had to stoop to a contemptible handout had to be either dissolute or cursed by the Almighty. Even innocents—the crippled, the blind, abandoned wives and their children—were included in the scorn; because it is poor stock, you see, that cannot support its own destitute members.

Taxpayers have been only too eager, especially in good times, to presume delinquency among relief recipients. To admit that economic hardship or other personal disasters beyond the control of individuals produce candidates for the relief rolls would require empathy, involvement and expense. But crude motivations alone cannot account for the present welfare system. Since the 1800's it has been *respectable* to treat paupers as pathological. Credit for this goes not to the business community but to those institutions that tradition-ally strike a moral stance, and so they are the proper targets of a book focused on the welfare poor and their principal enemies.

Though skeptics may disagree, the churches and trade unions, unlike business corporations, at least in theory are altruistic; they do not exist for material gain. For this reason, both groups enjoy certain governmental protections and exemptions from the laws. Each of the Christian denomina-tions, in its own way, purports to mediate between God and man. Labor spokesmen say they are called to achieve collec-tive justice for workers and most even add that, time per-mitting, they are also committed to the task of remedying other economic and social wrongs.

The organized bar, of course, is not in the same category as the churches and labor, but in the Anglo-American tradi-tion, the bar affects to place a low priority on profit-making and emphasizes its role as a stabilizing influence in society.

In short, all three groups contain within their respective

structures an idealism that is compatible with radical reformation of our welfare system, and an enormous potential for achieving it. In the past, however, all three groups shared not only an indifference to what went on in the public assistance sector but acquiesced in the system.

The churches, until this decade, concentrated on charitable enterprises that were not designed to disturb the status quo, and entrusted the shelter and feeding of paupers to economy-minded legislators and administrators. The labor movement in this country, which became a political power contemporaneously with the passage of the Social Security Act in 1935, has had a single-minded obsession with expansion of coverage and increased benefits under the Old Age Survivors and Disability Insurance provisions of the Act, as if such measures contained the solution for adequate relief for all workers under labor's jurisdiction.

There are other good reasons to link the churches, labor and the bar in a format of this kind. Since the summer of 1965, the War on Poverty has brought white representatives of all three groups into contact with each other and with residents of the urban ghettoes in new ways. Lawyers interested in counseling the poor have found themselves in storefronts and tenements engaged in a practice which extends beyond the traditional scope of a lawyer's duties. Priests and ministers have had to become experts on housing legislation and the use of economic weapons. A few union officials have helped organize welfare recipients; others have seen picket lines directed against them.

The provisions in the Economic Opportunity Act for free neighborhood legal services have provoked debates in legal circles over the need to revise the Canons of Ethics to conform to the requirements of ghetto practice, but there is also reason to believe that the traditional attorney-client relationship, for the middle class as well, is a thing of the past. Intent on maintaining an ersatz professionalism, the bar has progressively diminished the prestige of urban lawyers and made their services uneconomical for all except the very affluent.

Organized labor is still dominated by men who made their unions powerful and have grown old in their jobs. Few of them see that the onset of automation, the necessity to organize agricultural workers, minority-group demands for jobs and for representation in union hierarchies, indicate that the "father-and-son," craft-oriented Federation cannot survive in its present form.

The Christian churches in America face perhaps the most profound internal crises in their history. The new political ferment about economic injustice has been triggered in part by Vatican Council II, the popularity of the writings of Harvey Cox and Dietrich Bonhoeffer, and a brutal realization among Christians that the visible Church was not very Christian.

Finally, the bar, the churches and labor today suffer a common rejection by young idealists who regard the institutional commitments and pursuits as irrelevant. Certainly, the Wall Street firms will never have a dearth of qualified applicants, but a growing number of talented young lawyers are rejecting corporate practice for careers in the expanding public sector, and law school curricula are beginning to reflect this trend. The talent drain, still small, is, in terms of vigor and influence, nevertheless a threat to the legal establishment, which likes to believe it attracts the best in the profession.

There is no question about the jaded image of organized labor. The unions have continued doing business in the same old way while the times changed. Because of major strikes that threaten the public interest, trade unionism has encountered the periodic hostility of the general public and chronic cynicism about even the legitimate grievances of organized workers. Because labor projects a bureaucratic,

establishment front, unionists suffer the unequivocal disdain
of almost every young person sympathetic to the problems
of the poor. Blue-collar workers with young families and
large medical bills also have cause to question the sincerity
of a labor brotherhood that refuses to provide them with
government-financed medical care. In the process, unfortunately, labor's accomplishments tend to go unnoticed.
The AFL-CIO lobbied vigorously for Medicare, for example, and collective bargaining agents have helped achieve
racial integration in Southern plants.

The disenchantment with labor, as it affects the welfare
poor, is particularly poignant, because trade unionism is
probably the only institution in this country that possesses
all of the intangible ingredients necessary for a broad assault
on poverty—the theoretical commitment, the organizing
techniques, the political know-how—and some of the
physical resources like money, manpower and job opportunities. As Bayard Rustin and Michael Harrington have
often argued, the reformers, the poor and labor do need each
other.

As an institution, the Christian Church is probably most
threatened by the developments of the past few years. The
Church depends upon a timeless moral equation to justify
its existence. While a respectable number of unionists can
counter philosophical attacks with the reality of a good
contract, and liberal lawyers can take vicarious satisfaction
out of the social breakthroughs made by the Supreme Court,
the good works of Christians *qua* Christians make sense only
as elements of a plan oriented toward the Divine.

Accordingly, the charge of irrelevance that comes today
from thoughtful persons who, to varying degrees, still call
themselves Christians, as well as from outsiders, has produced evident panic among the Church hierarchies. With
his demands for reparations for past injustices against
blacks, James Forman has forced clergymen to question

their own vocations. The involvement of Roman Catholic and Episcopal priests in secular, controversial ghetto activities, usually without the explicit approbation of their bishops, are indeed among the phenomena of our times, but the turnover among them is staggering; moreover, as of this writing there are depressing indications that the Church hierarchies will continue to cling to pious rhetoric, imposing structures and tokenism on social issues in the hope that the storm will blow away.

There is no concrete evidence that more than a handful of churchmen are aware of the depth of the problem. The same black minister who reminded the white religious leaders of Alabama of their Judeo-Christian obligations in 1964 from a jail cell emerged in 1967 as the first powerful religious voice to denounce the Vietnam war. While most church leaders in 1967 found themselves uneasily justifying President Johnson's napalm, and the late Cardinal Spellman stood at St. Patrick's Cathedral reviewing a parade with marchers carrying signs that said "Bomb the Hell out of Hanoi," several hundred thousand secular Jews and Christians without the comfort of a reviewing stand marched for peace in San Francisco and New York.

Interestingly, even the formless "hippie" brigades have reproached the institutional Church with religious symbols in secular dress. At Columbia University's "Warmth Attic," barrels of money were to be given away to the needy, and at "New Christianity" headquarters in Greenwich Village an ice cream agape was available to all.

How does all of this relate to the welfare problem? The survival of ideology will depend on the adoption of radically new roles in the welfare drama by, if the reader will pardon the expression, major components of the so-called Liberal Establishment. On the other hand, while specific and drastic changes in the system are necessary, the ultimate "reform" of public assistance calls for the spiritual absorption of reliefers and their neighbors, the nonwelfare poor, into the body politic.

Hopefully, this book will help speed the process. It is important, it seems to me, for social workers to realize that they share in the humiliations heaped upon their clients. Lawyers must know that they cannot remain forever on Mount Olympus. Churchmen are blind if they do not see in the welfare poor the "other Christ" they so often preach about. Labor leaders cannot for long ignore the truth that they have members on the relief rolls, and the average citizen has a dim memory if he does not recognize his own among the sad faces of the welfare poor.

PART
ONE

THE
WELFARE
SYSTEM

CHAPTER
ONE

ONLY THE DESTITUTE
NEED APPLY

*Some people say when you're on welfare you're in
the gutter and no use trying to pull yourself out.*

—Mrs. Isabel Johnson, an AFDC recipient of
Brownsville, Brooklyn

I N ALMOST EVERY state an applicant for public assistance must be legally destitute in order to qualify. This
is the common denominator that helps to explain the
entire welfare system.

To be eligible for welfare, one must be impoverished, in
absolute need and with no other recourse. This condition
separates the recipient from the rest of us. Even a comparatively generous state like New York compels old people
with no savings and no income, and who own nothing except
the frame house they have lived in all their lives, to assign

even this poor asset to the Department. In order to understand why a black teen-ager leaves an AFDC home* to
hustle and die on the streets of Brooklyn, one must be able
to hear the First or Second Man in that family telling a
caseworker, "Lady, I got a wife and four kids and a job that
pays me seventy dollars a week. All I got to my name is a
thousand-dollar policy on my life. Christ, are you gonna
take that away from me too?"

It is the quality of going naked onto the dole that gives
welfare its end-of-the-road character. I once heard of a TB
sanatorium in Ireland that bore the caption "Home for the
Dying" in bronze letters over its front gate. So it is with welfare. It is true that not all who sign up for relief end their
days on the rolls. In fact, the relatively small number of
families headed by male workers tend to come and go. But
the mothers who remain and, too often, the daughters who
begin their own separate welfare careers after the first preg-

* Aid to Families with Dependent Children, a federal assistance program under the Social Security Act which since 1935 has provided
matching funds (according to a complicated formula which favors the
poorer states) to participating states. All states participate in the basic
program and pay at widely varying levels benefits to dependent, i.e.,
needy children and their guardians ("caretakers") in homes where the
breadwinner has deserted the family or died. Only twenty-one states
participate in AFDC-U, which provides matching funds for benefits for
dependent children of an unemployed father.

Prior to the 1962 amendments to the Act which emphasized *services*
to recipients, the program was known as Aid to Dependent Children
(ADC). In today's literature AFDC and ADC are used interchangeably.

The other less controversial "categorical" assistance programs under
the Social Security Act are known as Old Age Assistance (OAA), Aid
to the Blind (AB) and Aid to the Permanently and Totally Disabled
(APTD). In every state all of the programs are administered under one
statewide agency with local departments. State operations are subject to
the ultimate control of the United States Department of Health, Education and Welfare (HEW), but HEW traditionally has tolerated conflicting policies and practices among the states.

General Assistance or Home Relief refers to the locally financed, administered and controlled relief program available in some states to
needy persons, usually alcoholics, drug addicts, the prematurely senile or
intact family groups with low incomes, who do not qualify for one of
the federal programs.

nancy, accept welfare as a way of life because escape, for most of them, is out of the question.

Medieval Christians gave alms to "God's Poor" in order to purchase a corner of heaven for themselves. The Protestant and the secular reformers of Charles Dickens' time actually went so far as to make the System intolerable so as to discourage poor people, for their own sense of dignity, from going on relief. Ironically, our bland administrators are told by the legislators to distribute cash assistance to help reliefers to help themselves, but the present system has no more been able to stunt its own growth than its predecessors, and for essentially the same reason. A benefits program that permits its clients to apply only when all else has failed logically descends to a level of grants pegged at bare survival or less. In the desert only the cactus reaches for the sun. Only the very strong and angry recipients leave the welfare rolls.

We do not know whether to blame the monks or the liberals of nineteenth-century England for the tradition which denies our welfare children money for ice cream, toys and Saturday movies, but, however it began, such a system, in practice, must incorporate periodic and intensive investigations designed to establish or reject continued eligibility. The system becomes penal, oppressive and degrading as at best it seeks to pay no more than necessary to sustain life.

Unlike the citizen who applies for public housing and in a formal, impersonal way (usually by submitting affidavits) must satisfy certain criteria as to income level, family size and good character, the prospective welfare recipient must suffer wholesale invasions of privacy aimed at establishing that he or she is truly a loser in the economic game. The aged, the blind and the disabled have an easier time because they carry the marks of their eligibility. But the AFDC mother must do more than prove her poverty. No matter how proud or innocent of wrongdoing, she must establish to the satisfaction of the interviewer that no man lurks in the background willing or able to feed and clothe her children. In order to comply with the statutory requirement that her siblings are "deprived of parental support . . . due to the death or absence from the home of . . ." the welfare mother must confess, truthfully or not, that she has failed as a woman.

SIGN UP, TURN ON . . .

With receipt of the first check, the AFDC mother effectively drops out of society. She enters a world that pretends to satisfy her cash needs and in return exacts her freedom. In keeping her alive at a poverty level* but hopelessly dependent, welfare insists that the reliefer make public all of the details of her private life, from her latest quarrel with Con Edison to the name of the man who came one night to take her to the movies.

Workhouses are a thing of the past on both sides of the Atlantic. "Outdoor relief"† is now the norm, but we continue to keep recipients on desert islands in the midst of our cities because, like our ancestors, we refuse to accept that all of us help perpetuate poverty.

Separate treatment for the down-and-out began, of course, with the Elizabethan English. That crusty humanist Adam Smith described the early Settlement and Removal Laws as

---

* New York, New Jersey, California and most other states pay benefits at 100 percent of the computed "needs" (i.e., survival) level. Ohio and states in the South and Southwest pay benefits at a certain lesser percentage of need or impose "maximum grant" restrictions predicated on the size of recipient families. In the fall of 1969 the United States Supreme Court agreed to decide the constitutionality of maximum grants.

† This English expression refers to the exceptional practice, usually restricted to the lame, blind and aged, of paying assistance to needy persons, not in workhouses, but in their own homes.

an institution "peculiar to England."* What began as the Statute of Laborers† in the thirteenth century—a device promulgated during the Black Plague by landowners to keep able and scarce tenants down on the farm—evolved, with the growth of cities and large towns and the rise of a new class of urban poor, into laws designed to fix responsibility for the care of indigents on their place of origin. The poor man who sought to find opportunity elsewhere was returned with his family to their point of departure, sometimes on arrival and even before a search for work might have proved fruitless.

To this day, durational residence requirements and removal laws in forty states‡ encourage paupers to stay at home. Such statutes help impose a disproportionate burden on those states like New York which do not have them and which therefore attract more than their share of displaced peanut farmers from Georgia.

Welfare administration in this country on all levels of theory and operation continues to be hopelessly isolated from problems of automation, migratory labor, minimum wage laws, nonunion shops and racket unions. The War on

---

* Adam Smith, *The Wealth of Nations,* 140, 142 (Modern Library ed., 1937). For some centuries prior to the Protestant Reformation in England and the acquisition by the state of Church lands, poor relief, in a more haphazard but also more humane fashion, was administered by Church authorities. Secular relief administration, greatly influenced by the Spanish Catholic humanist Juan Luis Vives, did not begin to be systematized on the Continent until at least a century after the English Poor Laws. European relief, even prior to the modern welfare-state era, apparently never included the Anglo-American barbarities in its formal structure.

† (c. 1350) The Statute arbitrarily fixed wages and hours for each category of laborer and craftsman, forbade alms-giving, restricted travel and forced all idle persons to work at the established rates.

‡ In May, 1969, the United States Supreme Court in *Shapiro v. Thompson* declared residency requirements, permitted under the Social Security Act, to be unconstitutional, in large part because such laws impinge upon the right to travel. As a practical matter, however, it may be some time before the full impact of the decision is felt in day-to-day administration.

Poverty began in large part as a response to the failure of the Welfare System, but there are depressing signs that anti-poverty programs also will fail unless the owners of capital and labor permit the war to be waged elsewhere than in the racial ghettoes. Human misery in Brownsville results from cutbacks in medical assistance in Albany and Washington, sweatshop wages paid in midtown Manhattan, exclusion from high-paying construction work at the World Trade Center near Wall Street, etc.

In the past, professional social workers seldom spoke to caseworkers, economists, lawyers or politicians. Congress in 1935 consulted academics, labor leaders and, especially, businessmen about the Workmen's Compensation, Unemployment Insurance and Old Age and Survivors' Insurance titles of the Social Security Act but enacted AFDC *en passant*.

The legislators who prevailed on behalf of FDR conceived the separate titles of the Act as distinct income maintenance measures and would have regarded a comprehensive, interlocking package as pure socialism. The New Dealers believed that WC, UI and OASI, each in its own way, would go far toward solving the problem of on-the-job poverty and would in time draw the aged, the blind and the lame, along with most widows, into the social insurance scheme.

Arthur Altmeyer, Edwin F. Witte and other knowledgeable commentators have said that Congress in 1935 naïvely assumed that the poor children of abandoned mothers would disappear as a relief category. It seems more likely, however, in retrospect, that Congress simply ignored these children just as the locally financed predecessor to Aid to Dependent Children, the Mothers' Pension Laws, focused almost exclusively on the needs of (white) children whose fathers were dead. In 1933, 19,000 out of 22,000 New York women aided by Mothers' Pensions were widows. Across the country, Negroes constituted only about 3 percent of the total caseload.

However, the advent of the federal ADC program coincided with the beginning of a human rights–oriented era in Supreme Court thinking. Even the subclass of Negro illegitimates could claim the equal protection of the laws. HEW insisted, sometimes loudly, but usually in a whisper, that black children be included without discrimination in the state programs. Today, Negroes probably outnumber whites by an estimated slight margin on the national rolls. ADC is now more colored and more controversial than ever, and middle-class citizens who vote now more than ever attribute the size of the caseload to human failure.

THE MYSTIQUE OF POVERTY

Automation on the Southern farms plus the fact that children under eighteen and adults over sixty-five constitute about half of the American population are major causes, but, paradoxically, the destitution factor itself has contributed heavily to the burgeoning welfare rolls in the Northern cities. This has always been evident, however. The welfare population in Edwardian England trebled within three decades of the Poor Law Reform of 1834 in spite of and in large part because of eligibility requirements and budget levels intended to make cash assistance as unattractive as possible.

The refusal of Queen Victoria's relief officials to allocate funds to teach Irish farmers methods of crop control not only failed to assuage the human and the fiscal horrors of the Potato Famine; English brutality on this occasion drove a permanent wedge between two peoples.

Why, therefore, do we insist on this false economy? Rock-bottom poverty is a convenient badge for those who literally have no choice but to apply for assistance. If destitution were not the basic requirement, affluent citizens could less easily ignore the moral claims of those in every age in need of some help but able, though barely, to survive without relief.*

But even this is too rational an explanation. Tax monies do go into social welfare programs other than public assistance, but it is significant that costly housing projects, for example, or Food Stamp or Surplus Food programs, at least after initial enactment, seem to arouse much less passion among the voters than *cash* assistance. Paying a person the monetary equivalent of wages to do nothing shocks Anglo-American sensibilities. The act of handing a negotiable check or dollars to healthy men and women generates a collective insanity among the nonwelfare population that often precludes serious debate.

Perhaps an ugly worm in all of us wants to control the behavior of other humans. The White South uses man-in-the-house regulations to deny aid to the children of black mothers not so much because she bore illegitimates but to punish her audacity in asking the state to support them. These brutal rules have not curbed promiscuity; they *have* helped keep the Negro in his place.

Historically, welfare administration and the police power conjoined. When the town councils, parishes and boroughs in medieval England took over from the Church the burden of caring for paupers, relief and the removal of vagrants became intertwined operations. R. H. Tawney quotes a pamphleteer who wrote in 1646, "The general rule of all England is to whip and punish wandring beggars [and] to

---

* New York, California and one or two other states pay supplementary assistance to working men with low wages and many children, sufficient to bring them up to the poverty line. This is the "basic floor of income" concept advocated by White House Adviser Daniel P. Moynihan for the entire nation.

provide houses and convenient places to set the poore to work."*

Nonresident paupers were shipped back to their home towns. Taxpayers fed, clothed and sheltered local indigents to keep them from becoming public nuisances by begging or dying in the streets. Anticipating some of our own antipoverty measures, the English two hundred years ago sustained the poor in order to prevent riots.

Today, in many of our states the condition of being without funds makes a stranger criminally suspect. Loitering, trespassing and vagrancy are offenses that we usually associate with poverty. Vague penal provisions of this kind give legal justification to sending indigents on their way. Mississippi's welfare statute still calls for the removal of "strolling paupers." In most of the New York City Welfare centers, including a huge, modern building in Brooklyn, almost the first sign to greet the welfare applicant in otherwise stark surroundings appears over the door to the guard room and says "police."

BIG BROTHER AND BIG SISTER

The preambles to welfare statutes and regulations usually contain about fifty words of pious hope that financial assistance will "strengthen family life" and encourage recipients to become self-supporting. This bit of humanism, however, is then smothered by many paragraphs of advice to caseworkers on how to determine eligibility. Social work paternalism thus translates into an ugly investigative tool. The caseworker, who typically is a young white woman just out of college, believes she may take liberties with her client's

* R. H. Tawney, *Religion and the Rise of Capitalism,* New York, Harcourt, Brace, & World, Inc., 1926, p. 264.

privacy in ways never permitted to a claims' adjuster, for example, seeking to ascertain his insured's role in an auto accident.

Passive clients also hasten their own debilitation. Those active in the Welfare Rights Movement,* however, find it therapeutic to fight back. Isabel Johnson, Ellen Murphy and another AFDC mother had this to say at a meeting of Christians and Jews United for Social Action (CUSA) in Brownsville, Brooklyn, in May, 1967:

> MRS. JOHNSON: The worst thing about welfare, you don't feel like a real person by the time they get through with you. I'm not prejudiced, the black workers are just as bad as the others, but I do think sometimes it doesn't hurt as much to get insulted by your own kind.
>
> MRS. MURPHY: Yes, they got some real mean Negroes in welfare, but they should have more of them, good ones, that is.
>
> MRS. JOHNSON: You go down to apply, the Intake supervisor comes over and says, "Where did your baby come from?"
>
> MRS. MURPHY: The last one said that to me, I shot back, "Where did your Momma get you?" Another time a worker asked me, "Mizz Murphy, you got a boyfriend?" I said right away, "Do you have one? If you don't, you ain't dead yet, so you must be a fool."
>
> MRS. JOHNSON: You've got to tell them where your husband was born, and where *his* mother and father came from. They want to know, do you have any money in the bank? If you admit you have life insurance, you got to go home and come back with it.
>
> MRS. X: Even after they put you on a regular budget some workers will come into your apartment and stand with

* The movement is a product of the War on Poverty. Autonomous neighborhood organizations like CUSA, financed by the Office of Economic Opportunity, began to come into existence in 1966 to counsel recipients and advocate individual grievances. In a short time, the New York groups united into a City-Wide Coordinating Committee of Welfare Groups which itself affiliated with the National Welfare Rights Organization headed by a former Cornell chemistry professor and CORE activist, Dr. George Wiley.

their coats on while their eyes are going all over the place. Myself and a girl friend managed to put twenty dollars together to buy a fish tank and some tropical fish. I'm a diabetic and I can't get around too much, and I don't have any children, so the fish gave me something pretty to look at. When my worker first saw the tank she didn't say, "Missus, what a lovely thing to have." She said, "How much did it cost, where did you get the filter, who paid for the heater?" By the time that snotty kid was finished, those poor little guppies and swordtails must have been frightened to death.

A FAILURE OF COMMUNICATIONS

A benefits system that attempts to account for every nickel and dime delivered to a client entails reams of regulations. The New Jersey Manual of Administration contains five closely printed pages of instructions on how to deduct the 1968 increase in Social Security payments from welfare budgets.* Not surprisingly, the printed rules usually are more humane than practice in the field because many caseworkers in the big cities do not stay on the job long enough to master them.

The average caseworker in the New York–New Jersey area has a workload in excess of the legal maximums, and little time to analyze and memorize the printed directives. The usual budget formula relies upon a predetermined allowance (to which rent is added) intended to keep the recipient alive. A "special" or "supplementary" clothing allowance regarded by the departments as extraordinary is for the client with school-age children a necessary addition.†

---

* The statute does not permit Old Age Survivors and Disability Income benefits to be attached, but this does not prevent relief administrators from viewing OASDI as income available to the client and therefore justifying *pro tanto* a decrease in the welfare grant.

† In 1968, the New York City Department of Social Services instituted, on an experimental basis, a "flat grant" system whereby each AFDC

Since it is extra work for the caseworker to determine and process a client's eligibility for a special grant, there is a temptation to reject such claims, especially since the system exerts no real pressure on the caseworker to know the extent of entitlements. On the other hand, the conscientious and compassionate worker who wants to justify certain education allowances, for example, must do more than study her manual. She must present the case for her client forcefully enough to overcome resistance all along the line.

Do recipients cheat? The system is too tight to permit much fraud, but its niggardliness does compel most clients to exaggerate their needs. CUSA activist Shirley Wilson says:

> If you don't steal pennies from welfare, you won't live to talk about it. The home economist fixes prices for things like clothing and pots and pans by looking at sales advertised in the papers by the big department stores. She'll say it's good for a client to go look for bargains. But I can't stand in a crowd at Macy's at nine o'clock in the morning with a baby in my arms and two kids back in Brownsville getting ready to go to school.

---

family would receive automatically each calendar quarter a clothing allowance of fifteen dollars for each member of the family. The innovation complied in principle with progressive social work policy that recipients should be able to spend as they wished and should not be forced to beg for necessary items. Many unorganized recipients also benefited greatly from the flat grant.

Welfare rights leaders complained, however, with some justification that the clothing grant was too low and was motivated by a desire to undermine the movement and to reduce expenditures for "special allowances," especially clothing, won for organized recipients by the movement.

In the spring of 1969, the Republican-controlled New York legislature abolished the automatic clothing allowance along with traditional special allowances predicated on proven need, e.g., food for pets owned by the aged, and in addition instituted an exclusive flat grant system which raised budget levels for a minority of recipients but had the effect of lowering payments for the rest, including those in the socially critical category of AFDC mothers with teenage sons. The welfare rights movement protested the cuts with school boycotts and other direct action. As of the end of 1969, the constitutionality of the legislation was still being litigated in federal courts, and there also were indications that Albany was about to liberalize the measure.

You just can't make do on the food allowance, you know. Of course, you can't expect to live on steaks every day. You gotta go down on the hog a little bit too. In my family we get the surplus food, and we eat a lotta neck bones and red beans.

Some clients break the rules by taking a quarter a week out of the food money to pay for a life policy that you're not supposed to have. But most people, even if they are on welfare, want to be buried nice. An ADC mother, if she has a heart, lets her kids go to the Saturday afternoon movies out of the food money. Maybe (when she runs short) she buys her oatmeal and hamburger meat with the money she got to replace those towels the kids didn't really lose at school.

If you don't cut corners with welfare you have no pride left at all. Welfare makes a client cheat a little bit and sometimes the good caseworkers will even show you how to do it.

Say your worker knows you're really hard up for a new blanket. One of your kids had diarrhea and after you try to wash the smell out of the wool, you don't have much blanket left. The worker tells her supervisor. "No good," he says. "We gave her a bed blanket last year, the rules don't allow for another one right now. But you say she's on the level? All right. Her file shows she hasn't had a raincoat in five years. Write up an authorization for a raincoat. We pay her for a raincoat. She buys a blanket. Everybody's happy."

INCENTIVE FOR WHAT?

In 1966, New York City requested permission to institute an experimental incentive earnings program designed to encourage AFDC mothers to enter the work force by permitting them to add to the usual budget allowance a fair portion of their earnings.* The scheme that finally worked

---

* Prior to 1967, the Social Security Act required that almost every dollar earned be deducted from the budget. The 1967 amendments established the Work Incentive Program (WIN) which replaced more generous incentives permitted under New York City's program and under employment by recipients in the antipoverty programs with an exempt allowance for normal employment of $30 per month of earnings plus one-third of the balance.

its way through HEW, the Albany legislature and the State Welfare Department, though well-intentioned, was both inequitable and bizarre.

The incentive plan had to be justified as an economy measure designed to reduce the welfare body-count or at least the total monetary costs of welfare, and therefore was not open to those already employed. An AFDC mother who had *not* worked full-time during the previous six months could find a job and add the first fifty dollars of her monthly earnings plus one-half of the balance to her usual budget allowance. The employed Puerto Rican father, already on supplementary assistance because his full-time earnings could not support his family, might find himself with less total income than the AFDC family next door.

In the spring of 1968, the City Welfare Department announced that the program had been so successful that it might be expanded. Hopefully, the work incentive allowances have indeed stimulated reliefers who could and should work to look for jobs. On the other hand, at least one center in Brooklyn experienced a rash among "supplementaries" of discharges from employment, six months of idleness, and then reinstatement *by the same employer*. So much for economy.

The Work Incentive (WIN) provisions enacted by Congress into the Social Security Act in 1968 are no more rational. To begin with, they were included in a repressive, economy-minded package that included a "freeze" on the number of children eligible to participate in AFDC as well as the unique requirement that "employable mothers" be compelled to work at the risk of being excluded from the family's welfare grant.

The incentives are too low to motivate any except those already inclined toward employment. The program does not take cognizance of the social and economic harm befalling a mother whose baby-sitter fails to appear. WIN speaks of client rehabilitation but patronizes recipients by offering them "counseling" services and by assuming (incorrectly) that upward mobility employment is waiting for WIN referrals previously idle due to personal deficiencies.

Even a few extra dollars per week from a decent job added to the normal welfare allowance, with adequate child-care services provided, might in many cases be enough to provide a psychological impetus toward employment, but on its face WIN promises to create a supply of low-cost domestics, field hands, laborers on municipal projects, and fodder for New York City's low-wage industries.

To its credit, the New York City Department, though hampered by restrictions emanating out of Albany and by municipal budget considerations, has attempted through its incentive program and in other ways to give a measure of justice to the bulk of its clients. New York's factory employers, however, pay shockingly low salaries to working men with families whose protests cannot be amplified through a public official or honest union representation.

WELFARE WITH MILLSTONES ATTACHED

May the employed recipient save the money she earns? At what point is she no longer destitute and therefore ineligible in almost all states for cash assistance? The Social Security Act is silent on these matters and, apparently, HEW trusts the discretion of the individual states. California probably has the most progressive welfare statute in the country; its AFDC recipients are permitted to own realty valued at no more than $5,000 and the aged, blind and disabled, while on the rolls, may retain reserves of $2,000 for "future contingencies." Not so in New York.

New York's work incentive experiment went into effect in the spring of 1967. Subsequently, at least two lengthy articles in *The New York Times* described the program in glowing terms without at any point advising its readers that these recipients now embarked on new careers with welfare aid could not *save* their earnings. The New York City Department did not receive permission to change this rule until March, 1968. In the meantime, recipients bringing home extra employment earnings had every reason to believe they would be subject to fraud penalties *and* suspension from the rolls if they did not instantly spend their work incentive allowance.

It is also quite likely that most of the ambitious clients still labor under this disability. The directive authorizing a change in the general rule on savings, like most other benign policy statements from welfare administrators which might cost the taxpayers more money, appeared to be deliberately ambiguous. Clients, it said, have the right of "self-determination"; they may save from the recurring grant amounts planned to meet specific needs. But, theoretically, the Department provides for "needs" as defined by itself. It is virtually impossible to put anything aside from the basic grant, and no mention is made of saving from earnings. What, don't you understand the new policy, Mrs. ADC?

On the other hand, the directive also states that exempt income from work programs authorized under the Economic Opportunity Act "may be reserved or accumulated without any maximum limitations or time limit on the retention of such resources." Clearly, this cannot possibly mean what it says because no one believes that New York should or would permit an antipoverty worker with three or four thousand dollars in the bank to stay on the welfare rolls.

The system effectively withstands such paper assaults. Significantly, two days after the directive came down, a New York City court at the behest of Welfare Department attorneys ordered a former client to pay the Department $480 he held in a bank account while receiving assistance.

Despite the "change" in policy, New York caseworkers will continue to play Solomon with their clients' income and resources. Recipients, for their part, will still assume they are cheating by keeping *any* sum of money in the bank.

The administrative lie actually begins with the first application for relief. The federal and state statutes and literature distributed to clients by the state departments expressly advise the prospective client that cash assistance is intended to help carry her through bleak periods until she returns to economic health. Though mothers with small children are not likely, no matter how generous the assistance levels, to become self-supporting in two or three years' time, many others, only temporarily in need, would soon leave the rolls if given half a chance. The present system, however, makes aid available only to the hard-core destitute, and even these are saddled with the depressing obligation in New York and thirty-one other states of repaying the cost of assistance and care when monies become available to them.

The repayment obligation did not exist under the English Poor Law. New York did not have a recovery statute until 1930 when at the beginning of the Depression the Albany legislators braced themselves for the onslaught of a new type of welfare applicant, the small home-owner with no income and no cash savings.

The English statute, creating a "debt" out of the assistance transaction, was strictly construed by His Majesty's courts in this century to apply only to recipients who enter into a valid agreement to repay. Illogically, since the destitution requirement implies that the eligible recipient had no real choice except to apply in order to stay alive, New York and Massachusetts characterize application for and receipt of relief as a loan agreement. New Jersey defies common sense by insisting that aged clients actually execute a written promise to repay before they receive the price of a meal out of the public treasury.

Supposedly, all of the state plans must conform to the "self-help" objectives of the Social Security Act and the equal-protection requirements of the United States Constitution. But try to find a rational pattern among the state recovery statutes.

New York, which imposes the obligation on all categories of cash but not medical assistance, has the most stringent recovery laws in the country. Idaho, Ohio, South Carolina, Wisconsin and South Dakota collect only from the aged. New Jersey exempts only the blind whereas Colorado imposes the recovery obligation only upon blind recipients. Many states exempt the AFDC category; Tennessee, on the other hand, recovers only from abandoned mothers and children.

Repayment could almost be described as a Northern liberal phenomenon. Mississippi and most of the other Deep South states pay savagely low benefits but abide by the common law tradition which said welfare did not have to be paid back.

In many cases clients with nominal assets repay before they owe welfare anything, by assigning real estate, life insurance policies and personal injury damages claims to the department when they are accepted onto the rolls. New York law permits local directors to take assignments of realty "in their discretion" from AFDC recipients. But since none of the local departments are geared to apply social work considerations to individual cases, it is now the practice for Nassau County, for example, never to take such assignments, while New York City does so in almost every case. This disparity exists despite the fact that federal law requires a state plan to be uniformly applied in all parts of the state.

Dr. Charles Grosser of the Columbia University School of Social Work believes that the "rehabilitative" purposes of public assistance could be achieved in a better system.

Social work has the self-support and independence of clients as its *raison d'être*. Prominent members of the profession played large roles in enacting the 1935 legislation and subsequent amendments.

Grosser says, however, that in many cases where assets are possessed by a client, welfare not only fails to cure the client's income disability, but the attempts at recovery introduce a new pathology. To an elderly couple, a little stucco two-story house in East New York might constitute their entire estate and symbolize their life's achievements. If the mortgage payments on the house do not exceed a reasonable rental allowance, welfare will graciously declare the old folks eligible for relief, permit them to remain in the house, but take title to the property.

Ironically, the short-sighted recovery provisions, while depressing in themselves, also cause recipients to forego personal injury and other legitimate claims, says Dr. Grosser, because the bulk of the monies will not accrue to the clients.

New York exempts from the windfall a modest allowance that might keep the injured plaintiff-recipient off the rolls for a year at most, but, like the English of Dickens' time, the state refuses to allocate a portion of personal injury recoveries to help set up a client who is a trained dressmaker, for example, in her own business.

A CHANGE IN APPROACH

Welfare reformers have good reason to despair of ever getting public opinion on their side. During the past ten years, one distinguished nonpartisan commission after another has recommended drastic reforms in public assistance administration, but to no avail. However, this cause may be the rare exception—the federal open-housing bill also comes to mind—to the rule that legislators shall not rise above the bigotry of their constituents. There is still hope for President Nixon's reform proposal.

The evident waste of human and monetary resources that results from the present system, the studies that link poverty and welfare maladministration to riots in the racial ghettoes, have brought together on the reform bandwagon a curious but formidable coalition of good-government types and radicals of every political hue. A small but heroic band of liberals appeared for the first time in the Senate in 1967 under the leadership of the late Robert Kennedy, to vocalize the grievances of the politically impotent welfare poor. The economy-minded Congress gave a little and took away a great deal in 1967, but the cost of the war in Vietnam was a paramount consideration.

In recent years, reformers have zeroed in on procedural and substantive measures. The generic expression "negative income tax" refers to a more impersonal form of welfare benefits distribution, probably administered by Internal Revenue, that should enhance human dignity by ending the mutually degrading battles between caseworker and client. Emergency grants under most of the NIT proposals would still be made available through the welfare centers where caseworkers, trained in social work, would concentrate on the nonmonetary needs of the aged and the maladjusted.

Congress could complement an NIT system for chronic unemployables or at least begin the welfare revolution, like England three decades ago, by expanding the social insurance categories, with financing from general revenues instead of the retrogressive payroll tax, to include those with significant terms of service in the labor market.

Medical assistance in the nonwelfare manner, family allowances, increased accommodations in public housing projects, all available to both the poor and the not-so-poor— such benefits would jack up income levels or reduce the cost of living in the lower economic orders and help blend the welfare recipients into the total population mix.

The politically inflammatory expression "guaranteed annual income" actually describes the point of income eligibility for cash assistance for those who satisfy the other criteria—disability, abandonment, blindness, etc.—for the federal categorical relief programs. In reform parlance, GAI usually refers to a *national* income floor imposed by Congress on the states and financed in large part by the federal government. Such a guarantee would keep Mississippi Negroes from starving to death. It would help states like New York by encouraging the Southern poor to stay at home, and take much of the passion out of local anti-welfare attitudes.

But it seems to me that the logical place to begin is with welfare's destitution requirement. Oil millionaires receive depletion allowances and men like James Eastland qualify for farm subsidies on some vague public-benefit theory. In our increasingly restrictive society, a poor person who, by being totally dependent on the public weal, probably has more of a claim than any other class of citizen to benefits (in his case, not for profit but for purposes of survival), should be able to apply for his entitlements without crawling on the ground.

The welfare recipient, and especially the AFDC family, must be brought back into society. The poets of the New Left have discovered rightly that the isolation of the AFDC mother gives her a sad grandeur. Alan Keith-Lucas, a welfare administrator himself, wrote in his classic 1957 treatise on public assistance that the AFDC mother who exists on so little is the "unsung heroine" of our era. Shirley Wilson of Brownsville puts it this way: "You've got to give a woman a lot of credit for trying to make do on an ADC budget. There's other ways, not so nice, of making a living. You know what I mean."

CHAPTER
TWO

NO MAN IN THE HOUSE

There is another kind of violence, slower but just as deadly, destructive as the shot or the bomb in the night . . . the breaking of a man's spirit by denying him the chance to stand as a father and as a man among other men . . .

> —*Speech by Robert F. Kennedy at the City Club, Cleveland, Ohio, April 5, 1968, two days after the murder of Martin Luther King, Jr.*

IN THE WELFARE drama, the black woman occupies the center of the stage. With her hair in curlers, three or four children clinging to her torn housedress, the abandoned mother is the improbable object of vilification from taxpayers who believe they are financing her sinful life. At the same time, it is also the militants among the AFDC clients who in protest demonstrations in recent years have railed against the system and asserted the humanity of class and race on behalf of their brothers and sisters.

But where are the men? The husbands, lovers and adult sons of the welfare women stand in the wings. Shadowy but real presences in the lives of AFDC mothers, these men seldom appear on the case records and partake directly in the benefits of the relief programs to a relatively insignificant extent.

The Kerner Commission found that "the concentration of male Negro employment at the lowest end of the occupational scale is greatly depressing the incomes of United States Negroes in general. In fact, this is the single most important source of poverty among Negroes."*

The poverty of the female welfare applicant derives in large part from the disadvantages suffered by her men. The character of the AFDC mother, for better or worse, has been shaped by the psychic and economic harm that America has inflicted on the black male. The Southern states in particular sought to suppress any aggressive potential in the freed black man by using welfare policies among other devices not only to restrict his mobility but to diminish his manhood.

Harriet Beecher Stowe first described the process. Twelve decades later, in *The Confessions of Nat Turner*, William Styron, with much less precision, attempted to explain current black attitudes in the light of ancient wrongs. But the phenomenon of Martin Luther King memorial scholarships at white colleges in 1969 tends to obscure the fact that we still try to prove the inferiority of the black race by keeping all but a tiny minority of its members in their appointed place. Present-day welfare administration probably best illustrates the vitality of the comments made to a Negro literary society in 1884 by the popular writer George Wash-

---

* *Report of the National Advisory Commission on Civil Disorders*, 255 (Bantam ed., 1968).

ington Cable, himself a Confederate War veteran and a native of Louisiana: The racist "forbids the Freedman to go into the water until he is satisfied that [the Freedman] knows how to swim—and for fear he should learn, hangs millstones about his neck."

Blacks predominate in this discussion for a reason. Puerto Ricans, Mexicans and Indians are also injured by the American Way; but these last can and do advance themselves by blending far more easily into the general population than citizens of African descent. Upon them, White America affixes a color stigma as one method of excusing its sordid involvement in slavery.

Statistics compiled by unbiased federal agencies are available in abundance to show the gross disparity of earnings between black and white male workers. But even the most unsophisticated taxpayer suspects that human failings and other intangibles do not appear in many computations.

Conversely, the Moynihan Report angered black leaders by stressing illegitimacy rates to illustrate the deterioration of Negro family life. While the Report conceded the lasting harm committed by slave owners, not enough stress was placed on the effects of economic discrimination for more than a century after the Emancipation Proclamation. Daniel P. Moynihan, his critics believed, should have given some weight in his white-middle-class-oriented conclusions to the validity of a ghetto life style. The critics might have added that the Report also failed to stress the serious adverse impact of welfare policies on the psychology of low-income families.

Accordingly, the disproportionately high incidence of nonwhites on the relief rolls does not illustrate the depth of Negro poverty or economic oppression so as to excite white sympathies. Black indolence might be the cause. "It is their own fault." A better case can be made by focusing on the circumstances of the intact family units which, to all appear-

ances, have accepted most of small-town America's bourgeois values. In 1966 the median annual income for the 42
million husband-wife-children groups in the United States
was $7,722 as opposed to $4,628 for the nonwhite (3
million) component. While 6 out of 100 white families with
male heads are likely to become poor, the comparable figure
for nonwhites is 24 out of 100, only seven units below the
estimate for white families with female heads.*

These figures should indicate that deficient wages or unemployment drove the wives of these men toward the welfare centers. However, the white unionist, charged with
responsibility for maintaining brotherhood in the ranks, may
still retort that the workers we are discussing are honest but
stupid. Though faithful to their wives and children, says the
business agent, "When they're not raising hell about discrimination, they've got no push at all. They can't add two
and two. The colored guys are afraid of high jobs. They don't
even know you're supposed to stand the foreman [also a
union member] to a couple of balls and a carton of smokes
on payday." We win the argument by demonstrating that
the black worker who excels in doing all of the right things is
not permitted to finish first against white competition.

On Manhattan Island the political climate smells of
equality. Yet, according to the 1960 census, ten (29 percent) of the thirty-five Negro tracts that averaged high on
educational attainment and low on unemployment also fell
into the borough's lowest quartile for income.†

Statistics compiled by the United States Bureau of the
Census in 1966 reveal that at every educational level the
nonwhite earned substantially less than his white counterpart. Those liberals who cheer the rate of black progress

* Senate Subcommittee on Employment, Manpower and Poverty, 90th
Cong., 2nd Sess., Toward Economic Security for the Poor, 10 (1968).
† "The Negroes in the United States," Bulletin No. 1511, June, 1966,
U.S. Department of Labor, BLS, p. 11.

since 1960 should first dwell on the fact that in 1966 the handful of college-educated blacks, who do not relate to the welfare crisis, came within 19 percent of the median incomes of white graduates; but the greatest disparity, 39 percent ($7,267 to $4,418), occurred among adults with nine to eleven years of education, in other words in the group almost, but not quite, capable of finishing high school and chained, as a result, to unskilled or semiskilled blue-collar employment for the rest of their working lives.

The real shock comes, however, when we read that the black teen-ager who *is* ambitious enough to get a high school diploma earns less ($5,886 to $6,103) than the white dead-beat who completed only eight years of schooling.* Neither George Wallace nor the president of a New York plumbers local could explain away this statistic.

Forget for the moment about the farm laborers, the drug addicts, the school dropouts, the friends of Harlem author Claude Brown who acquired a police "sheet" too late ever to lose it. During the year immediately preceding the Newark and Detroit riots, young black men of good charac-ter (with only three dependents) had incomes perilously close to the welfare eligibility levels in New York and other states.

THERE'S ALWAYS WELFARE

Congress in 1935 said that it wanted cash assistance to be used to rehabilitate its beneficiaries, but the history of relief administration during the past three decades shows that on balance the congressmen and local politicians have profited most by exploiting the misery of welfare recipients.

---

* "Current Population Reports," Series P-60, No. 53, "Income in 1966 of Families and Persons in the United States," December 28, 1967, Tables 7 and 21, reported in *Welfare in Review*, March–April, 1968, p. 20.

On November 20, 1967, the Senate approved by a narrow margin an amendment, which did not pass into law, to the Social Security Act that would have prevented the states from disqualifying AFDC children because of the presence of a man in the house. Thirty-six senators, including Republican Minority Leader Everett Dirksen, voted against the amendment. On December 30, the Republican Coordinating Committee accused the Democrats of an "ugly crisis of failure" in legislating for the welfare programs.

Not all of the Democrats have clean hands. Senator Robert Byrd (Democrat, West Virginia) won national attention in 1965 and the praise of Vice-President Hubert Humphrey, among other progressives, for exposing fraud in the Washington, D.C., welfare caseload. Researchers who looked up the delinquents that Byrd had succeeded in knocking off the rolls found most of them working as prostitutes or living on skid row.

Due to the opposition of Robert Byrd, the District does not provide AFDC benefits to families with unemployed fathers.* Most students of the welfare system agree that this omission has a significant, though undetermined, impact on the breakup of low-income families. Senator Byrd, however, who also bemoans AFDC benefits levels as depriving people like himself of (low-priced) domestic help, attributes the rise in AFDC solely to promiscuity among the mothers. It is the women, not their husbands, says Byrd, who leave home with lust in their hearts, dragging their children with them.

It would be incorrect, however, to assume too close a correlation between family dislocation and the nonavailability of AFDC-U. The South did lose over 3.3 million nonwhites, over one-third to the Northeast, during 1940–

---

* AFDC-U has been available at the option of the states since 1961. The program was restricted by Congress in 1968 to families with unemployed *fathers* only, with substantial attachment to the work force. Eligibles must also choose between AFDC or unemployment compensation.

63.* New York, along with twenty-five other states, participates in the unemployed father segment of AFDC and in June, 1969, paid more than token average monthly family benefits of $282.80; but individual recipients under New York's basic "abandoned mother" program also received average payments that month of $65.65, as contrasted with $15.60 in Alabama and $10.20 in Mississippi.†

Translated, these figures suggest that while feudal Alabama and Mississippi give *some* encouragement to a black worker to leave home in order to qualify his family for AFDC, it is also evident that his departure will not present them with a bonanza. Low welfare benefits in a depressed economic context have driven poor blacks, including women with and without husbands, to the industrial centers of the North. A study of the New York City caseload made in 1966 by Professor Lawrence Podell found that the typical wife in the intact Negro family unit on welfare had been reared in the South and had migrated as an adult.

About 1950, the big, new expensive machinery began to appear among the cotton and peanut acres, reducing the need for field hands on the large plantations and at the same time forcing off their lands tenant farmers who lacked the necessary capital to invest in automation.

In keeping with the regional tradition, few communities in the South attempted to "rehabilitate" the displaced blacks. Instead, Southern demagogues, with more polish but less heart than Huey or Earl Long, beginning about 1951 set out on campaigns calculated to force unemployed blacks to leave home.

For every dollar of cash assistance the South has failed to pay its indigents over the past seventeen years, the region has sacrificed nine or ten dollars totaling countless millions

* "The Negroes in the United States," *supra* p. 2.
† Public Assistance Statistics, June, 1969, HEW, Social and Rehabilitation Service, National Center for Social Statistics, Tables 7 and 8.

in matching federal funds. But only reducing benefits levels
did not satisfy the needs of the New South. With pious expressions of concern over the rise in black illegitimacy,
Southern governors like Herman Talmadge of Georgia and
Jimmie Davis of Louisiana, to the embarrassment of state
welfare administrators, promulgated, among other measures,
"man-in-the-house" or "substitute parent" regulations. In
addition to restraining the amours of mothers by starving
their children, the regulations also were intended ostensibly
to afford equal protection of the laws to intact family groups
ineligible in most of the Southern states for AFDC-U or
General Assistance.

In 1968 the United States Supreme Court, in litigation out
of Alabama financed by the War on Poverty, faced for the
first time the question whether a state could terminate assistance to needy children solely because a man not their father
resided in their home, *in loco parentis,* with or without the
benefit of a preacher's blessing, or visited the home occa-
sionally for the purpose of copulating with their mother. In
King v. Smith the Court unanimously held that Congress did
not intend to substitute such men for the lawful parent whose
absence and failure to support entitles his children to relief
benefits, and thus deprive needy children of their statutory
rights.

Clearly, the South contributed to the relief problems of
states like New York that have no durational residence requirements and which in theory pay benefits that suffice to
keep recipients alive. Those sullen white workers in Boston
who scored points for George Wallace in 1968 evidently did
not know they were voting for one of the principal causes of
their discontent.

But the remarkable aspect of the postwar migrations is
that only a handful of the displaced blacks could have
headed north *solely* to apply for welfare aid. On the contrary, the White South made it virtually impossible for poor

blacks to remain in their home states and survive. Studies made in the North also show that most of the émigrés, both men and women, probably found jobs when they arrived.

The nonpartisan Moreland Commission, after examining the New York State welfare records for representative counties in 1961, exploded one of the many popular myths about recipients. The Commission found that state residence of less than one year in all categories ranged from a low of .07 percent to 7.3 percent. This profile emerged of the typical AFDC mother: black, with three children all under sixteen, who had been born in New York State or had lived in the state during the previous five years.

At best, the knowledge that work opportunities were available in Northern factories and that relief could be had if all else failed might have induced whole families forced off the land to start a new life together in another locale. In early 1968 I listened to a fellow passenger on a plane, a grower from Athens, Georgia, complain that radical changes in agricultural techniques had caused "good" Negroes to leave his county. "We get left with the dregs. You can't re-train these niggers for nothin'!" The disappointments that eventually were suffered by most of the migrants perhaps explains the sharp decline since 1963 in the outflow of non-whites from the South.

THE NORTHERN GRAVY TRAIN?

The nonwhite population of New Jersey soared from 323,744 in 1950 to 527,779 ten years later. In 1968 blacks constituted an estimated 64 percent of the population of its principal city, Newark. This inflow occurred despite the fact that New Jersey, like Alabama today, did not until early 1969 give AFDC to families with unemployed parents still on the premises. Four-person families in need because of unemployment or low wages in September, 1968, received under the locally financed General Assistance program average monthly payments of about $192. The comparable AFDC-U benefit that month in neighboring New York was about $232 (or a projected $2,784 for the year).*

Welfare, then, is hardly a financial windfall in either state for the employable male with a wife and children. Moreover, both New York and New Jersey make cash assistance as degrading as possible in a sustained campaign to discourage male reliefers. Isolated with most of their clients from the economic and social life of the city, oblivious of the paucity of decent-paying factory jobs in the New York metropolitan area, but acutely conscious of public pressure to cut costs, New York and New Jersey administrators pursue welfare policies that could only inflict serious damage to the male ego.

In *The Poorhouse State* Richard Elman observed correctly that the able-bodied indigent must spell out at the Intake desk in the welfare centers almost his entire life history, including any difficulties he might have had with the law. The man also must endure repeated investigations and is forced to accept job referrals that pay little and are themselves demeaning.

During a meeting in Brownsville in 1967 with a group of about 120 Puerto Rican strikers, I estimated on the basis of family size and income that more than half of the men present were eligible for supplementary cash assistance. When I suggested that the strikers apply for welfare, the audience responded with some boos and much silence. "Not even while the strike is on?" I said. Visibly annoyed, their leader replied, "No, Mr. Attorney, we don't want welfare even when we have nothing."

Incidentally, these men had struck, unlawfully, because

---

* *Welfare in Review,* January–February, 1969, pp. 48, 50.

their AFL-CIO union contract had failed to take cognizance
of a rise in the minimum wage. This was an incredible over-
sight, but even in ordinary circumstances wage increases
won by bargaining agents in New York City's marginal industries are not geared to minimum criteria for decent living. Usually the wage floors and the periodic nickel and
dime increases are negotiated with a view toward maintaining a modest distance between the factory average and the
statutory minimum wage; but such wage legislation has
never been viewed by economists or politicians as a device
for maintaining incomes above two-thirds of estimated survival levels.

During 1966–67, a period of unparalleled affluence for
most citizens of New York, almost 900,000 employees out
of 2.2 million in all of the city's industries had cash hourly
earnings before taxes of less than $2.25 per hour or $90 per
week or about $4,600 per annum.* On the basis of rough
estimates, probably at least one-third of these are in single-
income families.†

Is it paranoiac to imagine that a conscious conspiracy exists
in the New York political establishment to keep the voters,
incensed about rising welfare costs, from knowing that the
city has retained low-wage marginal industries by paying
welfare benefits to workers and abandoned wives? In
his Economic Report for 1968, Mayor Lindsay happily announced a decline in unemployment without mentioning the
rates of wages received by the newly employed. In the spring

* 2 New York State Department of Labor, Structure of Earnings and
Hours in New York State Industries (August, 1968).

† In manufacturing, where low wages in marginal industries are a
phenomenon in the expensive New York metropolitan area, only about
41 percent of the total of 867,000 employees in June, 1967, were
women. Since large families also predominate in low-income situations,
it is unlikely that more than a token percentage of the males employed in
factories also had wives with income from wages. *Employment Review,*
New York State Department of Labor, July, 1967, p. 27.

primaries of 1969, author Norman Mailer was the only mayoralty candidate to link welfare with low wages.

As late as April 30, 1969, over three years after the War on Poverty began to focus national attention on economic discrimination, a press release of the U.S. Department of Labor announced that five companies in the New York area had agreed, with the encouragement of federal funds, to launch job-training programs. For three of these companies, the "projected wage after training"—ranging from eleven to forty-five weeks—was an *average,* respectively, of $2.25, $1.96 and $1.87 per hour. This in a city that the Department of Labor said in 1967 had the second highest cost of living in the nation, where $10,195 per annum was required to maintain a four-person family at a "moderate living standard."

The New York wage structure presents a dilemma to those decent men in the labor movement who nevertheless refuse to acknowledge their share of responsibility for the welfare poor. Gains made in recent years by the welfare rights groups in New York City goaded Leon Davis in 1968 to strike for, and receive, a flat bottom wage of $100 per week for his hospital workers. Victor Gotbaum, of the state and municipal workers union, in a radical departure from universal past practice in this country, negotiated a minimum annual wage of $5,200.

On another level, Nicholas Kisburg, an intellectual who works for the New York Teamsters' Joint Council, has made a strong case in his frequent public pronouncements for raising the state minimum wage above two dollars per hour. But it is sad that he often does so by making invidious comparisons between the low-wage workingman and his sisters or abandoned wives on the welfare rolls.

Paradoxically, the low-wage situation in New York City combines with relatively high benefits levels and repressive practices to create a climate conducive to the breakup of poor families. But, again, it is perhaps a tribute to the human spirit that the availability of AFDC, especially in New York where intact families receive assistance at the same benefits levels as the other relief categories, does not motivate the abandonment; the welfare package simply eases the man's departure.

"Most men in low-income areas," says Professor Podell, "do not desert their families." The Podell study found that 60 percent of the AFDC women had been on welfare before the breakup. Contrary to the popular assumption, the typical husband of the abandoned mother in Podell's sample was not a drifter or a sluggard but a man with ambition, who probably married too young, decided the odds against him were too great, shirked his responsibilities and went on to make something of himself.

"No," says Ellen Murphy of Brownsville, "the black guy just don't sit down one day and figure out how much his wife and kids are going to receive from welfare after he leaves. He pulls out because the family has a tough time making ends meet on his salary. He comes home at night and it's nag, nag, nag. We need this. We need that. One day he gets disgusted all of a sudden and he just walks out. Sure, he knows welfare won't let them starve to death."

AFDC recipient Isabel Johnson has no hard feelings:

We'd both get aggravated over what we needed but couldn't buy and we'd start at each other's throat. I had a little job for a while, but he was out of work at the time and I was the only one bringing any money home. One day I went down to apply for supplementary. They said no—we lived in Jersey then and it was harder to get welfare. When I came home, wondering how to tell him, I found he had packed up his things and left two dollars for me.

THE SANCTITY OF THE HOME

In New York and New Jersey, administrators will par-
tially secure their investment in a welfare family by insisting
that the man in the house, in common law situations, submit
to formal paternity proceedings, even though the man publicly acknowledges his children as well as his obligation to
support them. Welfare, however, finds it expedient to place
the man under a court order so that he will be immediately
guilty of contempt if he abandons his charges.

I know of a couple with five children in Nassau County,
Long Island, who live close to the starvation point in a ply-
wood shack heated in cold weather by a coal stove. When
asked why the family did not apply for cash assistance, the
woman said, "I'm afraid that if I get him mixed up with welfare, he'll leave us."

Bright young men willing to marry AFDC mothers do
appear on the scene—especially if the women are comely
and have only one or two children. Presumably, the liaison
would reduce or erase entirely the woman's dependence on
welfare. But the system dampens such ambitions and defeats
itself.

If the woman needs a divorce, the department might frus-
trate a consent decree by appearing in court to demand back
alimony. In these cases the husband will assert his legal right
to refuse to pay because his wife has been unfaithful. This
actually happened in 1968 in Nassau County, New York,
with one of the most reputedly progressive welfare departments in the country. If the department had not finally capit-
ulated, an unpleasant trial might have resulted in a stand-
off, no divorce or remarriage and continued welfare
dependency.

New Jersey has a more restrictive divorce law than New

York and makes the defense of "recrimination" available even in actions for divorce grounded on "willful, continuous desertion for two years." The New Jersey Bar also imposes upon practitioners the quasi-medieval obligation of advising the judge before trial of any evidence of his client's infidelity.

In another important way New York and New Jersey discourage the remarriage of welfare recipients. Instead of Alabama's crude man-in-the-house rule, the more sophisticated Northern states utilize "substitute parent" regulations to achieve the same results. Children are not automatically disqualified because of the sins of their mother, but the family's budget allowance will be reduced, perhaps to zero, by inclusion of the income of the resident spouse or boy friend.

In theory, the man's income will not be "presumptively available" to the family if he categorically refuses to provide for children not his own. (The rules actually require him to say in effect, "We do not consider ourselves a single family unit.") Few men will be either so hardhearted or aware that they have a legal right to refuse to support. Caseworkers need not and few will volunteer to advise such men and women that separate budgets are available for the children. On the contrary, most workers, influenced by the American Protestant Ethic, assume that the man in the house, even with a salary of eighty dollars per week, *should* support someone else's children.

In New York City, Spanish-speaking recipients, with a high incidence of common law relationships among them, are more likely to insist on separate budgets than blacks. The black man, who probably has his roots in the feudal South, may not believe he can announce with impunity a semi-official marital status. It is also asking a great deal of a twenty-year-old, working his way through college, to marry an AFDC mother, then swallow his pride and tell welfare to

send a check to his wife for her kids because he will not pay
for their upbringing.

The system, of course, encourages promiscuity. In New
York City and Newark, one or more men may discreetly
visit the woman at frequent intervals without disturbing the
welfare status quo. Caseworkers, out of concern for their
own safety or to avoid extra work, are not eager, at least in
this metropolitan area, to pry deeply into the sex lives of
their clients. A well-intentioned handbook on the rights of
New York recipients which appeared in the city in 1968 first
recites the involved conditions—willingness to support, os-
tensible marital relationship, etc.—whereby the man's income will be included in the budget computation. The
handbook then concludes with this clear statement of advice
(and direction): "Remember, if a man just visits and sleeps
in the house now and then you can forget him. He does not
have to help support anybody." But will the children forget
him?

ANOTHER PECULIAR INSTITUTION

The man-in-the house and substitute parent policies have
added a special quality to the American welfare system. The
absurdities of the Poor Law Reform of 1834 preceded by
over one hundred years the advent of the race question into
relief administration on this side of the Atlantic; but when
White America found itself compelled by law to give equal
treatment to indigent blacks, the states, both North and
South, devised methods of evasion too degrading for Britons
ever to impose upon their own race.

The classic novel on Southern slavery *Uncle Tom's Cabin*
tells us why New York insists on emasculating its Negro
males. In her innocence, Harriet Beecher Stowe drew a
sketch of the War Between the Races that has survived the
Emancipation Proclamation, the New Deal and the emer-

gence of black separatism as a political force. Mrs. Stowe, in words that ring true today, has Augustine St. Clare chide Northerners for their hypocrisy: ". . . you loathe [blacks] as you would a snake or a toad. Yet you are indignant at their wrongs."

William Styron, in *The Confessions of Nat Turner,* aroused the ire of black spokesmen by implying that Nat's ability to read the Bible was an extraordinary accomplishment for a slave. Mrs. Stowe, in a work of fiction but with more historical truth, gave the world the character of Eliza's husband, George Harris, a handsome mulatto who invented a machine for the cleaning of hemp. Despite this accomplishment, Harris could not defeat the system from within because he was "in the eye of the law not a man but a thing."

The commandants of the Nazi death camps reportedly maintained esprit de corps among the guards by convincing them that their Jewish victims were less than human. We consign thousands of black men to the role of twilight lovers and fathers because, in the light of our history, it is important for whites to believe that blacks *are* inferior.

When asked if his slaves were honest, Augustine St. Clare answered, "Why, of course, they aren't. Why should they be? What upon earth is to make them so? . . . [Under slavery] cunning and deception become necessary, inevitable habits." The American welfare system assumes that its clients are incapable of leading upright lives. As if to prove the point, the system virtually mandates dishonesty as a means of survival.

Uncle Tom became a figure of ridicule for later generations of militants because he refused to break his master's trust by running away. But Tom acted out of a sense of pride; he was "self-respecting and dignified." Like the dark men who appear in the writings of James Baldwin and William Faulkner, Uncle Tom was both brother and father to the White South and, in his own eyes, a superior being.

The Black Power movement may resurrect this pride of race which, while trying to exist on a diet of theoretical equality under the law, died gradually from economic neglect. If anything, during the past five years, we have worsened the situation of the low-income black male vis-à-vis his women. Community action programs, for the most part, have developed female leaders. Corporations and law firms pay above scale for qualified black stenographers. Scholarships abound for Negro collegiates and law students. The high salaries awaiting these young men can only accentuate the bitterness of their blue-collar brothers who have lost ground to white men, with even less education, doing the same jobs.

Eliza was a pet of the Shelbys. Her mistress "adorned her beautiful hair with orange blossoms." But George's owner hated and abused his slave precisely for possessing those qualities White America says the Negro lacks. I once asked Bernice McLean of Brownsville to compare life in Brooklyn and Birmingham, where she was raised. "Not much difference. I worked for a couple that treated me good. They took me everywhere they went, even to the white movie house. Nobody could fuss with me while I worked for those people. Except I guess it's hard—real hard—on the black mens in Alabama. But then it's not easy for the mens up here either."

THREE

OLIVER TWIST ASKED FOR MORE

"What!" said the master at length, in a faint voice.
"Please, sir," replied Oliver, "I want some more!"
The master aimed a blow at Oliver's head with the
ladle, pinioned him in his arms, and shrieked
aloud for the beadle.

—*Charles Dickens,* The Adventures of Oliver Twist

OVER ONE HUNDRED and thirty years ago a cele-
brated English novelist told us almost, but not
quite, all we need to know to hate the present
American welfare system; however, we cannot update and
project his young hero as the spokesman for the current
generation of AFDC children because Oliver Twist was a
white English boy.

After adopting the British Poor Law formula for public relief, the states embellished its primitive framework with barbarities that are a direct outgrowth of our troubled racial history. In this country, those who regard cash assistance as a form of social control have tended to triumph in the traditional, continuing conflict with politicians and administrators who view welfare as a secular continuation of medieval Church charity.

"Man-in-the-house," "suitable home," "employable mother" and other economy measures unknown to the English began to appear among welfare regulations in the South not long after the federal government made it clear that blacks also qualified for assistance under the Social Security Act. However, since the needy child is the principal beneficiary of Anglo-American relief distributions, efforts to cut costs by discouraging applications, restricting eligibility and by reducing budget levels inevitably hurt him more than his father or mother; while intended to squelch the ambition of the black man, the American innovations, like the restrictions originating in England, achieved the results desired by adding to the misery of children.

TRANSPLANTED BRITISH HUMANISM

What we inherited from England is bad enough.

The Poor Law drew much of its character from the principle of "less eligibility." To this day, state administrators refuse to include in AFDC budgets allowances for comparatively inexpensive items such as plastic toys at Christmas, ice cream pops once or twice a week and Saturday afternoon movies. These omissions have symbolic importance. If nickels and dimes for childish pleasures were included, the welfare family might *appear* to be doing as well financially as the brood of the low-income worker who probably can afford no more than occasional luxuries for his children.

The low state of the British economy in 1847 called for additional material distinctions between reliefers and the working poor. That year, in an emergency move, the Poor Law Commissioners decided that children on outdoor relief (i.e., in their own homes) were not to be educated at all by the taxpayers. Even so, those children were fortunate by comparison with Oliver Twist and others stigmatized by their physical removal from society.

Betty Higden, in Dickens' novel *Our Mutual Friend,* expressed these strong sentiments about life in the workhouse: "Kill me sooner than take me there. Throw this pretty child under cart horses' feet and a loaded wagon, sooner than take him there. Come to us and find us all a-dying and set a light to us all where we lie, and let us all blaze away with the house into a heap of cinders sooner than move a corpse of us there!"

Influenced in part by the popularity of Dickens' social fiction, the reformers of 1834 intended to provide separate, and more humane, treatment for welfare children, but this did not come to pass. To use a choice expression coined by historians Sidney and Beatrice Webb, the English administrators, like their American cousins, continued to treat the poor in a "lump." The new workhouses soon reverted to the type of "general mixed institution" condemned in *Oliver Twist,* where kindly prostitutes, for relaxation, read bedtime stories to children.

As late as 1906, the Reverend Canon Bury, of the Brixworth Board of Guardians, testified apologetically at a public hearing: "I can see no way of treating [welfare children] less eligibly than the independent laborer's child except by bringing them into the workhouse."

In the early decades of this century England and almost

all of the American jurisdictions finally decided that work-houses cost more than they were worth, but the welfare label has been affixed in other ways.

YAH, YAH, YOUR MOTHER'S ON WELFARE

Even in regard to school needs, some welfare administrators (and school officials) follow insane policies seemingly designed to forever remind the AFDC child of his low state.

At a CUSA welfare rights meeting in Brownsville in April, 1967, I heard these comments from the ten or eleven mothers in attendance:

> When my child goes to the lunchroom his card shouldn't have to say welfare written on it . . . There's more children in there besides him that's eating, you know, and I don't think our kids should have to sit on one side of the lunchroom. They're all eating the same lunch and they're all children. Maybe they're on welfare because the parents can't help it, but, anyway, the kids aren't responsible.
>
> Sometimes a welfare investigator will go to see the principal and the principal sends him to the classroom; next thing the kid knows the teacher's saying, "Come here, Williams, this man wants to see you." The whole class knows what's up.

However, our welfare children, even in ghetto areas, stand out today in a crowd principally because of the clothing they wear. During 1967–68, I and law students Bob Jaffe and Joel Feldman, associated with the New York University Project on Social Welfare Law, conducted a comparative study of welfare policies and practices in Newark, New Jersey, and in Nassau County, New York. We found that, despite the wide diversities between the two areas in geography, racial mix and income levels, clients in both Newark

and Nassau complained most about inadequate clothing allowances for their children.

As in New York City, welfare rights groups in Newark
and Nassau have organized around campaigns for spring
clothing, back-to-school clothing, and special allowances for
the winter clothing needs of their children. Taxpayers who
foolishly believe that New York City welfare policies are
lavish should read the finding of Professor Lawrence Podell
of the City University in his study of the New York caseload: about 30 percent of his sample reported that they
sometimes kept children home from school because they did
not have the necessary shoes or clothes; 20 percent of the
mothers said they did so simply out of shame at the way their
children were dressed.

By all accounts, recipients across the country worry most
about the general harm the system inflicts on their children:
"Kids are cruel to each other. On the way to school, maybe
they'll get into a little argument; then one child says to the
other, 'Your mother's on the welfare. You eat welfare beans,'
and all that kind of talk."

The hurt deepens when welfare children reach their teens.
For the nonwhite, the usual crisis of growing up, relating to
girls and sex, adjusting emotionally to the black world that
surrounds him and the white world of opportunity that must
seem so near and yet so far away—this emotional travail is
intensified by the scarcity of part-time or summer jobs available to black teen-agers (or even to college students, especially in resort areas) that would have obviated the indignity
of wearing the same frayed pair of shoes seven days a week.

Several recipients have told me that they want their boys
to finish high school but that probably they'll quit at sixteen, get a factory job and a room someplace, and in words
like this exclaim, "Momma, now I can help both of us." But
the mother looks like she wants to cry when she says this is
going to happen.

THE NEXT GENERATION

Among the more egregious crimes committed by those who control American politics is perpetuation of the myth that welfare serves an able-bodied loafer sitting on his porch, drinking beer out of a quart bottle, and thumbing his nose at taxpayers on their way to work.

This man, where he does exist, probably will not be found on his or anyone else's porch but in an alley sleeping off a wine binge. Statistically, he is an insignificant element in the welfare caseload. In June, 1969, 3.7 million of the 10.2 million beneficiaries of the federally aided relief programs nationwide were over sixty-five, blind or permanently and totally disabled. The other 6.5 million fell into the AFDC category, and almost 5 million of these were children under eighteen.[1] General assistance, the locally financed program which, for the most part, services intact families not eligible for AFDC but in need of supplementary assistance because of unemployment or low wages, in September, 1968, had 834,000 recipients, at least two-thirds of whom were minors.[2]

More than half of the $540 million expended on cash assistance across the country in June, 1969, went to AFDC clients. The two "family" programs also accounted for most of the increase in cash assistance expenditures (a combined total for AFDC and GA, December, 1967, of 52 percent over December, 1966) that fanned the antiwelfare hysteria which found its legislative expression in the retrogressive 1968 amendments to the Social Security Act. When we discuss the welfare "problem," therefore, we are really talking about children who are almost entirely dependent upon the government for their present survival and, probably, the future direction of their lives.

1. Public Assistance Statistics, June, 1969, *supra* pp. 1–2.
2. *Welfare in Review,* January–February, 1969, p. 50.

Yet the myth about welfare persists and translates, even in the more liberal states, into policies and practices that baffle present-day administrators in England where it all began. Dr. Eveline Burns, an economist who seems to have devoted most of her professional life to establishing a cause-and-effect relationship between welfare and aberrations in the surrounding economy, said in 1960, "It is particularly shocking that the needy group which is treated in the most niggardly way in most states, the ADC category, is the one which contains the largest proportion of children, the citizens of the future for whom deep concern and affection is constantly proclaimed."

AFDC, around which all of the controversy swirls, has become in recent years, for all practical purposes and especially in the huge, volatile urban centers, a black program. Though nonwhite children constitute only about 14 percent of the underage population in the United States, more than 59 percent of them live below the poverty level. It has been reliably estimated that only slightly more than half of welfare children are black, but the activities of the welfare rights groups have exaggerated even this percentage in the eyes of taxpayers. Puerto Rican recipients have been largely apathetic about welfare rights. In some areas, especially in the West, white women have organized, but in the urban cores and the suburban belts of our big cities, white recipients have stayed home when their black sisters marched on City Hall.

IF YOU CAN'T PUNISH THE PARENTS

In 1942 about three-fifths of the states had laws requiring welfare homes to be "suitable" for the proper upbringing of children. Though phrased in moralistic terms, the suitable-home regulations, like most aspects of the welfare system, were exclusively concerned with saving money. Mothers found "guilty" of offending quite rigid standards of sexual deportment were permitted to retain custody of their children, but had to support them without welfare aid.

It was not until 1961 that HEW Secretary Arthur F. Flemming, in a rare display of strength, decided that the states could not have it both ways. If the home is in fact unsuitable, he said, then other arrangements must be made for the care of the children; otherwise, the family must continue to receive cash assistance. Congress in 1966 added the so-called Flemming Ruling to the Social Security Act, but the Southern states had available other less costly alternatives to reduce black participation in AFDC, in the form of work compulsion and man-in-the-house regulations.

Georgia's "employable mother" rule, explicitly enacted in 1952 to "discourage" black illegitimacy, did not face a court test until 1968: a three-judge federal court in Atlanta *unanimously* decided that the Georgia policy violated the equal-protection clause of the Fourteenth Amendment by arbitrarily discontinuing AFDC to black mothers when suitable seasonal employment for blacks was presumptively, but not necessarily, available. All aid had been denied these women and their children, even when their wages from stoop labor did not reach the pitifully low welfare budget levels. Georgia had promulgated this rule, but the rest of America had tolerated it for sixteen years. The rapidly rising crime rates, growing welfare caseloads, and the racial tensions in Detroit, Newark, Chicago and New York City, cities to which most of the children of those Georgia women eventually migrated, attest to the price now being paid for Northern indifference to the brutalities suffered by Southern blacks.

Needless to say, however, the South in these welfare matters offends only by its excessive zeal and crudities. Appellants attacking a New Jersey variation on the Alabama substitute parent rule, which arbitrarily assumes that a stepparent can and will support welfare children not his own, were recently denied review by the United States Supreme Court.*

States above the Mason-Dixon line traditionally have not compelled AFDC mothers to take jobs and leave their children with a baby-sitter, and they may be reluctant to do so despite the congressional intent expressed in the Work Incentive (WIN) legislation enacted by Congress in 1967; but the high regard in liberal circles for day-care centers and work incentive allowances sometimes leaves me with the uneasy feeling that a new variety of social work paternalism has arrived. Benign administrators and politicians seem to be saying that AFDC mothers, whatever their own feelings in the matter, *should* be out working.

In many cases, entry of the AFDC mother into the labor market may be the best thing for the family; but, obviously, the welfare "problem" is not going to be solved and, in fact, it may harm the psyche of the black male to reward his women for stepping into a man's world while ignoring the concomitant need to provide the black man with decent employment and to raise the level of his wages.

Northern administrators, in *their* isolation from the rest of society, get smug about Southern cruelty while applying Band Aids in the form of incentive allowances to only one manifestation of a much larger economic sickness that afflicts low-wage earners in cities like New York.

The "employable mother" also figured in the 1967 welfare legislation passed with the help of some liberals by a conservative coalition of federal legislators from the North

* The Court in October, 1969, however, affirmed on the authority of *King v. Smith* (the Alabama case) a lower court decision in *Solman v. Shapiro* which struck down a Connecticut regulation requiring inclusion of the stepfather's income in the budget despite the absence, as in Alabama, of a statute imposing liability for support in such cases.

and South. The vote for the package was so overwhelming as to stifle an abortive filibuster by a small group of Senate liberals. The 1967 legislation empowers the states, in their discretion, to compel AFDC mothers to take jobs.

However, children, rather than their mothers, were the more explicit targets of the legislative freeze in 1967 on the number of children of abandoned mothers on state AFDC rolls for whom the states could receive federal matching funds. It is, of course, significant that the most reactionary amendments in the history of the Social Security Act occurred in the face of a four- or five-year spate of progressive and informed criticism of the present system, but also at a time when AFDC appeared to have become a program for the relief of poor blacks.

ONE LAW FOR THE RICH . . .

Racial antagonism aggravates the widespread public disdain for the children of reliefers that Charles Dickens described so well. The late Jacobus tenBroek, a long-time professor of law at UCLA until his death in 1968, in his classic exposition of America's dual system of family law (one for the affluent and one for the poor), focused not on the South but on California. Moreover, said tenBroek, the California schema originally traveled intact across the country from New York where, as in England, the family law of the poor was within the exclusive jurisdiction of the legislature. There it stood "in sharp contrast" with the legal succor available to the rest of the community.

In child custody and adoption litigation, most family court judges will bend the statutes to achieve desirable social benefits for children in the disputes presented to them. It is also a fair generalization that our jurists are obsessed with the notion that, except in cases of extreme unfitness, children should stay with their natural mother. But seldom do American courts have the opportunity to apply humanistic legal principles on behalf of welfare recipients. This is so because judges lay down equitable edicts of this kind at the behest of lawyers, and most lawyers charge fees for their services.

Welfare children appear in Family Court when the Welfare Department seeks to have their mother declared unfit and the children removed to a shelter. More frequently, perhaps, judicial determinations intimately touching the lives of welfare children occur in child support and paternity proceedings where the overriding concern of all parties (except the infants) is fixing monetary liabilities. In Nassau County in 1967, until legal services attorneys appeared in the case, the Welfare Department was prepared to force an AFDC mother to file a paternity petition against the true father of her baby. The court proceedings would have disgraced all concerned, including the woman's husband and their four children, all of whom lived in the same house.

Justice Justine Wise Polier of New York, in an unusual decision in 1965, gratuitously frustrated a state's attempt to reduce its welfare costs in favor of the best interests of a three-year-old child. In *Matter of Higgins,* Justice Polier refused a request from the Michigan Department of Social Welfare that New York retain technical custody and liability for the *possible* cost of caring for Samuel, orphaned in New York but then quite contentedly living with an aunt in Michigan. Neither the child nor his guardian was on welfare, but Michigan preferred to further disrupt a child's home life rather than take the chance that the state at some future date might be forced to support this infant citizen of New York.

The *Higgins* controversy helped publicize a brutal administrative practice. Samuel, like other children similarly situated, might have spent many months in a shelter instead of his aunt's home, if the New York court itself had not provided the funds necessary to pay for Samuel's transportation to Michigan. The New York Department had refused to do so until New York and Michigan were able to execute a "gentlemen's agreement" to the effect that Samuel would never burden Michigan's welfare rolls.

Justice Polier took note of the hypocrisy that coated an essentially coarse transaction: "While conclusions disapproving the home by the receiving state are often couched in terms of the child's welfare, the rejecting report is generally based on the economic circumstances of the relatives who have offered to accept the child. The comparative benefits to be derived by the child from living with relatives or being placed in an institution are rarely, if ever, weighed. Without any independent assessment, the Department of Welfare of the sending state accepts the negative decision of the receiving state. In fact, it rarely asks for further consideration of the child." (259 N.Y.S. 2d at 881.)

SOMEBODY ELSE'S CHILD

Samuel, in the *Higgins* case, of course, was black. The racial component in the welfare caseload, in my opinion, permits administrators to injure their clients in order to placate taxpayers who might be less cost-conscious if economy measures were directed at their own kind.

Oliver Twist, on the other hand, clearly belonged to the English people. Orphaned, illegitimate, a chattel of the state, denied educational opportunities, Oliver admittedly toiled among a lower order, or, more correctly, an inferior *class* of Englishmen; but still he belonged to the race, and his betters could not pretend that Oliver did not exist. Charles Dickens, in the interest of reform, permitted Oliver's friend in the workhouse, Little Dick, to die young in order to remind his readers that their neglected kinsmen might be waiting, in eternity, for a reckoning.

When, shortly after World War I, trade union spokesmen and the liberal intelligentsia began to accumulate political power in England, they cut through the pieties to demand fair treatment for all poor citizens, whatever the cause of their indigency. On this side of the Atlantic, those who purport to speak for blue-collar workers, until last year (and then only on the national level), refused to accept any responsibility for the welfare poor. While ideological disdain is the paramount factor, I do not believe that American labor could have sustained its indifference to happenings in the welfare sector if the bulk of our 5 million AFDC children were Irish, Italian or German.

Moreover, it is a truism that a pure brand of Jeffersonian democracy flourishes in many parts of the South, applicable to all citizens except black people. Ironically, our own children suffer additional harm as the result of American egalitarianism. Because we cannot tolerate the notion that underprivileged *classes* exist in the Land of the Free, we dole out crumbs to black children pretending they are only shadow figures on the other side of town. We also lie to them and to ourselves by telling the children, from a distance, among other things, that their budget level is adequate, their mothers are trollops and their fathers lazy black animals.

But suppose, for the sake of argument, that everything White America says about the parents of the AFDC child has a basis in fact. What about *him?*

In 1968 a conservative Catholic publication, the *Brooklyn Tablet,* had an anonymous caseworker advise its readers that children were "pawns" used by unscrupulous parents to con the Welfare Department. However, the *Tablet's* expert, like other reactionary critics of the system, left unanswered the all-important question. Suppose, in fact, it is true that

children are meal tickets for bums on welfare; is it Christian
to hit back at the parents through the children?

Since 1969, the Christian message on war, birth control,
poverty and race has sounded rather thin; it may be more
socially useful to speculate upon how the AFDC child will
repay his "debt" to society. Crime by juveniles in the United
States in 1968 increased by 60 percent over the 1967 figure.
No studies are available, but it would be foolish not to believe that welfare poverty has been a galvanizing force.
During the Depression years, poor Jewish boys became
gangsters in Brownsville and Irish and Italian kids robbed
grocery stores for cartons of cigarettes. In Brooklyn neighborhoods now paranoiac about "crime in the streets," the
same sociology impelled black youths to take their places.

During the past year New York City television stations
featured a delightful child in a public-interest commercial
designed, apparently, both to instill and to demonstrate race
pride. When asked his color, the boy would reply, "I am
black. I am beautiful."

After the age of innocence has passed, about eight or nine
years from now, if that child does not embrace a more negative and violent doctrine of Black Power, no thanks will be
owing to this generation of white Americans.

CHAPTER
FOUR

SERVANTS OF THE POOR

I F CHILDREN ARE the principal victims of the present welfare system, then its paradoxes are best illustrated by employees like the Brooklyn case supervisor who is ashamed to tell people in his old neighborhood that he works for the Welfare Department. The attitudes of self-contempt and client hostility to be found among so many of the college graduates who distribute cash assistance benefits have no parallel in other government agencies, or, for that matter, among prisoners and their guards.

On another level, the character of the social work profession* itself has been flawed by the ambivalent role forced

---

* Professionals hold M.S.W. degrees received from graduate schools of social work after a two-year course of study that combines class and field work almost in equal proportions. In addition, the Academy of Certified Social Workers confers certification (similar to C.P.A. status, for example) and some states, like New York, require as a prerequisite to certain positions in public employment licensing restricted to holders of M.S.W. degrees who have also satisfied written and other state requirements.

upon its practitioners in the public assistance sector. Trained to act as a bridge between maladjusted individuals and their environment, social workers, by default of the other professions, have had exclusive theoretical responsibility, not fully exercised, however, for those "pathologicals" whose rehabilitation depends less on expert guidance than on cash in hand.

In a real sense, social work spokesmen are the only communication links to the outside world available to welfare administrators and caseworkers. These last are included in the same total isolation from politics, labor and economics imposed by the system upon recipients.

A SPLIT VOCATION

In the Anglo-American relief scheme, the bureaucrats traditionally have had the unhappy task of satisfying those forces who view cash assistance as a way of easing human want and those who insist that welfare be an instrument of social control. In our time, Washington has forced state and county relief officials to serve two masters.

President Franklin Delano Roosevelt, a fiscal conservative himself, consigned the public assistance titles of the Social Security Act to the watchdog House Ways and Means and the Senate Finance Committees. Since 1935, therefore, Old Age Survivors and Disability Insurance has co-mingled with tax legislation. Those amendments affecting its poor sister, Aid to Families of Dependent Children, are always cemented into the OASDI package in a context which relates less to social needs than to balancing the government's books.

FDR also acquiesced in the desire of Congress not to give jurisdiction over the Social Security Board to Madam Frances Perkins and other "radical" overseers of the Department of Labor. Even the Finance Committee saw the incongruity of separating functions so closely related. "This type of legislation," the Committee reported, "the world over is almost invariably under the direction or supervision of the labor department or its equivalent."

Early in the history of the Act, when the populism of Huey Long threatened to invite fiscal irresponsibility by the states in making relief expenditures, Congress decided that public assistance administration should be removed (if not insulated) from partisan politics. Moreover, welfare reforms of all kinds were not to disturb existing power balances nor intrude, for example, upon national agricultural or labor policies. Congress thus effectively created the unnatural isolation booth in which both clients and welfare personnel find themselves today.

Forced to be nonpolitical, those charged with maintaining the survival income levels of indigents became politically naïve. Alan Keith-Lucas and Charles Schottland have criticized welfare professionals for ignoring the truth that politics is the stuff of life. Representatives of the public agencies and the social work schools have been conspicuously absent from the halls of Congress and state legislatures where citizen groups rightfully lobby for legislation benefiting specific causes or clients.

In fact, most of the state and county administrators probably are not social workers and, in an inverted way, are actually quite political. Appointed by the Executive branch, these men, as Keith-Lucas says, are responsive to public opinion only when their programs are threatened. It would also be foolish to suppose that the same officials are not sensitive to the impact of voter reaction to welfare policies on the political fortunes of their sponsors. A department director in a suburban county where the cost of relief was an inflammatory issue in the fall, 1968, election campaign privately admitted to me that he would not institute a work incentive program until the polls had closed.

Even the social workers probably would agree with former New York City Commissioner Mitchell Ginsberg that his was a dual responsibility, to the taxpayers for economical operations compatible with the legislative intent, and to the clients for distribution of their entitlements. During his tenure and afterward, Ginsberg may have been the most outspoken critic in the country of the present welfare system, but even he has been noticeably wary of attacking New York state and city regulations which are shot through with contradictions.

In the spring of 1969, another reform-minded official in the Department told me that he hoped the Albany legislature would pass a bill sponsored by Assemblymen Peter Berle and Joe Dowd freeing stepparents of financial liability for assistance given to another man's children. I asked if the Department had supported the legislation. He replied, "We couldn't do that because your bill will cost the City money." Why then had the Department's Advisory Council on Public Welfare said nothing? The answer, of course, is that the Council, over one year after the appearance in the New York area of welfare rights activists, scholars and client attorneys, was composed exclusively of representatives of private and religious charitable agencies, other civic organizations and Morris Iushevitz, an official of the Central Labor Council, who also sat on the Board of Education, where in 1968–69 he voted consistently with the UFT against Ocean Hill-Brownsville. All of these, having little or no interest in reform of public assistance, could also be counted on not to disturb the Department's operations.

Litigation challenging welfare policies usually, but not always, encounters token resistance from the defendants, most of whom probably rejoice when the plaintiffs succeed. At the same time, candor is not considered a virtue among bureaucrats in this field and, as Edgar May (author of *The Wasted Americans: The Cost of Our Welfare Dilemma*) and

I separately discovered, welfare officials in the New York–
Northern New Jersey area are notoriously reluctant to co-
operate even with university-sponsored studies of their programs.

Until a few years ago, the national organization of administrators, the American Public Welfare Association,
maintained a cautious attitude toward progressive reform
measures in public assistance. As late as 1966, Gilbert Y.
Steiner described APWA as having a "split personality,"
unsure whether, as the collective voice of its membership, its
first obligation was to advocate clients' rights or efficient,
well-financed operations.

In an exhaustive and generally praiseworthy study* sponsored by APWA in 1961, M. Elaine Burgess and Daniel O.
Price overlooked a pattern of savage, compulsory "employable mother" regulations in the Deep South with the comment, "Apparently there are better work opportunities for
Negroes in rural areas."

At its 1967 annual convention, however, the Association
brought controversy under its roof by inviting civil libertarians and activists as panelists and by giving space to the
National Welfare Rights Organization to distribute its literature.

In May, 1969, George Wiley of NWRO—a few weeks
after James Forman demanded "reparations" from churches
—without much opposition from the public officeholders
and administrators and private agency professionals in attendance, disrupted a social welfare conference in New York
with the claim that social work professionals owed money
to the welfare poor.

At the peak of the government bureaucratic plateaus,
HEW appears to be a supervisory agency that will tolerate,
for prudent reasons, widely conflicting policies in state plans

* *An American Dependency Challenge,* Chapel Hill, University of
North Carolina Press, 1963.

for cash assistance that bear no relation to the purposes of the Social Security Act. The HEW Manual of Administration sometimes reads like a social work textbook while retaining a certain ambiguity as to whether its idealistic expressions are binding on the states.

In times of political crisis affecting public assistance HEW seems to bury its massive head in the sand until the storm has passed, then emerges to lick its wounds. A department publication, *Welfare in Review,* in 1968 blithely referred to the most repressive welfare amendment ever enacted by Congress—the freeze on the number of AFDC children entitled to federal support—as a mere effort by the legislators to reduce the cost of the program. During the 1967 legislative debates, HEW Secretary Wilbur Cohen incurred the wrath of his colleagues in the private sector—the schools and charitable agencies—by advising the legislators that the proposed amendments were "regrettable but necessary." The freeze and other punitive measures were necessary in order to insure passage of the OASDI increases which, as usual, were part of the legislative package. In 1968–69, in separate litigation attacking New York's welfare repayment obligation and Louisiana's policy of paying AFDC recipients less than survival benefits, HEW took the (at best) arguable position that Congress did not intend to restrict the states in these matters.

But even that branch of the social work profession which is truly immune from political pressures—the academic— is not altogether blameless in the welfare drama.

EAGER, BUT ALOOF

Law schools are often accused, with some justice, of attempting, for the sake of image, to carve out a course curriculum larded with disembodied legal principles that have little to do with scholarship, the unfettered search for truth

in the classic sense, or with the actual practice of law. However, since the law is but another branch of human relations,
upon graduation attorneys find that their professional attitudes and interests are greatly influenced by the clients they
serve.

Not so with social workers. Until the current protest-
oriented era, its practitioners, and the social work literature,
evidenced a remarkable detachment from the external forces
—labor unions, employment cycles, wage legislation—that
have a direct impact on the economic well-being of their
clients. To an attorney, this aloofness is particularly surprising because social work, more so even than the law, is a
hybrid of several academic disciplines. Its exponents must
have had significant contact on the undergraduate and graduate levels with the work of psychologists, sociologists and
criminologists, to name only a few. In recent years, the faculties of some schools, including New York University and
Columbia, have also felt the need to offer courses in "legal
rights" to their students.

According to Gilbert Steiner (writing in 1966), however,
social work education normally does not include exposure
to the significance of economic trends or personal income
statistics. Few social work instructors tell their students
about the political aspects of welfare, the legislative process
or lobbying. Perhaps as a consequence of this intellectual
lag—except for Alan Keith-Lucas and the militant pronouncements of Richard Cloward, Frances Piven and Richard Elman—the most persuasive scholarship in public assistance during the past two decades has been produced by
economists Eveline Burns, Robert Lekachman, Robert
Theobald and James Tobin, political scientists Daniel P.
Moynihan and Gilbert Steiner, and by lawyers.

We are still in dire need of studies to establish, for example, what most of us surmise, that the present system *does*
encourage family breakups and discourages remarriages

among recipients, that low factory wages and relatively high welfare benefits *do* create a kind of Speenhamland* situation whereby cities like New York subsidize marginal employers and racket unions. Few economists and scholars in other disciplines undertake such endeavors beyond the stage of analyzing raw statistics because, it is generally agreed, the nitty-gritty of public assistance belongs to social work.

The schools probably give short shrift to the causes of economic dependency because so few of their graduates make careers out of public assistance. The Moreland Commission in 1963 found fewer than 100 graduate social workers employed in *public* welfare agencies in New York State. This deficit was due to a general shortage of social workers and more attractive opportunities elsewhere. A legislative committee reported in 1967 that while the state's private agencies had vacancies ranging from 10 to 15 percent, the public units, including the New York City Department, which needed 574, had a total of 4,708 known vacancies in graduate social work positions. This need contrasted sharply with the fact that in March, 1967, only 2,400 certified social workers (i.e., holders of M.S.W. degrees who have satisfied written and other state requirements) were present in all of New York and in 1966 only 1,617 full-time students were enrolled in the state's nine graduate schools of social work.[†]

The federal government, of course, has the money to provide scholarships, specifically for caseworkers on leave of absence from county welfare departments. With the help of government financing, the colleges also could help alleviate the shortage by granting bachelor's degrees in social work. Undergraduate training and accreditation of this kind presumably would attract entrants into public assistance em-

---

* In 1795, the District of Speenhamland, near Newbury in England, fixed a "rate in aid of wages" to be paid by the community to bring agricultural workers up to a prescribed minimum living standard.

† 1967 Report of the Special Senate Committee on Manpower, p. 45.

ployment who would be better qualified and have more
interest in casework than the mélange of temporarily unemployed accountants, actors and lawyers (some of them quite
sincere and competent, however) that presently pass in and
out of the welfare centers.

Assuming that Congress, prodded by the Nixon Administration, does begin to throw benign glances toward reform
of the welfare system, unless leaders of the social work
profession declare total war on the present manner of
income maintenance, they will continue to have difficulty
persuading their junior or senior members to make careers
out of public assistance.

Today, even professional social workers in the ranks of
caseworkers are not immune from the sense of depression
that afflicts so many people involved in the system. In view
of their involuntary isolation, even from the mainstream of
social work activity among the charitable agencies, professional status does little to erase the stigma that rubs off the
clients onto the workers. Like the transient caseworkers, the
social workers leave in droves for more prestigious employment in the private sector.

In Newark, Nassau County and New York City, the at-
trition rate in 1968 averaged about 30 percent. A study
made in 1964 of New York City caseworkers showed that
the trainee most likely to remain more than one year with
the Department was a married female who had graduated
from a "South Atlantic" (i.e., Negro) college and had scored
low on the Civil Service examination. In other words, a composite portrait emerged from the study of a career caseworker whose other opportunities were sharply limited.*

It takes no research, of course, to ascertain that caseworkers primarily dedicated to the needs of their clients can
be found in public assistance employment; but if they re-

* *The Welfarer*, July–September, 1966, p. 1.

main for periods of years, and retain their equanimity, they probably ignore social work doctrines in order to keep their clients alive.

IF YOU WANT TO BE A BASTARD

In 1967, while on a trip to Arkansas for the Columbia Center on Social Welfare Policy and Law, I complained to a high-ranking welfare official in Little Rock that "visitors" (i.e., caseworkers) in a rural county were threatening to cut off grants to those families participating in a SNCC-sponsored boycott of the local segregated high schools. The official, a trained social worker, deplored such conduct and promised to bring it to a halt. Later, however, we were both indignant (and embarrassed) to learn from her superior that Arkansas law requires school attendance by minors as a prerequisite to receipt of AFDC benefits.

During the NYU study of civil liberties problems in welfare administration, students Jaffe, Feldman and I interviewed clients, lawyers and caseworkers.

In Nassau we found that social work principles, to the detriment of the clients, tended to obfuscate necessary pragmatic considerations. The expressed need for professional detachment ("do not overidentify") led to a general failure to empathize with clients' difficulties. The sound advice not to permit clients to become dependent on the worker translated in practice into a reluctance to do *anything* for recipients. For example, instead of phoning a doctor for a medical report on a disabled applicant, the worker could justify ordering his inarticulate client to do so on the grounds that this sort of thing was "rehabilitative." Client lawyers could be ignored because they intruded upon the warm worker-client relationship. On the other hand, "cheating" by clients had to be uncovered at all costs, not to replenish the public treasury, but to acquaint clients with the necessity of conforming to accepted standards of conduct.

The truth, of course, is that rehabilitation is impossible when destitution is an initial and continuing requirement and budget levels barely sustain life. The system blatantly encourages amateur fraud by administrators and caseworkers as well as clients. The worker-client relationship in the social work sense seldom exists in public welfare.

Mrs. Elaine Shulman, a psychiatric social worker, had had peripheral but agreeable contacts with public welfare while employed with a private agency. After six months of daily contact with the Department, however, while on the staff of the Nassau Law Services Committee, Mrs. Shulman told me she would discourage graduate social work students from entering public assistance employment unless, perhaps, the schools made a much greater commitment of faculty and students to field work in the public sector. "The System," she said, "corrupts social workers."

In Newark, the administrator of the categorical programs leaves much to the discretion of his workers. On balance, this approach seems to benefit the clients. While acquiescence in a request for a special grant means extra paper work, aggravation from the client might be worse, and the home economist will usually agree to such requests unless, in the words of one caseworker, "you panic her by asking for too much at one time."

In Newark the "good" caseworker "pushes" a claim through the bureaucratic labyrinth. He only comes to visit a client when absolutely necessary. Newark caseworker Ricky Lissek says, "If you want to do the right thing for a client you learn the rules, then you look for loopholes or you bend the language and you beat your supervisor over the head with it until he approves your request for extra clothing. Then your client might wait three days for the check to be sent out, or if it is an emergency you can carry your memo

through every step of the process and deliver the check your-
self the same day." Why don't all the workers learn the rules?
"Their supervisors don't tell them they're supposed to," says
Ricky's colleague Connie Brown.

"If you want to be a bastard," said one supervisor, "you
can try to find out if her boy friend is giving her money, but
who wants to bother? The Department won't give you any
medals for looking under a client's bed, and, let's face it,
who has the guts for that sort of thing?"

Welfare practice is almost always more restrictive than
the written statutes and regulations. It takes less effort to
deny a claim for benefits in close cases than to search for
administrative loopholes to justify payment. The "good"
caseworker in Newark accepts the present reality of the system and, without illusions, attempts to live with it. She masters the manual of administration to justify special allowances
for education, children's clothing, etc. If the need is critical
and valid but technically disallowed, she and her supervisor
call it by another name and submit the authorization.

We also found, in our study, a different breed of caseworker in Newark. Whereas in Nassau, the quasi-profes-
sional pose of the workers probably acerbated the prejudices
they brought with them from their Irish and German middle-
class environments, their counterparts across the Hudson,
like the New York City group, tended to be Jewish, Negro
or Italian, and very much influenced by the radical move-
ments of our times.

In both areas, the administrators refused to permit us to
interview caseworkers. In Nassau, our client and lawyer contacts failed to produce any workers willing to volunteer, but
in Newark we had an adequate (for our purposes) sampling
of young militants eager to help change the system. Some,
like Ricky Lissek, had civil rights backgrounds and others,
admittedly, were more interested in revolutionizing society.

When the Students for a Democratic Society (Tom Hayden's Newark Community Union Project) unit in the predominantly black Central Ward began to fade in 1967, with the advent of Black Power, Connie Brown and about five other associates of Hayden, who of course had since endorsed black separatism, gravitated, naturally enough, toward jobs in the Essex County Welfare Department. When I met them, the SDS caseworkers seemed as baffled by the system as the rest of us and even less certain than the welfare rights organizers about how to destroy it.

Connie and her friends were surprisingly low-keyed about the deficiencies of their employer and the prejudices of their co-workers. They included themselves in the criticism ("All of us should be required to report to the Center every day when in the field") and seemed more ready to place primary blame for client grievances upon the impersonal welfare *apparat* which, they felt, sapped the energies of all its human components. Allan Gould might have uttered the last word of the despairing rebel when he said, "Poverty becomes boring after awhile. Nothing seems to change."

In New York City, the welfare experience, like everything else, may be atypical; but many among the hundreds of new caseworkers recruited by the Department in 1966–68 were kin, like Connie Brown and her friends, to the wave of student and recent graduate activists who brought Columbia to a halt or worked for Senator Eugene McCarthy's Presidential candidacy.

The welfare component of the New Left in New York City gave new vitality to the reform-minded leadership of the caseworkers' union, Social Service Employees Union, and like their outnumbered brothers and sisters in Newark brought both compassion and flair to welfare employment. At the intake units in the Brooklyn centers, for example, if a caseworker calls amiably for "*Mrs.* Smith," she probably wears a miniskirt and long hair. The male caseworker, with a similarly respectful attitude toward his clients, might appear with a beard and sandals.

Even in New York, the new breed of caseworker constitutes a distinct minority on the staff and, of course, not all of them remain. But the activist element makes up in energy and dedication what it lacks in numbers, and enough of them have stayed long enough, assisted by replacements, to inject a breath of life into a dormant system. One cannot see these young people educating clients about welfare or arithmetic on their own time late at night in sections of Newark and Brownsville, where even white and black policemen refuse to walk alone, without feeling that whatever changes take place in welfare, the system, like politics, will never be the same again.

A PECULIAR RESPONSIBILITY

The militants, whose idealism seems to focus both on the Vietnam war and on domestic poverty, have also made their way into the schools of social work. There, because of a climate increasingly sympathetic to their views and, more particularly, because of a growing sentiment among some social work teachers that welfare poverty is their special concern, the new student idealists stand a better chance than older caseworkers of making deep inroads into welfare poverty.

Men and women on the faculties who for years have been arguing for greater emphasis on the "community organization" component of the curriculum have welcomed professional trainees not too timid about their careers to participate in antiwar demonstrations. This generation of students has been able to choose field work placements with organizations as diverse as the American Jewish Congress, the American

Civil Liberties Union, and the Nassau Welfare Tenants' Co-ordinating Council.

Hugh Wilson, a fairly successful chief rights organizer in Nassau, and a graduate social worker himself, believes that helping people to help themselves by radicalizing their social and economic milieu is a return to the pristine faith of Edith Abbott and other social work pioneers.

As with the caseworkers, the reform-minded graduates of social work schools are a vocal minority in a profession that supplies trained social engineers to probation departments and mental institutions, as well as private adoption agencies. But the private agencies, with all of their resources and prestige, have also been moving toward a greater recognition of their responsibilities to society at large. Most important, however, wherever they are, social workers see themselves, and are regarded, as being among the professional "do-gooders" whose talents, like those of architects, have emerged in recent years as particularly helpful to the resolution of the urban dilemma.

Students at Chicago's School of Social Service Administration published for several years a *Guaranteed Annual Income Newsletter* which may have been (until discontinued in 1969) the most valuable, concise periodical on economic developments in welfare poverty. In New York City, the faculties at Columbia and NYU stand somewhat to the left of their colleagues in the other disciplines. During the spring, 1968, demonstrations on Morningside Heights, Columbia's School of Social Work took second place only to Architecture in voicing support for the cause of democratic reform. At NYU, early on the morning of the April Mobilization for Peace, a large contingent of faculty and students breakfasted at the home of Dean Alex Rosen before boarding buses for Washington. Professors Richard Cloward and Frances Fox Piven of Columbia, who successfully advocated a costly "special grants" campaign in New York City as a tactic to bring down the system, have walked with recipients in picket lines at City Hall.

Ironically, the "community organization" sector, growing in strength with the temper and needs of the times, has brought a fresh crisis of identity to the social work profession which fought for years to achieve prestige status for its practitioners. The CO people argue, however, that in the past academics ambitiously, but unnecessarily, devoted much of their efforts to carving out a distinct body of knowledge for their curricula. The newcomers also contend that during the past three decades the tone has been set by workers in the private agencies who probably overreacted to the public image of their profession that derived from cash assistance employment and which was dramatized derisively in the Broadway musical *West Side Story*.

To this outsider, it also seems that the marvelous synthesis of diverse streams of knowledge that do or should go into the social worker's training will always serve to differentiate him, even in the fluid and volatile racial ghettoes, from his co-workers in the legal profession and in the ministry. Moreover, while the social work activist perhaps lacks the prestige and, therefore, the equivalent power to effectuate change that priests and lawyers bring with them into poverty neighborhoods, the same social worker will have less difficulty persuading *his* colleagues in the private agencies or elsewhere that their common vocation not only tolerates but insists on work among the poor.

TWO

THE
LAWYERS

CHAPTER
FIVE

KEEPING THE POOR
IN THEIR PLACE

*The law not only regards life and member and
protects every man in the enjoyment of them, but
also furnishes him with everything necessary for
their support. For there is no man so indigent or
wretched, but he may demand a supply sufficient
for all the necessaries of life from the more opulent
part of the community, by means of the several
statutes enacted for the relief of the poor.*

> —*Blackstone,* Commentaries on the Laws of
> England*

THE MODERN PUBLIC welfare system, which began
with the English Poor Law Reform of 1834, migrated to the United States during the next three
decades; though battered, it remains remarkably vigorous

* Book I, chapter I, "Of the Absolute Rights of Individuals" (12th
ed., London, 1793), p. 131.

today, and could not have survived at all without the force of law. The courts provided the moral coercion needed to join Social Darwinism, Protestant Christianity and American chauvinism in one nationwide formula for the care and feeding of the poor.

An almost forgotten jurist may be more responsible than any of his more illustrious fellows for the present condition of the welfare poor. David Josiah Brewer served as a justice of the United States Supreme Court from 1890 until his death in 1910. The influential Yale sociologist William Graham Sumner, who once said, "There are no rights. The world owes nobody a living," died the same year. Brewer, a Yalie himself, symbolizes, from the standpoint of the sans-culottes, the best and the worst in the American legal tradition.

THE IDEAL AMERICAN

This phrase appeared in the title of a magazine article eulogizing Brewer. Among liberal scholars Brewer has the reputation of being a conservative on the most conservative bench in Supreme Court history, but in his lifetime, Justice Brewer was famous on several continents as an expert on international law and was known to be a champion of women's suffrage and a foe of both labor and corporate monopolies. A deeply religious and stoic man all his life, David Brewer left the comfort and prestige of the Eastern legal establishment—he was a nephew of David Dudley Field of New York—to make his career in "Bloody Kansas."

Brewer also lectured extensively and became an unofficial spokesman for the Court during his tenure. Even after his death, Brewer's philosophy undoubtedly influenced the unveering "interventionist" course followed by the Court which caused Oliver Wendell Holmes, from 1905 to his retirement in 1932, to dissent in over 40 out of 180 decisions nullifying in the name of substantive due process state and federal laws that sought to regulate business activities.

Justice Brewer deserves to be remembered by the historians, not because of his family connections or intellectual gifts but because he rationalized and refined the coarse prejudices of the American Establishment at the turn of the century, which in the words of Clinton Rossiter was "politically, socially, culturally, and in the most obvious sense, antiradical." Brewer was able to do this because in addition to his other assets, qualities of mind and prejudices, Brewer's strength of character reflected the peculiar values most admired by his generation.

In Brewer's time, what was good and wholesome for the judges was at least palatable for America. But the Court majorities in those years also took a paranoiac view of themselves on the legal barricades defending rugged individualism against the disciples of Karl Marx. Oliver Wendell Holmes, dissenting in a 1906 decision which declared unconstitutional a New York statute limiting employment in bakeries to sixty hours per week and ten hours per day, reminded his brothers that the Fourteenth Amendment did not enact Herbert Spencer's "Social Statics," i.e., the doctrine of laissez-faire carried to the extreme of barring state regulations in education, welfare, labor-management relations, etc. The other judges, however, noted darkly that "this interference . . . with the ordinary trades and occupations of the people seems to be on the increase"; they went on to imply sinister motives on the part of that hotbed of Bolshevik intrigue, the Albany legislature.

Brewer's Court is best remembered for its clever adaptation of the due process clause of the Fifth and Fourteenth Amendments to protect property interests. A sympathetic critic quotes his hero's description of the ideal government as "that which protects to the fullest extent each individual, rich or poor, high or low, in the possession of his property and the pursuit of his business." This is a nice equation between the classes, except that few among the poor are likely to require this kind of protection. In addition, Brewer's egalitarian philosophy permitted him to sacrifice the intangible "property" rights of workers to labor under safe conditions or to organize collectively, to the overwhelming right of a businessman to operate without interference from the state.

We may also surmise that Brewer, like some of his successors on the bench today, would balance to her detriment the civil rights of an AFDC mother against the obligation of a state to reduce its welfare costs.

David Brewer, the strict Calvinist, also accepted as hard dogma the fact that few people in any community would possess its wealth, but he did not attribute this to either fortune or human malice. Brewer, along with Sumner and Spencer, believed that the masses are "unwilling to endure that long self-denial and saving which makes accumulation possible." In order to justify restricting the Good Things of Life to a few without impairing the capitalist system, Brewer and others like him had to link in their own minds poverty with dissolute or slothful living.

In another one of his Yale lectures, the judge noted that the phrase "over the hill to the poorhouse" reflects the imperfection of human law, but proceeded to emphasize his Christian notion that "to every right-thinking person" the obligation to care for the aged parent is as sacred as any. In other words, for those parents and children that matter, the poorhouse will not be a problem.

The passage of time, of course, has made much of Brewer's thought obsolete. It is impossible any more for a jurist to isolate himself on Mount Olympus when modern communications media flood his senses with evidence that there is economic exploitation, that the oppressed minorities are rising, and that the Old Order faces its most serious threat in American history.

But despite the changes there are still, and always will be, many men in the Brewer mold in the financial power centers of our civilization and in the lily-white Christian suburbs of our large cities. Furthermore, Judge Brewer's enduring reputation among legal scholars probably should rely most on a much-cited opinion by the jurist in 1875 when he was a justice of the Kansas Supreme Court. To this day, *Griffith v. Osawkee Township* expresses the prevailing law among most of the states and the federal government that only the rejects of society are entitled to public assistance.

DEFINING THE WELFARE POOR

In *Osawkee,* Judge Brewer voided an act of the Kansas legislature authorizing a bond issue for the relief of drought-stricken farmers. This, he held, was unlawful legislation that intended to benefit a "special class" of citizen. In so doing, Brewer brilliantly articulated the states' obligation to relieve the poor in natural law terms which, in context, accommodated the principle to the American regard for unaided, individual achievement.

Said the judge, "the care of those unable to care for themselves is among the unquestioned objects of public duty . . . in obedience to the impulses of common humanity, it is everywhere so recognized." However, only the "pauper" may draw from public funds. For the government simply to aid all poor persons would require the state to "equalize the property of its citizens." Those who today wonder why relief payments under the Social Security Act do not achieve the "self-support" objectives of the statute should read *Osawkee.* There, Judge Brewer further defined the pauper as one "entirely destitute and helpless and therefore dependent upon public charity." The prospective recipient not only must be in want but "unable to prevent or remove such want." Brewer thus gave judicial sanction in the United States to the hallowed English notion that must have crossed the Atlantic on the *Mayflower:* that the proper objects of relief were the lame, impotent and decrepit of society.

Brewer translated the secular, liberal concept of the English reformers of 1834 into terms compatible even today with practice in most Christian sects. So, too, Congress in 1935 expressed the pious hope that payments under the public assistance titles of the Social Security Act would provide the means and generate the desire among recipients to get off the rolls. At the same time, the legislators imposed the statute upon a relief foundation universally rotted by Brewer's "destitution" rationale. In 1939, Congress, codifying this principle, expanded its own paradox by amending the Act to compel the states in determining need to take into consideration "*any* other income and resources."

LAWYERS STAY AWAY

To anyone familiar with the *Osawkee* decision, it is not surprising that social workers, until a decade ago, would have nothing to do with lawyers. According to the 1957 classic by welfare administrator Alan Keith-Lucas (*Decisions about People in Need: A Study of Administrative Responsiveness in Public Assistance*), the "social work professions have the same attitude to the law as they might to a dangerous weapon: useful, certainly, if one has control over it but otherwise best not played with." It was the rigidity and, to them, the alien quality of the legal process that turned off the social workers.

Only lawyers profited from the dreary business of settlement and removal litigation which is one of the scandals of relief administration in this country. Social workers stood aghast while counsel debated whether John Jones had established a legal settlement with his dependents in X before coming down with diphtheria. In one case a dispute between two counties in Wisconsin over liability for relief payments totaling about ninety dollars dragged through the courts for almost two years.

Having criticized the role of the judiciary and the legal profession, generally, in social welfare, it is only fair to describe the other side of the coin. For the most part, the courts approached public assistance tangentially; they were seldom asked to confront and decide substantive issues directly affecting clients' rights. Until recently, a body of Poor Man's Law never had a chance to develop because it was unheard of for attorneys to appear at welfare centers or at eviction hearings.

Until the War on Poverty began, the legal profession, in the context of the traditional attorney-client relationship, quite rightly could not be viewed as a vehicle for any kind of social change. Lawyers still are a luxury for all except the wealthy and an unfortunate necessity for all classes. Public benefits programs which require destitution (cash assistance) or near-poverty (public housing) as an eligibility requirement, together with their attendant and pervasive indignities, were not likely to attract even the most idealistic practitioners.

The Legal Aid Societies performed commendably in representing indigents in civil and criminal cases but because of limited resources and ideological orientation, focused on individual grievances rather than test cases designed to aid poor persons as an economic *class*.

Moreover, an indigenous paternalism among social workers and an understandable desire to carve out a distinct and honorable profession generated antagonisms toward other disciplines, especially the law, which by encompassing many aspects of human relations in its scope, always presented a potential threat to social workers unsure of the boundaries and the content of their own terrain.

Several years ago Elizabeth Wickenden of the National Social Welfare Assembly and a national spokesman for reform-minded social welfare professionals persuaded Edward Sparer, the legal director of Mobilization for Youth, to devote his full-time efforts to welfare client representation. Shortly thereafter, other attorneys financed by the legal services component of the Economic Opportunity Act, as well as older groups like the American Civil Liberties Union, the Scholarship, Education and Defense Fund for Racial Equality and the NAACP, Inc., Fund, began to enter the field.

The War on Poverty also coincided with the growing dominance of the activist, community-organization sector of the social work profession. Whereas the old one-for-one, caseworker to client, social work approach saw attorneys as an unnecessary and nontherapeutic obstacle, Dr. Charles Grosser of New York University and Dr. Richard Cloward of Columbia and other younger men and women oriented to group work came to regard lawyers as allies in the cause of client rehabilitation, which is of the essence in the social work vocation. They saw legal representation as a useful instrument to resolve the conflicts of disadvantaged clients with society.

ANARCHY IN THE WELFARE SECTOR

If "rehabilitation" is the key word of the social work profession, then "order" best describes the lawyers' hangup. Private practitioners, in particular, by training and necessity are positivists. They are in love with precedent. The practicing lawyer wants to be able to tell his client what the law is and generally resents judicial uncertainties, vague statutes and abrupt departures from the norm. Even government, union and corporation attorneys are obsessed with the need for uniformity of application of statutory law and administrative regulations.

Furthermore, while not every lawyer is a civil libertarian and some are capable of fantastic balancing acts when it comes to individual rights against the interests of the state, legal training predisposes a man to abhor arbitrary or objectively unreasonable conduct by public officials, particularly when directed, for no good reason, at a single individual or class.

The most jaded practitioner who ventures into the field of public welfare administration expresses surprise at the almost complete absence of a rule of law. He finds hard-pressed state and local directors spending most of their time recruiting personnel for unappetizing, underpaid jobs, or lobbying for policy changes or for funds for politically unpopular programs. The more candid among them will admit that they have little time for protection of clients' legal rights; nor, for that matter, are they necessarily informed about practices in the field which may violate express departmental policy, humane and otherwise.

Since economy is a paramount consideration in public assistance, caseworkers in every state complete endless forms to insure federal reimbursements and for the benefit of legislators, while they and their supervisors play God with human needs. For caseworkers often are a law unto themselves. Policemen, court clerks, parks department guards, sanitationmen, all are notorious for making their own rules or dispensing instant justice, but seldom with the authority enjoyed by caseworkers. Even Alan Keith-Lucas, a professional welfare administrator and no friend of attorneys, conceded the need for tighter controls over caseworkers who, he said, "are apt to find in the law what they wish to find in it."

Paradoxically, from the client's point of view the good caseworker may be an actor marking time until his next stage offer who could not care less whether the client lied about her "missing" blankets. The truly diligent worker, who might equate his role with that of an auto claims investigator, is despised. There is a need for test-case litigation in public welfare, as in civil rights matters, both as an educative process and in order to establish legal beachheads. But the fact is that the daily concern of most recipients involves the denial of benefits under *existing* administrative policies and practices.

So insensitive is welfare administration to basic concepts of clients' rights that most lower-echelon officials are also oblivious to the power of lawyers to make trouble for them. Phone calls are not returned. Letters are not answered. Most welfare centers in New York City, including the new ones, do not have public telephone booths. Whatever the intention, this practice has the effect of inconveniencing the attorney (as well as his client) and discouraging return visits.

I once made an appointment to visit a supervisor at a Brooklyn center. My secretary, confirming the appointment, was told that Mrs. X has an interview with Mrs. Y (my client) but not with Mr. Graham. He may be present, said Mrs. X, but he may not participate. At the center we were kept waiting an hour until a subordinate appeared who seemed more intent on interrogating my client than discussing the case with me. He promised to phone me with their decision. Instead the supervisor phoned my client and she, somewhat inarticulately, relayed the decision to me.

In this case, I and Marty Garbus of the American Civil Liberties Union ultimately filed a complaint in federal court alleging, among other things, a violation of the right to counsel. The city and state welfare commissioners expressed astonishment at the need for such action. The right to counsel, they said, was implicit in New York welfare administration. Was it explicit anywhere, I asked, knowing that the official manuals contained nothing on the subject? I was referred to a transmittal letter sent to the centers by the New York City Commissioner which said that a "representative" may "appear" at all "quasi-judicial" proceedings. We settled this aspect of the litigation with a comprehensive stipulation agreed to by the city and state welfare departments permitting recipients to be represented at all conferences affecting their benefits by counsel of their choice. Counsel was to be directly notified of all decisions in the matter. Only a few months later the stipulation was rejected, no reason being given, in a federal suit brought by the Nassau Law Services Committee attacking denial of the right to counsel in that county.

This controversy illustrates the built-in communications problem in this area. It involved City Commissioner Mitchell Ginsberg, perhaps the most reform-minded administrator in the country (who is now the top antipoverty official in New York City), and State Commissioner George K. Wyman, who as consultant to the Ad Hoc Committee on Public Welfare was instrumental in the passage of the progressive 1962 amendments to the Social Security Act.

A RIGHT TO WELFARE

It would be wrong, however, to attribute the preoccupations of administrators and aberrations in the field entirely to the absence of representation. Rather, much of the explanation lies in the Poor Law tradition of contempt for the clients. As late as 1941, a New York court described old-age assistance as "charity" and the person accepting it as having "consented to the provisions of the law under which charity is bestowed" (*Wilkie v. O'Connor*).

The appeal process in categorical (federally financed) assistance, which includes "fair hearings"* mandated by the Social Security Act, is a good argument for the proposition that welfare is a right hedged in by procedural safeguards, rather than a handout. In practice, however, fair hearings held in libertarian New York City, where one-fifth of the nation's lawyers have offices, would shock the freshman class at the University of Alabama Law School. The public is not admitted. Often the attorney is not permitted to examine the case record to be used against his client. Cross-examination is available but often cannot be utilized because the case-worker probably will not appear at the hearing. Only select decisions are reported by the State Commissioner for public use and seldom constitute what the lawyers call *stare decisis* (i.e., precedent). The recommendations of the hearing examiner are not furnished to the client or her attorney.

The benign social work concept of "confidentiality,"† intended by the Social Security Act to protect clients and the social work relationship, in the context of the existing system usually operates to the client's detriment. Like other policies intended for good purposes, confidentiality has been distorted into another instrument of social control by

---

* "Fair hearings," a statutory term of art, are available to all persons aggrieved in any fashion by the actions of local welfare officials in respect to federally financed benefits. (New York for the past two years has extended the right to a fair hearing to the general assistance category.) The hearings are conducted by examiners appointed by the State Commissioner and decisions issue in his name. The statutory fair hearing is usually held some weeks after discontinuance of assistance, for example. After much agitation by clients' lawyers for reform, the State Department in 1968 issued a new regulation providing for a hearing *de novo* prior to the suspension or termination of benefits before another supervisor in the local department. With typical inconsistency the state permitted the local departments to adopt an alternative procedure which in effect gave clients no more right to a "prior hearing" than they had before. New York City for lack of manpower chose the alternative, which was later declared unconstitutional by a federal court.

† The Social Security Act prohibits disclosure of welfare records except to authorized public officials. Some courts in New York have interpreted the requirement literally to deny access by a client to her own records for use in litigation, etc.

denying access to individual clients' records or to facts about the system generally to lawyers, journalists or others intent on positive reforms.

For example, the social work emphasis on "rehabilitation" does represent a civilized advance over the attitude expressed by the United States Supreme Court in 1841 that paupers are a "moral pestilence" (*City of New York v. Miln*). But if this approach—happily seized upon by legislators as promising reduced costs as clients are taken off the rolls—does not suggest previous delinquency, it does contain the implied warning that we can write off the true pathologicals on the relief rolls as well as those who will require permanent assistance because of large families, low wages and family breakups.

Since the best impulses of the orthodox social work approach seem to have been used to gull the legislators into voting for greater appropriations for work training and other services for clients on the false promise that economies would result, it is not surprising that our representatives, seeing no return for their money, reacted, albeit despicably, by freezing the number of children on the AFDC rolls as of January, 1968. (Congress later reversed itself and revoked the freeze.)

Moreover, the concept of rehabilitation, the cornerstone of the 1962 amendments, tended to dilute the argument that an individual who qualifies has a right to receive public assistance without strings attached.

Today, the new social welfare lawyers and the activists in the social work profession emphasize, instead of rehabilitation, the need for a legal rights concept and cash in hand. A variety of commentators, among them Justice William O. Douglas, equate, for purposes of entitlement, the client's due process right to appeal his conviction because of his poverty with the statutory, constitutional or common law right of a person not to die in the streets or in a Mississippi cotton patch because of *his* poverty.

Significantly, the new social work attitudes were reflected in the Report of the President's Advisory Council on Public Welfare delivered to the Secretary of Health, Education and Welfare in June, 1966. In addition to procedural protections designed to insure prompt and courteous treatment, the Report recommended that adequate benefits, consistent with society's standards for income maintenance, be "available on a dignified basis as a matter of legal right."

From a lawyer's point of view, the 1966 Report was a remarkable document for several reasons. It presented legal rights as the core requirement if public assistance was to achieve either economic or social objectives. To those libertarians unfamiliar with the law of public assistance, it must have been a shock to read that such rights are not recognized in practice. The Report also cloaked legal rights in substantive legislative proposals.

These recommendations by a national cross section of expert technicians, administrators, and representatives of labor, business and the professions appointed by the President of the United States to date has been totally ignored by the Congress and timidly implemented in part by HEW and state welfare officials.

The Advisory Council Report also implicitly adopts the *parens patriae* views of seminal-rights theorist A. Delafield Smith. Smith wrote in the forties and fifties that the scope of a citizen's "Right to Life" expanded as his access to natural resources contracted and as his dependence on the government for support increased. Smith went so far as to suggest that the Roman Empire collapsed because its rulers never conceived of establishing an economic security system as a matter of legal right.

Smith's thinking sounds radical only if one does not know that in 1793 the respected jurist Sir William Blackstone wrote that even the most wretched citizen had a right to demand not "survival benefits" but the "necessaries of life."

While Blackstone lamented the fact that "miserable shifts and expedients" had been adopted from time to time, we may conclude, nevertheless, from his informed writings and those of Charles Dickens and the Poor Law historians Sidney and Beatrice Webb, that the Dark Ages for welfare recipients did not really begin until the Poor Law Reform of 1834.

Ultimately Congress may be more responsive to the "Right to Life" concept than the judiciary, but at the present writing this seems doubtful. Recent Supreme Court decisions, striking down residence requirements and "substitute parent" regulations restricting the receipt of welfare benefits, have been magnificent instruments of reform.

But faster progress could have been made if both the legal and the social work professions had heeded Smith's call two decades ago for the greater involvement of lawyers in public welfare. Test-case litigation educates judges and administrators. Judges, as well as administrators, must be battered out of safe but tepid channels of thought. The rights concept, no matter how explicitly defined by the courts, is meaningless in practice if lawyers are not available to pressure and, by their mere presence at the welfare centers, to coerce administrators to focus on elemental fairness in distributing benefits.

However, day-to-day welfare administration is such that those are misguided who see the legal process, as it now exists, as the overwhelming answer to the prayers of the recipients.

Until the distributions system is changed radically, diligent caseworkers will continue to look for men's shoes in the AFDC mother's bedroom. At a federal court hearing in the District of Columbia in an OEO-sponsored case seeking to uphold the right to privacy, two welfare investigators blithely admitted that it was their practice to move fast through an apartment until the client began to complain vociferously. Then they left the scene. However, the investigators said, few clients were bold enough to object at the outset of the search and less than 1 percent refused them admittance to the dwelling.* As late as May, 1969, the New York City Department terminated recipients who denied welfare investigators without warrants access to their homes.†️ It is difficult to assert one's civil liberties when dependent on the aggressor for food, clothing and shelter allowances.

After the welfare test-case period has reached its peak, perhaps ten years from now, the contribution of the legal profession to reform will be as limited as the cumbersome tools lawyers must employ in their work and the archaic system within which they must function.

The day-to-day grievances of recipients will continue to vary from locality to locality and from caseworker to caseworker. Despite the impression conveyed by much of the legal literature, the typical welfare client problem is substantive. It should not require the exclusive services of an attorney. The use of law students working under an attorney's supervision to make phone calls, write letters and appear at the centers and at fair hearings is more economical and probably more efficient. Furthermore, this kind of experience, as opposed to opening windows and running errands for partners in a firm, will enrich a law school career and educate in the problems of the poor the men and women who may go on to become tomorrow's Establishment figures.

Lay advocates also can be easily trained by attorneys in client "representation." Since most of the welfare grievances involve budget computations or the failure of a new caseworker to understand existing policies, lay advocates of reasonable intelligence—including, and perhaps especially, former and current recipients—can perform a distinct, ongoing, quasi-legal service. At the very worst, the advocates might unduly harass the conscientious caseworker but, even here, the same worker will be pressured into reading the rules

---

* *New Republic,* October 21, 1967, p. 13.
† This practice was subsequently declared unconstitutional by a New York federal court.

and checking more often with her supervisor. At best, such advocates employed in legal services or community action programs will sift out unmerited complaints and so earn the trust of the diligent caseworker; by their access to and their ability to use a telephone, these client representatives can bridge the gulf between the nether world of the AFDC mother and the professionals who have difficulty relating to her and her problems.

If it is good for a poor person to have his own attorney, it may be even better for the AFDC mother to hear Bernice McLean of Brownsville, a home relief recipient, winning a point with a welfare supervisor or tearing into the food stamp program at a client organizing rally.

It may come to pass, therefore, that after the new-old legal principles are engraved on the welfare center doors, the ultimate contribution of the legal profession to public assistance will be a massive, grass-roots education program. The knowledge, on the part of AFDC mothers, of their rights and the ability to protest their denial at least may take their children out of the welfare dependency cycle.

At the moment, however, the large question is to what extent the successors of David Josiah Brewer are willing to commit their prestige and resources on behalf of the poor.

CHAPTER
SIX

CHANGING THE IMAGE
---

*The Economic Opportunity Act and its provision
for the legal services program is . . . perhaps the
most important evidence that law is again coming
alive as a living process responsive to changing
human needs.*

> —*Justice William Brennan addressing the Con-
> ference on Legal Services Programs in War-
> renton, Virginia, November 15, 1966*

THE NEW INVOLVEMENT of the legal profession with
the poor seems out of character only to those who
misunderstand the role of the Anglo-American
lawyer. The conservative reputation that the profession
rightly has acquired derives only in part from the attorney's
obligation as an "officer of the court" to sustain society's
rule of law. Pillars of the Bar, as a class, appear to be intent
on maintaining the status quo only because private practi-

tioners of necessity must go where the money is, and the poor are always elsewhere.

How he earns his fees does not necessarily describe the attorney. Philosophically, there is room on the same side of the Bar for the man who argues in the Supreme Court for General Motors and for the man who tries to persuade a district court judge that pacifists wearing masks have a constitutional right to picket Saint Patrick's Cathedral. Moreover, practice in the common law mode ordinarily does not permit the lawyer to maintain a safe distance between himself and his paying client. Like the Teuton chief who articulated the grievances of his tribe to an enemy band as a hopeful and orderly way of forestalling a blood feud, the Anglo-American advocate is less an instrument of justice than of redress for one of the antagonists. Consequently, the American lawyer, wherever he practices, must identify not only with his client's cause, but also with his client.

At the same time, in a free-market economy, the practicing lawyer delivers himself and his time only in proportion to the fee he may expect. Small practitioners who handle minor criminal cases have made an art out of not getting to know their clients. For many, the beauty of a lower-court criminal practice is that a plea of guilty signals the end of the trial attorney's case and of all contact with the defendant. It is, however, one of the proudest boasts of the entire profession on both sides of the Atlantic that the criminal advocate in theory, if not always in practice, and especially where serious charges have been leveled, goes all out for his client. The defender who admits to doing less would be denounced even by the most reactionary of his brothers at the Bar.

In the noncriminal area, a restrained, impersonal approach does not satisfy the needs of corporate clients who demand ongoing representation. For them, the able practitioner must understand and speak their language; sometimes he must be more than a technician when the bargain is about to jell over the second martini. So, too, the attorney who wants to lend his skills both to remedy the immediate problems of poor clients and to eradicate the root causes of the criminal activity and civil disorders must be willing to suffer the incoherence, delusions, the smells and the dirty streets that are indigenous to storefront practice.

Assuming that the reasonable monetary needs of the Poor Man's lawyer are met by government financing, there is no theoretical obstacle under our system of law to his rendering the same quality and kinds of service available to the affluent. The total involvement of lawyers in ghetto practice as instruments of the War on Poverty is more than compatible with the American practitioner's vision of himself; it may also be vital to the survival of our cities.

TUNING IN

The theoreticians of the Economic Opportunity Act linked the new legal services operations to community action programs and emphasized their *neighborhood* aspect. Former OEO Director Sargent Shriver characterized legal services financed by the War on Poverty as "one of the crucial components of any broad and effective program for remedying slum conditions." The theory is that the federal monies will be spent best not by providing counsel in the traditional, colonial manner but by giving the poor legal strength with which they can identify. A practitioner in a Brooklyn storefront who looks to Manhattan for his instructions and leaves his work area by nightfall will not satisfy the leaders of the poor or help solve their basic problems.

William Stringfellow demonstrated in *My People Is the Enemy* that it is possible also for a lawyer to maintain his professional poise while dispensing legal advice on a Harlem streetcorner or while noshing over local politics at Frank's Restaurant on 125th Street.

Stringfellow also anticipated the legal services component of the War on Poverty with his low-keyed approach to the practice of law in the ghetto. Motivated by his Christian commitment, he moved quietly into a slum neighborhood in East Harlem and waited for the other residents to get used to seeing him around. Stringfellow eventually won the trust of the community because, unlike most visitors to the ghetto, he did not come on strong, had something to offer and evidently planned to stay awhile.

It is expected that the new programs will operate law offices somewhat more structured than Stringfellow's but in the same genre. Storefronts will be utilized wherever feasible in order to permit easy and casual access off the streets. Investigators will assist attorneys in gathering factual data and in locating missing landlords. Social workers will lend their expertise on technical matters, such as the fine points of welfare regulations, in communicating with clients, and, in general, reminding attorneys that the law, as the late Judge Jerome Frank often pointed out, is a very fallible instrument of redress.

The one aspect of the new approach which impresses Mrs. Elaine Shulman, a psychiatric social worker with the OEO legal project in Nassau County, is the "availability" of the lawyers. "The people know that they can wander in anytime. They might have to wait a while but they know they'll get service and nobody's going to get too mad at them for being late."

The neighborhood offices are to maintain "client" files rather than case files. These will reflect the ongoing attorney-client relationship and will permit the lawyer handling the latest grievance to review quickly the client's legal history and his life situation. The "one shot" aspect of much of private practice is the single complaint leveled, sometimes unfairly, against the Legal Aid Societies:

The next time you appear in court you got a new Legal Aid lawyer. He don't know you and you got to tell him your whole story all over again—like how your husband left you three years ago and you got to raise three teen-agers all by yourself with some welfare help and one of them is heading for the electric chair and that's why you are in court all the time.—Mrs. S., member, CUSA-Saratoga Avenue, a welfare clients' group.

In addition to getting to know their clients, their families, where they live and how they live, the OEO attorneys will be expected to attend civic council and block association meetings, social affairs, tree-planting ceremonies, protest rallies, etc. Most important, because of their involvement, the new lawyers presumably will gain an appreciation of the "subculture" of poverty described in detail by Oscar Lewis as well as the "culture," sometimes referred to as the "Swing" or "Soul," of the racial ghetto.

The Poor Man's lawyer also must maintain double standards; he must, if he wants to keep both his sanity and his professionalism, insist on order in his own affairs yet tolerate a large amount of confusion that gathers around his clients.

Poor clients are notoriously ungrateful. In the eyes of a welfare recipient who does not know the difference between due process and equal protection but does know she suffered an injustice, the lost case may be a sellout. All of this, of course, is deplorable, but the attorney, like the social worker, cannot begin to help in the ghetto by bringing his middle-class world with him.

Said Vinnie Negron, of Brownsville, from behind his Fu Manchu beard and dark glasses during one of his many encounters with antipoverty bureaucrats, "You tell me we forgot to submit our proposal in on time. Sure we forgot, but that don't mean we're gonna ask your forgiveness and crawl, begging for the money. It's your President, baby, not mine, that's droppin' flames on those poor bastards in Vietnam."

HAVING YOUR OWN ATTORNEY

Legal services, like the community action programs, also call for the "maximum feasible participation of the poor." While it is true that some spokesmen for the OEO point of view, given to naïve sloganeering, have helped create a red herring, the reaction of a New York court and the City Bar Association to the mere possibility that laymen might have an effective voice in the new corporations almost bordered on the paranoiac.

Because of the misgivings of the legal establishment, the neighborhood legal services component of the War on Poverty did not begin operations in the largest, most politically liberal city in the nation until the spring of 1968,* three and

---

* In early 1966, Mayor John Lindsay's antipoverty agency, the Human Resources Administration, requested permission of the Supreme Court of the State of New York, Appellate Division, First Department, to establish an umbrella corporation, Community Action for Legal Services, Inc. (CALS), to channel funds to and to exercise some supervisory control over semi-autonomous legal services offices located in poor communities around the city.

Professing concern for efficient operations, the Bar Association intervened to request the Court to modify the proposal to permit only the existing Legal Aid Society to provide the new legal services for a period of three years.

If this happened, said OEO, no federal funds would be forthcoming. The Court, in November, 1966, without a hearing or calling the parties to a conference, and in a lengthy opinion that defies reasoned analysis, rejected the city's proposal and directed the parties to resubmit a new proposal clarifying the scope of the lawyers' activities and the respective roles of law students, social workers, and representatives of the poor in the program. (*In Re: Community Action for Legal Services, Inc.,* 26 A.D.2d 354, 274 N.Y.S.2d 779, 1st Dept., 1966.)

After lengthy negotiations, William Fry and George Nicolau of HRH, OEO and Bar Association representatives and former MFY Legal Director Edward Sparer agreed on a revised program without substantial ideological changes whereby CALS would have loose control over eight independent neighborhood corporations employing a total of about 100 lawyers. Two-thirds of the members of the boards of directors of the parent and subsidiaries were to be lawyers representing Legal Aid, the City and County Bar Associations, and the poor. The Court approved the revised proposal, without opinion, on October 10, 1967.

one-half years after the Economic Opportunity Act made federal funds available for this purpose. The delay cost the poor of New York $10,000 per day, or over $3.5 million in OEO financing.

Echoing the sentiments of leaders of the organized Bar, the Appellate Division, in rejecting the original proposal, expressed the fear that lay control of the program might cause lawyers to engage in "political lobbying and propagandistic activity." The proposal, said the Court, could be construed to permit "the indiscriminate mingling of social goals and legitimate legal practice."

To this day no one knows precisely what conduct the judges intended to proscribe. Were rent strikers or recipients arrested for sitting-in at welfare centers to be denied representation available, for example, to the upper-middle-class members of Students for a Democratic Society arrested at Columbia? The tone of the decision suggested that the Court believed it had a sacred trust to protect *the idea* of an attorney-client relationship that has changed little since the time of Queen Elizabeth but which in fact is incompatible not only with the legal needs of the poor but with much of present-day practice.

For example, in every firm there are attorneys who prepare pleadings, try cases and research the law, and there are others who spend most of their time discussing strategy with clients, mediating on their behalf with legislators and government agencies and negotiating with opposition attorneys. While engaged in the latter type of activity, the attorney often wears several hats. There is sometimes a thin line between advice and direction, especially when the attorney also owns stock in the client corporation. Today, men who once served in high government office are partners in the most respectable Wall Street firms. It would be foolish to suppose that their impressive earnings derive from an ability to educate clients on the fine points of the antitrust laws.

Needless to say, no one construed the New York program as an economic threat to those who speak for the organized Bar. Wall Street is not likely to lose clients to Mobilization for Youth.

Many local practitioners, on the other hand, especially Negroes and Puerto Ricans presently located in ghetto areas, do see the advent of OEO-financed lawyers both as competitors and as potential threats to the equanimity of their major clients, the landlords and the small banks. They are, of course, correct on the second count, but it is only too evident that few attorneys make a living representing dispossessed tenants or testing, in court, the rights of welfare recipients to privacy or adequate budget allowances. These cases along with "marital" litigation predominate under the new programs. The eligibility levels ($3,500 for a family of four and $500 for each additional dependent), though more generous than Legal Aid in the past, are not likely to attract many nonwelfare clients. Even the English "Judicare"-type program, also favored by the American Bar, whereby private practitioners are paid fixed hourly fees by the government to represent poor persons, is not likely to attract experienced attorneys who know they must acquire corporate retainers in order to survive with a fair measure of comfort and security.

Instead, the Establishment opposition to CALS reflected the fears of men, middle-aged and older, emotionally wedded to an elitist image of their profession. Whatever the activities of the senior partners, young lawyers must avoid personal or controversial entanglements and must be content to wait for the clients to come to them; the apprentice attorneys must have earned some distinction at the right schools and must be willing to spend long hours serving in the shadow of the partners for more than adequate compensation and the right to attend cocktail parties at the Harvard Club. For their part, law students in the big firms to this day must be content at best to research the law and prepare rough drafts of pleadings and briefs.

While it was consistent for the legal establishment to opt for a viable program—lawyers are not doctors, after all—the democratic tone of the OEO formulation was disturbing to the senior Wall Street crowd. Their idea of a sound program resembled, as closely as possible, the structure and methods of the Legal Aid Societies which have played the same role vis-à-vis the organized Bar as the civil rights unit of the AFL-CIO Executive Council to the Federation, the National Catholic Welfare Conference to the Roman Church, and the private welfare agencies to the rest of society. They give us vicarious absolution.

To the Association of the Bar of the City of New York, the presence of a successful competing system of legal services on the bases advocated by Jean and Edgar Cahn, Edward Sparer and lawyer-spokesmen for the New Left threatened to disturb a formidable hierarchy of values.

A GRUBBY LOT

The late Perry Miller in his brilliant volume *Life of the Mind in America* pointed out that the legal profession has come a long way in the last hundred years. Toward the middle of the nineteenth century, lawyers were still considered by rich and poor alike as unlearned technicians who charged fees that were highly disproportionate to the services rendered.

Unlike his European counterpart, trained in the civil law tradition, who is expected to be able to digress during a plea in a rape case into a discourse on why the wisdom of Seneca or a decision by one of Justinian's magistrates should determine the fate of his client, the American practitioner is a captive of a common law system which in essence is not too far removed from the formalized resolution of disputes under the Dooms of Aethelbert (circa A.D. 600).

Despite periodic reforms, the waste of time and effort in the present court system, especially in the big cities, makes modern practice highly uneconomical for the middle class as well as the poor. State court pleadings in Philadelphia must be translated for the New York practitioner ninety miles away. Some lawyers would rather part with their wives than the expression "Now Comes . . ." at the head of an affidavit.

Mort Cohen of the South Brooklyn Legal Services and I represented a group of parents in a relatively uncomplicated suit arising out of the 1968 teachers' strike. In addition to typing expenses, salaries, etc., it cost the War on Poverty about $300 to Xerox (a cheaper alternative to printing) the thirty copies of our briefs and record required by the Appellate Court. In litigation attacking New York's welfare repayment obligation before a federal judge known for his sympathy for the poor and for the legal services program, the clerk of the Court charged the American Civil Liberties Union $28 for one good copy of the decision dismissing our complaint.

According to Charles Dickens, the son of a man who served time in a debtors' prison, the English practitioner of the last century also had an image problem, and for the same reason. Dickens was fascinated by the impact of laws and lawyers on the lives of the poor. To him, the profession had a "phrase and a fee for all the contingencies of human existence."* In the opening chapter of the novel *Bleak House,* Dickens uses the physical presence of the fog to depict the murky legal atmosphere in a courtroom: ". . . lawyers with mountains of costly nonsense piled up before them . . . mistily engaged in one of the 10,000 stages of an endless

---

* William Holdsworth, *Charles Dickens As a Legal Historian,* New Haven, Yale University Press, 1928.

cause, tripping one another up on slippery precedents, grop-
ing knee-deep in technicalities . . . and making a pretence of
equity with serious faces, as players might."

To his credit, the great English legal historian William
Holdsworth acknowledged the truth of Dickens' antilawyer
attacks but remarked, disingenuously, that "Dickens has
little to say of the ordinary barrister." In other words, the
novelist was not talking about the lawyers Holdsworth knew;
he simply was describing those members of the profession
who serviced the poor.

According to Perry Miller, David Dudley Field and other
leaders of the Bar managed by mid-nineteenth century to
refurbish the image by consciously identifying the best impulses of the legal profession with the American version of
the Christian Way of Life. Miller described the process in
these words:

> Despite their noble endeavors to make the Common Law
> appear a systematic wisdom, to invest it with the halo of
> Blackstone, lawyers could never quite fumigate it of the smell
> of the grubby. It *had* grown up by accident, out of low con-
> tention. To shed upon it the light of the sublime was a tricky
> enterprise. But once the Common Law could be caught up
> into the superior effulgence of natural law, of the law of na-
> tions, then it also could be covered by the Canopy of Chris-
> tianity. By this manner, the profession could evade the charge
> of hardheartedness.*

MISPLACED FEARS

In the light of subsequent developments, the CALS im-
broglio appears to have been a wasteful quarrel over words.
Liberal lawyers who expected the worst were surprised to
see that the City and local Bar Associations appointed men
to the various boards of directors who were either resigned

* Perry Miller, *The Life of the Mind in America—From the Revolution to the Civil War*, New York, Harcourt, Brace & World, Inc., 1965.

to or sincerely committed to the OEO legal services approach. The Poor Man's lawyers have achieved a few significant victories in test cases and have rendered competent and responsible services to poor persons in their own communities. But while the program has siphoned away many bright recent graduates from the Wall Street firms to the dismay of the establishment,* CALS to date has realized only a small portion of its potential without revolutionizing society or radicalizing the New York Bar.

In retrospect, it was not likely that men and women would place so little value on their attorney status that they would jeopardize it on capers in the ghetto. The thought of Ivy League graduates assaulting the Canons of Ethics at the behest of Black Nationalist demagogues would be laughable, except that this sort of thing intolerably delayed the commencement of the OEO program in New York City.

Major Owens,† on one critical occasion, and a CUSA delegation led by Father James Regan on another, picketed the City Bar Association building; but Owens tried and failed to interest the citywide federation of antipoverty groups in a massive, peaceful assault in Manhattan and the other boroughs. It is a sad fact that while the poor communities knew they wanted a neighborhood-type legal service operation that would involve them to some extent, they could not get passionate about it. Perhaps more so than most laymen, lower-income groups do not relate at all to how a lawyer conducts his business. The mechanics of legal services were in 1967, and still are, esoteric to them, and for this reason the success or failure of local programs will depend heavily on the commitment of the attorneys who do the work and the

---

* This phenomenon is directly responsible for current annual beginning salaries of $15,000 or better as well as slowly increased opportunities for women law school graduates and other minorities.

† Owens at the time was executive director of the Brownsville (antipoverty) Community Corporation. He later became Commissioner of Community Development for the Human Resources Administration.

attorneys who actively help shape policy on the local boards of directors.

In the last analysis, even if the lay representatives in no way *control* the policies of the local programs, it may be more important that by their mere presence on the board of directors, they know it is *their* program in the sense that it is both for them and among them. I am not aware, for example, that representatives of the poor in the Nassau County program have influenced the day-to-day operations, but it is quite impressive to hear welfare recipients and community action employees refer to the OEO personnel headed by Director Allen Redlich as "our" attorneys. This means that the attorneys service no one else, and that the local poor go to them with all their problems because they trust them not to stool to the welfare department.

THE MAN IN BLUE

The gut difference between the middle-class white and almost any Negro living in a "deprived" area is found in their attitude toward the law. Despite occasional minor conflicts, the former, on balance, identifies with the forces imposing order on the community; but to the Negro civil servant, for example, the policeman and other agents of the Rule of Law are unavailable when needed and annoyances otherwise.

To the poor black or Puerto Rican, however, the law is almost always his enemy. His economic situation throws him into frequent contact with bored, incompetent and overworked lesser officials of government agencies—caseworkers, unemployment insurance interviewers, probation officers, truant officers—and with their counterparts in the private sector—bill collectors, utility company clerks, process servers.

In the words of former Attorney General Nicholas De B.

Katzenbach, to the poor man, "statutory provisions and administrative regulations are a hostile maze, established as harassment, at all costs to be avoided." Poverty generates an impotence before the bar of justice that diminishes in intensity as a citizen ascends the economic ladder. It often manifests itself in a paranoia which sees labor unions, Con Edison and the politicians in active hostile coalition.

For most poor blacks, however, the man on the beat is their first and most constant contact with the Rule of Law. For several reasons the initial encounter is usually unpleasant, and thereafter the policeman tends to personify the outer boundaries of a discipline imposed on the ghetto by the Man Downtown. The ghetto dweller fears it because it is alien to him and also because he does not grasp its complexities. The employer class, the unions, City Hall, are hostile forces in a vaguely defined way; the man in blue, however, is a tangible presence in a racial slum whether in his role as arresting officer or as the silent partner of the crooked merchant, the slumlord and the marshal.

How will the OEO legal units help remedy this situation? According to Judge Raymond Pace Alexander of Philadelphia in a decision upholding that city's OEO legal program,* the major contribution of legal services may be instilling "greater respect for and confidence in the American police by the slum dwellers . . . with the greater protection of the American poor person against all the evils under which he has suffered in the abuse of legal process, both civil and criminal, the 'law' (as the police are known to him) will no longer be his enemy."

It is unfortunately true, however, that at the present time, the neighborhood lawyers in New York and elsewhere are not permitted to engage extensively in criminal practice. The limited funds available and the possible economic threat to

* *In Re: Community Legal Services, Inc.,* May 10, 1967.

small practitioners are responsible for this limitation. Harold
Rothwax, the director of the Mobilization for Youth program and himself a criminal law specialist, argues that the
theory of ongoing representation dictates that, at least in
minor cases, only the attorney who knows from past contacts the family circumstances and economic situation of the
delinquent should appear with him in Criminal Court. In the
whirlwind trial pace of justice distribution in the big cities,
where young lives are altered after a half hour's testimony
and three minutes' reflection by the presiding judge, most
jurists probably would be relieved to know that the defense
attorney will not lose sight of his client.

In *Les Misérables* the legal process hounded Jean Valjean
because he stole a loaf of bread. Because of the thin line in
welfare administration between petty cheating by an AFDC
mother for the sake of her children and "fraud" within the
meaning of the penal statues, it is also foolish not to permit
the OEO attorney who has welfare practice all to himself,
rather than the criminal specialist, to appear with a recipient
accused of willful fraud.

Some of the current proposals, including CALS, do permit representation at the police precinct level, and this is
important. Neither the Supreme Court nor the police commissioner, for that matter, can really assure observance of
judicial formulae in the squat, brick building with the green
exterior lamp and the melancholy air at East New York and
Rockaway Avenues in Brownsville. The awareness among
policemen that committed legal services lawyers will give
prisoners the kind of representation that the police know
from experience other lawyers will refuse to render even for
a fee, may deter more false arrests and police brutality than
any reviewing agency.

Even if the client, after he is booked and fingerprinted,
must be referred to a specialist prior to arraignment in court,
the local man need not leave the case. As in any other re-

ferral situation permitted by the Canons of Ethics, the OEO
attorney can continue to act in a nominal capacity as co-
counsel and thus keep an eye on the work of the litigator. In
addition, the OEO man's contacts and familiarity with the
neighborhood may enable him to assist the specialist by finding witnesses who might know, for instance, that the com-
plainant in a rape case is a prostitute, narcotics addict or
sometime police informant.

A CONTROVERSIAL EDUCATION

It is ironic, in the light of the CALS controversy in New
York City, that Congress explicitly expressed its intent that
legal services should include the "preventive law" approach.*
    In the long run the presence in the ghetto of citizens alert
to their legal rights and obligations may be one of the more
lasting memorials to members of a profession that often has
reason to doubt the social efficacy of its work. Except for
test-case litigation in welfare and public housing, which has
snowballed since OEO money became available, in Poor
Man's Law it is the *threat* of litigation, the *presence* of an
attorney in the case and not the end results of the legal
process itself, which resolves most disputes.
    The OEO lawyers will perform their assigned role in help-
ing to eradicate the root causes of poverty by advising poor
people singly or in groups concerning their legal rights. This
calls for the distribution of informational pamphlets, visits

---

* "The Committee feels that authorizing legal services for the poor is
an effective way of opening exits from poverty . . . An essential ingredi-
ent of most programs is an educational effort to apprise eligible people of
their rights and responsibilities . . . Indeed, the broader the range of
public information activities concerning the availability of legal services
and the recognition of the legal problems that confront the poor every
day, the greater the benefits of the program." (Legislative History of
Economic Opportunity Amendments of 1966, P.L. 89–794, House Report
No. 1568, 3 U.S. Code Cong. and Ad. News 4285–6.)

to tenements to address rent strikes or to community action centers to tell welfare recipients about *their* rights and obligations. Some leaders of the Bar in New York expressed concern that this education process smacked of "barratry," a hoary expression used to describe the vaguely discredited practice of stirring up litigation.

Martin Mayer in his book *The Lawyers* came down hard on the "doctrinaires" of the War against Poverty. He accused the OEO leadership of refusing to consider the social consequences of their litigation.* Certainly attorneys deeply involved in ghetto group representation before, during and after the grievance arises are not at liberty to disregard the possible immediate consequences of their advice and representation. Volunteer lawyers in Brownsville in 1966 discovered to their dismay that the economics of slum housing are such that rent strikes and petitions to the city for rent reductions in controlled buildings, might persuade some title owners simply to abandon the premises. "You want me to repair the building? You can have the building!"

But I doubt if mistakes of this kind are made by full-time practitioners who know what they are doing, because they have had time to learn. Moreover, after three years' activity, the War on Poverty has begun to produce booklets, handbooks and other materials for storefront operations that permit OEO attorneys to take a national perspective on Poor Man's Law. Nancy Le Blanc, of Mobilization for Youth, utilized her landlord-tenant experience to prepare a paperbound pamphlet complete with forms that departs from orthodox legal literature by telling the reader not only what

---

* During the 1968 strike, Mayer in a *New York Times Magazine* article sided with the United Federation of Teachers against Ocean Hill-Brownsville. Referring in *The Lawyers* to what must have been one of the more ambiguous and costly opinions ever written (*Matter of Community Action for Legal Services, Inc.*) Mayer remarked, "considering how busy these judges are, it was an astonishingly well-informed opinion."

the law is in the statute books but also how it relates to a pragmatic resolution of a tenant's problem.

The proliferation of administrative agencies during the past three decades shows that legislatures and the profession recognize that public policy in certain areas can best be effectuated, not by the courts, but by trained experts. But even here lawyers may still be necessary to complement the activities of government agents. The gross violations of individual rights that occur daily in welfare administration is proof enough of what happens when lawyers are not around to disturb comfortable arrangements.

"Why don't they stick to their business?" said a press release from the office of Governor Ronald Reagan, referring to the California Rural Legal Assistance program. Senator Robert Byrd (Democrat, West Virginia), Chairman of the Appropriations Sub-Committee for the District of Columbia, expressed his indignation in this curious outburst: "What business do these [OEO] lawyers have to question the [welfare] department's regulations? I'm not against fair hearings but I'm not going to sit by and watch our agency attacked . . ."

Whatever the motivations of Messrs. Reagan and Byrd, there is good reason to believe that the California program will reveal in the courts how the growers of that state, with the passive or active cooperation of public agencies, have exploited farm laborers. The D.C. unit, by exposing the legal skeletons in welfare administration, may well make a joke out of Byrd's perennial forays against "fraudulent" recipients in the District.

But the most obtuse and bigoted legislator will soon learn that while the United States Supreme Court and the American Bar Association will permit Congress to reasonably restrict the cases a Poor Man's lawyer might handle, they will not tolerate limitations on the types of defendants he may sue.

GETTING BACK AT THE MAN

Members of the profession can also be useful agents of the poor in their struggle for power. Lawyers, says Major Owens,

> are needed desperately and we are grateful for their services. But, like priests and ministers, they must see themselves as "technicians," performing specified tasks for which they qualify by their training. The white lawyer, or the black lawyer for that matter, who steps over the line into policy areas or tries to play politics or acquire a following within the Brownsville Corporation, will not be welcome. We who have been elected or appointed to speak for poor people have had our fill of paternalism. We are wary of professional outsiders who think they know what's best for us and for the poor.

On this question of power, it is also of note that among congressmen, legal services continues to be one of the most popular of the OEO programs. Whereas many legislators, with varying degrees of sincerity, like to argue that allocations for community action are a waste, the same men and women will help attorneys for the poor to battle the status quo. In fiscal 1967, over 300 legal services units received $30 million from Congress or 4 percent of the antipoverty expenditures. In late 1969, the Senate increased the Nixon Administration request for legal services from $58 to $74 million.

It may be that the voting margin in Congress is provided by attorneys knowledgeable, to the point of cynicism, about the deficiencies of the legal process, or conservatives who think they see a measurable return for the federal monies. I believe, however, that the answer lies in an implied recognition by Congress that many citizens become and remain impoverished because the law gives them a bad time. Under this theory, even Albert Quie of Minnesota concedes that the racial ghettoes are exploding with grievances which can be articulated in language politicians are able to cope with and channeled by neighborhood lawyers into nonviolent avenues of redress.

The Senate inquiries into the Newark riots of 1967 sought to fix some of the blame on community activists on OEO payrolls, but the probers readily admitted that Oliver Lofton and his legal services unit in that city probably helped prevent greater tragedies. Yes, the lawyers "solicited" affidavits from residents who complained of police brutality, but this detoured much of the racial hate away from white patrolmen.

Paradoxically, however, by focusing on long-range solutions to slum problems, the OEO legal units, unlike traditional private charity, over the long haul may be of more benefit to society as a whole than to the poor.

THE LAW STUDENTS

Several states, including New York and Michigan, anticipated the War on Poverty by permitting third-year law students to function, under certain restraints, in a quasi-lawyer capacity in Legal Aid or legal services corporations. The OEO units in those states usually provide in their budgets for students to work part-time during the school year and full-time in the summers at a wage rate of about $2.50 per hour.

While I know of no scandals involving the student lawyers, the experiment has had its share of controversy. The role of the students and the precise limitations on their activities figured in the judicial apprehensions about the CALS program. The vested-interest point of view appeared in a bill that passed the New York Assembly in 1967 by a startling vote of 90 to 18. The legislation would have prevented third-year law students from appearing, under the guidance of senior attorneys in legal services corporations, with clients in minor court cases or at welfare hearings. Credit for defeating the bill in the upper chamber is owing to responsible officials of the Wall Street-oriented City Bar Association and faculty members of the New York University School of Law.

With several honorable exceptions, almost every assemblyman from New York City, including the Negro legislators, voted for the bill. When I asked one of the Brooklyn delegates for an explanation, he gave me the official Democratic party line. He said, sanctimoniously, that the poor should receive only the "best" legal services. It meant nothing to this legislator that Congress will never provide sufficient funds to make client representation at welfare centers feasible on a large scale for lawyers and that no private practitioner will do it for free.

To date, the student-client experience has been mutually rewarding. The nature of ghetto legal activity is such that a reasonably intelligent law student may perform unromantic but invaluable services. Since much of welfare representation involves visits to the centers, and frequent telephone calls coupled with an ability to explain departmental policy to a caseworker who might be on the job only two weeks, the time of a student working on welfare matters under a lawyer's general supervision can be spent economically. Whereas the graduate attorney, with pleadings to prepare and briefs to write, might be ready to explode waiting at a center for his client or the caseworker to arrive, the student, free of his library chores, could profit from the experience.

In housing matters a student, perhaps with less authority than a lawyer but with more confidence than a community leader, can advise tenants' associations as to their rights and obligations under rent-withholding provisions in the law. Few welfare recipients know, for example, that a New York statute (the Spiegel Act) permits the total abatement of the rent of a welfare client living under housing conditions dangerous to health and safety.

Effective rent strike representation also calls for time-consuming title searches by persons familiar with the difference between a bond and a mortgage. It is also necessary, in cases where a client alleges "sewer service," to thumb through court records to find the affidavit which says where the summons was delivered to the defendant.*

Pre-graduation experiences of this kind also will help satisfy the idealism which in 1967–69 focused on peace and poverty and agitated probably every campus in the country. Law students were no exception. Dean Robert McKay of the New York University School of Law in his September, 1967, address of welcome to the freshman class acknowledged that a curriculum weighted with commercial law courses will disappoint the new breed of student anxious to know more about the public sector. Unfortunately, as late as the summer of 1969, student idealism contrasted sharply with the reluctance of most faculty members in the New York area and elsewhere in the country to give course credit for field work activities or to volunteer their own invaluable expertise to the storefront attorneys.

The OEO legal programs permit students to become embryo lawyers, salve their consciences, find their identities,

* In 1969 U.S. attorney for the Southern District of New York, Robert Morgenthau, provided perjury indictments against several dishonest process servers. In a raid on one service company, investigators found six thousand affidavits of service signed in blank, indicating at best the assembly-line nature of the operation conducive to cheating by the servers. Because of the difficulties of proving nonservice, state prosecutors had never taken action in this area. In a typical case involving a low-income defendant with a residence address in a racial ghetto, it might be cheaper for the defendant to pay or to agree to repossession of the purchased article than to hire an attorney.

Thurman Harris of CUSA once received notice of a sheriff's judgment levy for $200 which he allegedly owed to a small furniture store. Thurman never had been in the store and had received no prior service in the action. The matter ended when I advised the collection attorneys that Thurman appeared at the address listed in the affidavit of service, the headquarters of his employer, about twice a year and not on the date he supposedly was serviced there.

reject their parents, or whatever, while rendering technical service to the poor. A serious problem for many student activists, both North and South, is finding a proper role to play in the racial ghettoes. The failure of many upper-middle-class white college students to become involved in ways that will not conflict with the concept of "self-determination" or the ambitions of ghetto politicians or the need for expression among young black men and women, had much to do with the decline of the civil rights movement.

The white law student, however, has an easier time because, like the graduate lawyer, he is a classless, a-racial commodity. Like a doctor, he is a trained technician with a precisely defined role, and, therefore, presents no threat to the aspiring indigenous.

Eight students sponsored by the Law Students Civil Rights Research Council, who worked during the summer of 1966 in slum areas in Brownsville and East New York, did not learn much about drafting complaints, but at the end they concluded the experience had made them better human beings. The students visited slum tenements to encourage the formation of tenants' associations and guided rent strikers to the housing court. (One who helped a tenant file a criminal complaint against his landlord heard himself denounced as a "Communist" by a clerk of the court.) Most often, however, the future lawyers simply hounded welfare caseworkers by telephone on behalf of aggrieved recipients in storefronts operated by Christians and Jews United for Social Action (CUSA), a local community action organization.

These white students, two of them women, also attended evening meetings, went on bus outings with their "clients," and by accepting invitations to parties in the community effectively demonstrated that the concept of Black Power, at least at the grass-roots level, does not exclude all outsiders.

Jed Eisenstein and Fred Weisberg, VISTA volunteers in

New York University's graduate law school (class-field work) program who were assigned to Red Hook during the 1968 teachers' strike, established a close rapport with black militant Gloria Oliver. When at a local school board meeting, Gloria, under extreme provocation, flung a water bottle at an agitator from the right-wing Jewish Defense League, the two young men followed her to the precinct house and overnight jail and then appeared with Mort Cohen of the South Brooklyn Legal Services at Mrs. Oliver's arraignment.

Undoubtedly, many of the students will continue in legal services activities after graduation, but a fair number of students and young lawyers will move out of the ghettoes into private foundations, labor unions, administrative agencies and prosecutors' offices, where they may function as a leaven for desirable social change. By getting to know the poor, they will probably learn more about themselves. They may also never find life quite so lively again.

Steve Wizner of MFY tells the story of a group of hippie clients who were scheduled to appear in court. Since their usual adornments included guru robes, wooden rosary beads and painted faces, Steve asked them if it would unduly compromise their principles to dress for court in shirts, suits and ties. No, the hippies were only too happy to oblige. When Wizner arrived in court the next day he saw eight of his clients in the front bench wearing dark suits, white shirts and dress ties—beneath striped faces and thick strands of wooden prayer beads. The attorney, who wanted an adjournment anyway, got one without difficulty. "Take them out of my sight," said the judge.

THE HOPE OF THE MIDDLE CLASS

The possibility that the legal arm of the War against Poverty may accomplish radical reforms on behalf of the poor, in the long run will also redound to the advantage of that sector of the profession that services a middle-class clientele. Just as successful protest demonstrations organized in the ghetto neighborhoods have encouraged small home-owners to form block associations in order to more effec-tively agitate for better municipal services, so too will legal successes in indigent cases enhance the image of the lawyer outside the slums. Even the American Bar Association, which only a few years ago denounced the British system of free legal aid as "socialistic," has adopted a similar point of view.

Hopefully, the advent of a neighborhood-based legal services system will aid in revamping outmoded legal pro-cedures generally and in encouraging more widespread use of group practice for those well above the poverty line but too poor to afford effective and continuing legal representa-tion.

Today, it is generally conceded that though indigents can-not even begin to think about hiring a lawyer, middle-income people in the big cities, especially, will also think twice before doing so. The cost of an urban lawyer's services—except for real estate closings where cash in hand or a new home tend to give a glow to the transaction, or personal in-jury litigation where almost everyone recovers—for most citizens is usually disproportionate to the results achieved, and therefore a luxury item.

The fault in most cases is not attributable to the lawyer himself. He has no choice but to charge for the many hours he spends in a lower court, not to speak of the discourtesies he endures, waiting for a calendar call on a single claim worth one or two thousand dollars. The fault, instead, lies with an archaic and rigid system which, in practice, imposes a sacrosanct attorney-client relationship on all except the truly affluent.

PART

THREE

THE
CHURCHES

CHAPTER
SEVEN

GOD'S POOR

The Church is the Church only when it exists for others. To make a start, it should give away all its property to those in need . . .

—*Dietrich Bonhoeffer,* Letters and Papers from Prison*

THE YEAR 1969 may go down in history as the year black militancy challenged the pretensions of the Christian churches in America. When James Forman of the National Black Economic Development Conference strode uninvited into the chancel of New York's Riverside Church on May 4 to demand millions of dollars in "reparations" for blacks, he in effect made a sophisticated attack upon the most vulnerable of our major institutions.

Forman's manifesto forced thinking Christians to examine the nature of their beliefs. Were they committed to a theol-

* New York, Macmillan, 1967, p. 201.

ogy revolutionary in content or to one which called for weekly distributions of spiritual balm? According to Arthur Moore, editor of the United Methodist publication *World Outlook,* the "screams of rage" directed at Forman "may result from the exposure of a moral nerve." More so than university presidents confronted with disruptive student demonstrations, the men of God had the unhappy choice of either calling the police into houses of worship to oust black communicants with real grievances; or by submitting to negotiations and payments, the religious leaders would thereby acknowledge a specific debt owed to the black community.

Executives of the National Council of Churches resolved their dilemma by urging members to tolerate Sunday morning demonstrations not constituting a "clear and present danger" to human life. The Council also appointed a committee to negotiate with Forman. Some Protestant churchmen, including one or two black ministers, denounced Forman. Others invited him to appear at their assemblies.

Predictably, official Roman Catholic response was almost universally negative, with Terence Cardinal Cooke of New York taking the hardest line of all: the Black Manifesto, he said, is "contrary to our American Way of Life." It seemed curious for a Prince of the Church of Peter to make a secular, chauvinistic reply to a demand for justice, but the Cardinal also erred both on grounds of American history and the Canon Law of his Church.

Professor Graham Hughes of New York University draws an analogy between the "sporadic outbursts of genocidal rage . . . displayed towards the Indians and the settled, institutional policy of slavery applied to the Negro"* as one of several justifications for compensating blacks as well as Indians out of the general revenues.

* Graham Hughes, "Reparations for Blacks," *New York University Law Review,* Vol. 43, December, 1968, pp. 1063, 1064.

When directed at the churches, the term "reparations" is somewhat inexact in that it conjures up the image of blacks as a separate nation instead of an exploited element of the American Christian community. If the Manifesto is construed to seek *restitution* of property wrongfully denied the black man, then, as we will see, Forman's demand rests on a moral and legal foundation no orthodox Christian can ignore.

RECONCILING RHETORIC WITH REALITY

The Gospels, of course, are replete with admonitions to perform corporal works of mercy. There is also reason to believe that the early Christian communities were obedient in their fashion to the Master's command, "Give to everyone who asks of thee!" (St. Luke 6:30) However, around A.D. 1100, after the Church emerged from the Dark Ages a tradition sanctioned by law began to develop among the faithful which regarded the poor as a *class* set apart by God for the salvation of the affluent.

Individual beggars accepted handouts asked and offered in the name of the Lord. Persons of means purchased a piece of heaven with each donation. Since the emphasis was on the donor's obligation to relieve, poor people became a depository of good works. The distribution of alms to all who knocked at the kitchen door became a way of life for monastics.

Because the element of ultimate self-interest was paramount, the practice of almsgiving conjoined in time with the purchase of indulgences and helped fire Martin Luther's passion for reform. The ethereal character of medieval charity caused some twentieth-century historians to accuse the Church of ignoring actual need or willingness to work and thus propagating generations of English beggars.

Erich Fromm has described the world in which these acts took place.* It was a highly structured society. Man was not free in the modern sense to choose among different avenues of self-expression. The Church helped to keep all men in a kind of bondage that was only dimly apparent to them; at the same time she eased temporal suffering with the promise of eternal life. Professor Brian Tierney, an authority on ecclesiastical jurisprudence, in an excellent treatise, defends the early English Church against the charge of haphazard relief measures.† Tierney attributes the quality and extent of almsgiving in the High Middle Ages (A.D. 1150–1350) not especially to the force of the New Testament, but rather to a sense of embarrassment among canon lawyers who had difficulty reconciling the accumulated wealth of the Church with the spartan teachings of men like Ambrose and Chrysostom to whom the Sermon on the Mount was faint music still ringing in their ears.

As a consequence, the lawyers developed a practical doctrine of charity with the rationale that the Church held its possessions "in trust" for the poor; but this did not imply common ownership with the concomitant right of control. Legal title to all property was vested in the corporate Christian body. The canonists also acknowledged, as compatible with the nature of man, social classes for civilians and a hierarchy for churchmen, together with the appropriate emoluments.

However, medieval communism did call for a sharing in time of need. Since a beggar simply asked for his daily portion, who had the right to question his sincerity? The first stirrings of the "rights" concept in English Poor Law administration can be attributed to the insistence of the early

* *Escape from Freedom,* New York, Holt, Rinehart & Winston, 1941, pp. 58–59.
† "Medieval Poor Law: A Sketch of Canonical Theory and Its Application in England," Los Angeles, University of California at Los Angeles Press, 1959.

nineteenth-century radical William Cobbett that relief was the altered product of the lands formerly held by the Church in trust for the poor and since confiscated by the government. More directly, James Forman made his claim for restitution upon churches that have prospered from tax exemptions.

In the light of our current debates over the "means test" and other qualifications for the right to receive public assistance, it is intriguing to read in Tierney's work how logic drove the medieval canonists to espouse a rights concept that the Socialist Workers Party has not yet dreamed of. A compilation of papal decrees, canons of Church councils and opinions of the early Fathers which first appeared in A.D. 1140 contained a separate section devoted to the law of poverty and the entitlements of the poor. Whereas the well-to-do could and should resort first to the secular tribunals for redress, indigence qualified a person for easy access to the ecclesiastical courts. Since it was no disgrace to be without means, the testimony of a poor man was not to be rejected in *any* court. While the aggrieved indigent had no action at law, he could publicly denounce in church the rich man who refused to give him alms.

It is significant, however, for our purposes that Professor Tierney relied to some extent for the root source of his contention that organized Church charity was both humane and practical upon the same man whose teachings on the Christian law of poverty were codified by the medieval canonists.

St. Ambrose was a fourth-century lawyer, mystic, musician and diocesan administrator. He is the clerical counterpart, though on a grander scale, of David Josiah Brewer, the American judge whose Calvinism permeated his decisions with such devastating effects. The compartmentalized nature of charity in the highly structured Christian Church, currently under assault from within, cannot be fully appreciated without some mention of the towering figure of Ambrose, the

Bishop of Milan. He helps to explain why the Christian
churches should make reparations to blacks and why the
Roman Catholic, among others, will refuse for insular reasons to do so.

A CHRISTIAN HUMANIST

Ambrose was the son of comfortably situated Romans
who lived in Gaul at the time of his birth in A.D. 333. Like
many other aristocrats ambitious for advancement in the
Imperial Civil Service, Ambrose chose for his vocation the
practice of law, but at age forty, while prosecuting attorney
of Milan, he was elected by popular acclaim to fill the vacant
bishopric of that city. His intimates included the famous
rake-hell-turned-Platonist, Augustine of Hippo, who wrote
in his *Confessions,* "Thus I came to that city [Milan] . . .
and to Ambrose, the bishop, known throughout the world
as one of the best of men."

Immediately upon his consecration the new bishop do-
nated all of his personal wealth to the Church. Later he
ordered the diocesan gold and silver vessels broken into
pieces, then melted into bars and used to ransom Roman
soldiers captured by the Goths. Unlike the Stoics, Ambrose
regarded poverty with compassion. Whereas Cicero urged
his disciples to reciprocate kindness with kindness, Ambrose
ordered his affluent constituents to participate in the misery
of the poor.

Ambrose categorically rejected the notion of private property. "Nature," said he, "has poured forth all things for the
common use of all men . . . Nature created common rights,
but usurpation has transformed them into private rights."
The pristine Marxist cautioned the landowner, "You are not
making a gift of your possessions to the poor person. You
are handing over to him what is his . . ." This sort of thing,

incidentally, reappeared in 1967 in the papal encyclical *Progressio Populorum* and caused the *Wall Street Journal* to rebuke Pope Paul for making a sharp swing to the Left.

In refreshing contrast to modern relief administrators, the Bishop of Milan ordered his almoners to go look for needy persons too ashamed to apply for relief. But Ambrose also did not believe in throwing money away. Since fraudulent receipt of alms reduced the funds available for poor relief, Ambrose warned his agents not to be taken in by the expertise of professional beggars.

In other respects, Ambrose encouraged or instigated those Christian reforms which generally elevated the dignity of man and refined the quality of life in pagan Rome. Infanticide was abolished. Manual labor became a worthy enterprise. Women acquired a higher status in society. Secret marriages between free Christians and slaves were considered legitimate by the Church even though such unions were forbidden by secular law.

Ambrose also favored the abolition of capital punishment. Though he believed in "just wars," such conflicts should be waged only to protect Romans against aggressors. Ambrose, the lawyer-bishop, also argued for the due process rights of criminal defendants. The aesthetic side of this incredible human being produced quality poems and hymns and introduced religious "praise of God" music into Church services.

ONCE A LAWYER . . .

Perhaps because he lived at a time when the civilized world was in a state of rapid flux, Ambrose ruled his diocese as if he were chief judge of Milan, principal defender of the faith and advocate of the best interests of his Christian constituents. Ambrose was also a fanatic who came down hard on the sins of the flesh and condoned the burning of a synagogue by Christians as an act of faith.

During his entire tenure, Ambrose played a game of one-upmanship with the emperors. He alternately praised, begged and threatened with spiritual reprisals for the purpose of establishing a close union of Church and State whereby certain legal prerogatives, including exclusive recognition, were accorded his corporate client for many centuries in Western Europe.

It is foolish to look for a latent psychosis to reconcile Ambrose's brutal legalisms with the humane intelligence that made charitable endeavors a meaningful avenue of Christian expression. Both facets of his character are quite compatible with orthodox Christian belief. Even today, the insistence upon a special brand of salvation within a visible Church structure at best leads logically to a de-emphasis on concern for the plight of those alien to the one true faith.

A STRAW MAN

Accordingly, Professor Brian Tierney in his able defense of the medieval Church seems to miss the point. Tierney summons the canonists to answer the charges against their client, but it is the *law* of charity itself which is under attack.

Charity as a separate and complete legal obligation of the Christian community, which is most evident in the Roman sector, actually has been a mixed blessing for both the Church and society. The tradition produced in Saint Vincent de Paul, "the Father of Organized Private Charities," a rare combination of asceticism, administrative shrewdness and compassion for the poor. Whatever else may be said about them, the long line of Church orphanages, asylums and hospitals *have* catered to physical as well as spiritual needs in a generally humane fashion. It is noteworthy, for example, that despite the political and social conservatism of American Catholics, the Roman Church sponsors more than fifty of the two hundred or so maternity homes for unwed mothers in the United States, including some with postnatal facilities.

It is this humanistic tradition of organized charity which Professor Tierney apparently chose to defend against the assaults of secular liberals. The legal codification of this tradition first occurred during a period characterized by Tierney as "one of the greatest flowerings of the human intellect and spirit which the world has ever known." One requires little objectivity to balk at the mere suggestion that conditions improved for the welfare poor after the Reformation.

However, the principal objection to the distribution of food, clothing or shelter under religious auspices, whether in the High Middle Ages or today, is twofold:

(1) the motivation is "selfish," i.e., to spread the faith or to prepare a place in heaven for the donors; and

(2) the relief transaction is not designed to disturb the social conditions which gave rise to the need for succor.

Another valid criticism is ordinarily overlooked by the secular liberals and, for that matter, by the recipients themselves, who are not obliged to question the source of their good fortune. The charitable impulse of the institutional Church is so legalistic, so compartmentalized, that it is easily satisfied by donations to the poor box or, vicariously, by the full-time endeavors of others. It need not, and does not, permeate the lives of those who call themselves Christians.

On balance it is fair to say that for the philosophical origins of the modern welfare system we must look to the Protestant reformers and to the Catholics for an explanation of the increasing isolation of the welfare recipient from the rest of society.

THE PURITAN ETHIC

Not all modern historians agree with the classic thesis of R. H. Tawney that Protestantism is to blame for the inherent defects of capitalism. But no one denies that the Puritan emphasis on individual responsibility and the Calvinistic notion of predestination guided the Poor Law architects of 1834 in their belief that paupers, for their own spiritual good, should be humiliated off the parish rolls.

Among other things, Martin Luther stormed against the practice of compulsory charity and organized alms distributions which he and his followers saw as degrading to human nature. According to Reinhold Niebuhr, Luther reflected a major weakness of the "religiously inspired social spirit," which is always subject to the temptation of "sacrificing effectiveness to spontaneity and social usefulness to purity of motive."

Luther felt that Christian love should not be institutionalized; but in the process of destroying the law of charity, the Great Reformer inadvertently threw out good deeds as well. Even Luther deplored the abrupt cessation of private almsgiving which followed hard upon the confiscation of Church properties.

In England, the new doctrine coincided with the advent in the middle of the sixteenth century of the secular relief theories of the Spanish Catholic humanist Juan Luis Vives. Vives visited King Henry VIII in 1521 at a time when monarchs all over Europe were deciding that Church charity was both inadequate in itself and a poor model for civic officials to work with.

The Spaniard reportedly impressed Henry, and later all Christendom, with the novel theory that public authorities had a duty to the community to provide for the destitute.

Poverty, Vives said, leads to slum conditions and rebellions. On the other hand, human dignity and economic considerations were to be reconciled. Adequate budget levels, a ban on begging and work requirements for the able-bodied poor were basic to the plan.

Vives divided indigents into three classes: (1) those in hospitals and almshouses, (2) homeless beggars and (3) the "honest and shamefaced poor in their own homes." An accurate census, therefore, was an indispensable prerequisite to the inauguration of this scheme in any municipality.

With the help of John Calvin, the theories of the Spanish reformer as translated into the English Poor Laws became in time a wholly secular enterprise. Calvin's hard view of life gave rise to the doctrine that the fundamental purpose of Christianity was to regulate conduct. Human failures who ended up on the relief rolls were, therefore, peripheral objects of Christian concern.

Quoting Paul, Calvin preached, "If a man do not work, neither shall he eat." With the greater assumption of relief obligations by the community, English citizens were only too eager to equate poverty with dissolute living. The mass of indigents, they said, contained many who in some way had broken the laws of God. Like prisoners, they were to be sheltered and fed, not for their sake but for the good of society and at the least possible cost to the taxpayer.

There were, of course, many exceptions. The "honest and shamefaced" poor undoubtedly were cared for by the trades guilds or by local overseers who waived harsh regulations in particularly bad times. In fact, "widespread abuses" of this kind triggered the Poor Law Reform of 1834.

But the dreary chronicle authored by the Poor Law historians Sidney and Beatrice Webb contains this descriptive general comment by Chief Justice Sir Matthew Hale in 1659: "It seems to me that the English nation is more de-

ficient in their prudent provision for the poor than any other
cultivated and Christian state." Oliver Cromwell, we are
told, was content to wage war only on people and not on
poverty.

In this country, the Protestant ethic, the doctrines of the
classical economists and Darwinian natural selection syn-
thesized in the person of the Yale sociologist who, from his
seat in New Haven, probably had a greater influence on the
shape of our modern public welfare system than any other
American. It was William Graham Sumner who said:

"THERE ARE NO RIGHTS. THE
WORLD OWES NOBODY A LIVING."

Sumner, who became the secular saint of the well-to-do,
was born in New Jersey in 1840, the son of an English
laborer. Though ordained in the Episcopal ministry, Sumner
spent most of his life as an academic. While teaching sociology, he acquired a national reputation in economics and
political science as a rigorous advocate of hard money and
laissez-faire governmental policies.

In a Hobbesian way, Sumner believed that moral results
follow acquisitive impulses in the economic struggle. Since
millionaires are the product of natural selection and the
poor are life's failures, it was mischievous for the state to
attempt to alter income distribution.

Like his contemporary Justice David Josiah Brewer,
Sumner's Christian view of America had racist overtones.
Mass immigration, with its boatloads of poor Italians and
Jews, was destroying the "American Type." Like English-
man Herbert Spencer, Sumner abhorred expansions in the
public sector. Voluntary charity, he said, was infinitely pref-
erable to government relief measures which penalized
thrift and rewarded indolence.

Tawney may be correct in saying that the sense of spiritual independence generated by the Protestant virtues is the foundation stone of democracy and political freedom; but, unquestionably, the same virtues made America a highly unsympathetic haven for all indigents, including the aged, the blind and the disabled.

With men of the caliber of Sumner of Yale shaping the social attitudes of every class in the United States above the poverty level, in the light of these Protestant virtues, it is only surprising that the public assistance system today is not more corrupt than it appears to be. What *is* difficult to understand, however, is the willingness of the Christian churches to follow the Yale sociologist *en masse* into the cozy world of private charity and away from the grubby precincts of the truly poor.

OUR OWN KIND OF CHARITY

In the case of Roman Catholicism, church charities after the Reformation became more parochial in outlook with the passage of centuries. After the breakup of Christendom the canon law obligation to relieve suffering again became intertwined with the defensive "one-true Church" mentality of Ambrose's time.

The prerogatives of Church agencies were to be guarded against governmental interference. In the United States, Catholic Charities sought to protect its clients against immoral notions being propounded by secular humanists and the godless social work disciples of Sigmund Freud. The role of the Church in combating poverty during the past three decades became simply another facet of the Church's war on the non-Catholic world.

On another level, it is probably inevitable that any human institution that depends heavily on the force of law for its survival as an intact *institution* takes the chance of creating a Frankenstein monster. The rule of law as an end in itself is the rich uncle of our common law tradition. Its influence is disproportionately greater than the sentiments it arouses.

As late as 1961, the Reverend Swithun Bowers, director of the School of Social Work of St. Patrick's College of the University of Ottawa, published an essay entitled "What Is Catholic in Catholic Social Work?"* Father Bowers explained that since the purpose of human life is to be found in God, this is the context for Catholic social work, "This alone gives ultimate meaning to its activity." Whether helping to resolve marital difficulties or planning for the future of a dependent child, the client must be assisted in setting "goals within the framework of life's ultimate destiny." Father Bowers regretted that nonsectarian social work seemed to have lost sight of the original purpose; for some seculars the only goal of social work was a new use of self by the client.

If this was not enough to chill the ecumenical spirit, the spokesman for the Catholic viewpoint went on to deplore some Catholic agencies that differed only negatively from their secular counterparts in that "morally wrong practices, e.g., birth control, divorce, extramarital relations, are not countenanced as solutions to a difficulty."

In other words, this is charity with strings attached. Whatever the wishes of the client, the services or monetary benefits he receives are designed to push him toward heaven along a sectarian avenue. But, more important, this social work approach places the natural law, as interpreted by house theologians, theoretically ahead of what is best, here and now, for the individual client.

After reading Bowers, one gets the impression that even

* "A Symposium, the Catholic Church and Social Welfare," ed. Marguerite T. Boylan, Greenwich, 1961, p. 18.

lay social workers, some of them trained professionals, in Catholic agencies must have signed on as soldiers of Christ. I doubt if many Catholic lawyers would dare to admit at a Bar Association meeting that they declined out of obedience to Church law to pursue the best course of action for their client.

Certainly in some cases, for the therapeutic health of a woman and her children and for the good of society, birth control, divorce and extramarital relationships *will* be desirable solutions. I know of a stable common law union in New Jersey that almost was shattered by the rigid moralism of an Irish Catholic judge. Joe and Lois had been living together out of wedlock for ten years. They could not marry because her first husband was in a New York prison and New York at that time permitted divorce only on grounds of adultery. Lois, a nice person, would not take that dirty legal route. Joe was the father of two of Lois' four children, but he worked steadily and took good care of the whole family. Joe fell sick, however, in 1967 and the family was compelled by need to apply for supplementary assistance.

The caseworker, following departmental policy, suggested that Lois commence a paternity suit "for the sake of the children." The couple agreed. Welfare prepared the court papers. Judge —— found Joe "guilty" of an unnamed offense (fornication and adultery, however, are crimes in New Jersey). The judge ordered Joe to contribute fifty dollars per week to the support of his children. He also sentenced Joe to a year in prison but suspended the sentence on condition that Joe leave the home.

The embarrassed caseworker brought Lois and Joe to Mrs. Annamay Sheppard of the local OEO legal services unit. Three months later, with Joe still out of the house, the attorneys won a reversal from an appellate court but only on technical grounds. Joe returned to his family pending a new determination by the welfare officials who, incredibly, had argued against the appeal.

What if the family had gone for aid to a Catholic Charities office? We may surmise that people like Joe and Lois, whether Catholics or not, probably know enough about Church law to stay away. If they do go, they must find out soon enough that he who expects to be rehabilitated by Catholic social workers must first satisfy certain arbitrary standards. Accordingly, Catholic Charities, like the parochial schools, intentionally or not, manages to avoid most of the "hard" cases.

On the other hand, it is my impression that the casuistry which is a real though subordinate element in the Roman tradition permits some local deviations from the letter of the law.

MEASURED INDIGNATION

Gilbert Steiner, in his important contribution to the poverty literature,* made the observation that "the approach of organized, private welfare agencies to public assistance is typified by caution and by an apparent determination to maintain a suitable distance."

Church and secular charities played the same dormant role as organized labor in formulating the Social Security legislation that made FDR a world hero.

Professor Steiner credits Catholic Charities, on the national level, with being the most active and effective lobbyist for improvements in categorical (federally supported) assistance. The secular agencies typically saw fit to comment *by mail* on the major reform amendments to the Social Security Act proposed in 1962. Steiner points out, however, that

* *Social Insecurity: The Politics of Welfare*, New York, Rand McNally, 1966, p. 11.

even Catholic Charities has carefully guarded its share of the market. The 1962 bill was generally understood not to disturb the widespread municipal practice of purchasing certain local welfare services from religious and secular private agencies.

It is also true that lobbyists for the major denominations, along with representatives of the AFL-CIO, were among the most vigorous opponents of the repressive amendments of 1967. Undoubtedly each team had both the formal and sincere backing of its principals. The passage of the amendments showed clearly, however, that this was not enough.

Legislators as a group respond to moral pressures only when translated into concrete political realities. The Civil Rights Bill of 1964 carried in the wake of John Kennedy's murder in a Southern city, but the national mourning brought an army of clerics and lay Christians openly into the civil rights arena for the first time. Their powerful presence, on behalf of legislation aimed primarily at the Deep South, caused Senator Dirksen to conclude that enforced racial equality was an "idea whose time has come."

Prepared statements may be persuasive intellectually and good for public relations purposes, but it is people who enter the voting booths. George Meany, or his lobbyists, do not speak for John DeLury and his New York City sanitation men. The National Catholic Welfare Conference does not express the sentiments of rank-and-file Catholics nor, as a practical matter, of many of the bishops who *are* in a position to sway congressional votes against cuts in the AFDC program but whose parochial concerns, like those of local union leaders, are far more compelling.

The Catholic role in attempts since 1960 to reform New York welfare law and practice is quite revealing. In that year, the Right Reverend Monsignor George H. Guilfoyle, executive director of Catholic Charities in the Archdiocese of New York, at the outset of his prepared statement to a legislative subcommittee on public welfare, expressed his personal conviction that in New York "the overall administration of the public assistance programs has been essentially sound and praiseworthy." Guilfoyle repeated this appraisal in 1962 before the Moreland Commission.

Guilfoyle meant what he said. The Monsignor was most concerned that the policy-making powers of the Board of Social Welfare, a broadly representative body, not be transferred to a single commissioner appointed by the governor. Though he did not say it, Monsignor Guilfoyle undoubtedly was afraid that a new commissioner, free of bipartisan pressures, might make birth control devices available to AFDC mothers.

The Moreland Commission's investigation resulted in a report indicting virtually the entire system of welfare administration. In 1962 the spokesman for the Federation of Protestant Welfare Agencies, Henry G. Hotchkiss, urged the Moreland investigators to reject proposed residency requirements, restrictions on benefits to unwed mothers, general use of vouchers and more stringent investigation procedures. The Federation also recommended more funds for more caseworkers and for information programs aimed at community understanding of welfare. Mr. Hotchkiss also stressed the close correlation between rising caseloads and economic factors.

The late Cardinal Spellman's charities' representative also made the hopeful but startling comment in 1960 that OASDI benefits, which he characterized as a "right" contrasting with the welfare "dole," together with private insurance programs, would soon cause public assistance to wither away. Because of this dream, which most legislators discarded about twenty years earlier, the Monsignor argued strongly against federal participation in general assistance. Such aid, he said, would eventually stifle state, local and private programs of "insurance and self-help."

What about general assistance? New York pays benefits pegged at the bare survival level to both general assistance recipients and participants in the federal programs. Largely because of financial-political pressures, which would be eased by greater federal participation, New York does not include in the welfare budgets allowances for Christmas toys or Saturday children's matinées. As a consequence, *good* mothers on welfare lie and cheat for a worthy cause. Some will whore, on occasion, in order to buy presents for their children.

What do you say, Monsignor, to this real-life Negro father of eight children? Bill —— was told four years ago by a Newark caseworker when he applied for a GA hand-out that he would be doing his family a favor by leaving home. In that way, she said, the man's wife and children would be eligible for AFDC.* When Bill, who had a drink-ing problem, did abandon his family two years later, his wife and children were both sorry and glad to see him go.

In 1966, Charles J. Tobin, secretary of the New York State Catholic Welfare Committee, speaking for all the bishops in the state, reversed their official position in sup-port of relatives' responsibility laws. Abolition had long been advocated over the bishops' opposition by welfare experts who believed that such requirements had the effect of persuading elderly people not to apply for assistance or of turning father against daughter-in-law. The change, said Mr. Tobin in 1966, was now compatible with "our Judeo-Christian heritage" and enabled the faithful "to provide aid and support for those near and dear to us, through our vol-untary religious conviction rather than by legal require-ment."

Mr. Tobin's theology may be confusing but in context his strategy was quite clear. The bishops' spokesman was

* New Jersey, until January, 1969, did not pay AFDC benefits to families in need because of unemployment.

principally concerned in 1966 that Church-operated nurs-
ing, maternity and old-age homes be eligible to participate
in the Medicare and Medicaid programs, both of which he
incorrectly described as being within "the framework of
our social insurance system." Mr. Tobin traded relatives'
responsibility to the liberals for aid to Catholic Charities and
in the process betrayed his ignorance of the fact that Medicaid was a public assistance program.

In the light of this history, it is not surprising that Albany
legislators have not responded to the drastic reform measures suggested by secular liberal economists and social
workers during the past ten years.

Moreover, we are not now discussing the role of lawyers
or even labor leaders, whom sophisticated legislators have
no reason to believe represent the poor. Poverty is the mission field of the organized religious charities. Why should a
conservative Catholic Republican from upstate New York
believe that an AFDC mother in Brownsville puts out in
order to send her kids to the movies, when the Church of
the Poor, the organization which purports to be the conscience of humanity, refuses to tell him so?

To the contrary, Albany Republicans in a party-line vote
in the spring of 1969 arbitrarily slashed AFDC budgets and
denied medical assistance benefits to needy persons with
incomes slightly above the poverty level. The category of
recipients that suffered most (a mother with three teen-age
boys lost about $200 per year) is probably the one with the
most social problems. The Republicans defended the cuts on
the broad grounds of inefficient administration. Reform
Democrat Albert Blumenthal replied, "May God have mercy
on the soul of everyone in this chamber."

State Senator John Marchi a few weeks later defeated
John Lindsay in the Republican mayoralty primary in large
part because he voted for the bill and, unlike Lindsay, was
generally identified with reactionary politics. A deeply

religious man, Marchi could not conceivably have adopted such a brutal stance if his Church had denounced the welfare economies in the same tones that have so effectively blocked abortion reform in New York.

But this is an old story; administrative practices that in their conception and execution are degrading to the Judeo-Christian view of man flourish in almost all of the states with no cry of protest from the leaders of organized religion.

The AFDC mother, once numbered among God's Poor, arises from the table at the new Christian agape as the symbol of all that is wrong with our society.

Some of the Christian churches will reject James Forman's demands with equanimity because over the centuries the un-Christian notion crept into religious practice that the various denominations hold material wealth in trust only for their own constituents.

CHAPTER EIGHT

THE SANCTITY OF
THE STATUS QUO

. . . and so let Christ come leaping out of you . . .

—*from a sermon in a Brooklyn Roman Catholic Church*

IN THE CATALOGUE of Christian virtues, the one most identified with the visible accomplishments of the People of God is prudence. While few churches publish financial reports, prudence as a clerical *modus operandi* has resulted in real estate and corporate holdings so extensive as to seriously weaken the tax base of New York and other urban centers desperately in need of revenues. The organized "structure" required to manage Church wealth and "credibility gap" have become terms of opprobrium in the past three or four years among both avant-garde believers and secular critics.

As with other large and stable institutions, the best interests of the Christian churches since the era of Saint Ambrose have been served by preservation of the existing order.
But while General Motors, being a completely human institution, must take some chances, the otherworldly focus of
Christianity has made passivity on social issues a success
formula for the churches, if not for society.

From the perspective of a Nazi prison cell, Pastor
Dietrich Bonhoeffer viewed the corporate manifestations of
Christianity as another kind of prison, with walls built of
iron rules and regulations that insulated believers from the
social concerns enunciated in the Gospels.

Giant houses of worship and ostentatious rectories co-
exist with an otherworldly innocence about the root causes
of poverty. In this country, fulfillment of the command to
go forth and preach the Good News across a wide swath of
society has given the Church an excuse not to revolutionize
that society with meaningful Christian teachings. God's
favor manifests itself in the acquisition of material resources
and the enrollment of souls who will never be scandalized
by having their bigotry denounced in a Sunday sermon.

The virtue of prudence has smothered countless reforms.
Its principal product, the insipid sermon, is an integral part
of the Christian tradition in this country. One seldom hears
a discourse from the pulpit on Sundays that relates to something more controversial than beating a child in anger.

In Catholic homiletics, God is the law and Christ is love,
but only the law comes through loud and clear. Though the
most skilled of preachers repeats the Saviour's name twenty
times in a sermon, he cannot prudently relate Christ to this
life.

The Italian Communist film director of "The Gospel According to Saint Matthew" had no difficulty depicting Jesus
as a social revolutionary. The late novelist Nikos Kazantza-
kis also pointed out, to the consternation of the Greek

Orthodox hierarchy, that Christ lived for a time in this world and while here ate, drank, schmoozed a little, and perhaps on occasion stared with appreciation at a pair of full hips swaying past Him on a dusty road.

Christ also was born and died a Jew. The Christians came later. When labor organizer Cesar Chavez was asked why he wears a mezuzah around his neck, he replied, "Christ might have had one; He certainly didn't wear a cross." For this reason, it is particularly important for priests and laity reared in the Irish-German tradition to dehumanize Christ in their sermons. If they brought Him to life, they might find themselves conjuring up the image of a Semitic-looking son of a Hasidic tailor in Williamsburg, Brooklyn, who got a job with VISTA and is now organizing welfare recipients, who wears his hair full and sandals in the summertime, hates the war and believes in civil disobedience.

In both the civil rights movement and the War on Poverty, young Jews served tours of duty in urban storefronts and country schoolhouses while Christian laymen were still asking each other at meeting after meeting, What can we do to make our faith meaningful? But the Jew tends to identify with the exploited. The Christian, and especially the Catholic, escapes into the law. Paradoxically, the modern Jew, who is cool toward religion, betrays a quasi-religious yearning for the brotherhood of man. A minority of young Catholic priests find in their theology an excuse for toppling the institutional Church. Portions of the same theology reportedly shaped the radical humanism of Michael Harrington, Mario Savio and Tom Hayden, all of whom proceeded to leave the Church. The typical progressive Catholic who remains signs petitions against the war in Vietnam and spends most of his free time trying to reform his parish Holy Name Society.

My experience has been Roman Catholic, but reports of Protestant pastors being ejected from their pulpits for preaching against race hate suggest that it is only the preachers and not the congregations that have deviated from the norm in those cases. I also have passed too many announcements of Sunday sermon topics like this one, "Take the hinges off your mind," posted at Protestant churches. The success of bland clerical politicians like Dr. Norman Vincent Peale and especially Billy Graham, who has yet to require of his converts a change of heart toward the Negro, is added evidence that the indifferent sermon is a nonsectarian phenomenon in this country.

The virtue of prudence has created the clerical credibility gap. In Vatican circles, and as practiced by more sophisticated types, the art of making pleasant conversation while saying nothing can sometimes be a delightful performance. But on the grass-roots level, the man of God who essays this sort of thing is usually too crude to pass off his double-talk as honest pretence and too simple to understand that he is twisting the truth.

In reply to my question at a civic meeting in Brooklyn, a diocesan education official said that proposals for achieving parochial school integration by bussing or altering parish boundaries were drastic steps that should be preceded by an educational campaign. You cannot legislate proper attitudes, said this representative of the most authoritarian church in the world. Was such a campaign in progress, I asked. "Well, I know of a priest in Bensonhurst who got into a mess of trouble with his people by talking about integration." Was the diocese itself sponsoring a racial education program? The answer: No. The year: 1968.

A priest who was a friend of the official said to me afterward, "You know he's not that conservative. He has to talk that way. He's really on your side." But, I asked, he lies in public to defend his bishop? "I wouldn't put it that way."

It is an easy guess that a generation of young people, whatever their politics, who have reached maturity since the

Second Vatican Council, the War on Poverty and the black revolution, are not likely to be as sympathetic as their parents to the public relations problems of clerical bureaucrats. Don Haymes, a young bearded minister of a congregation of the Churches of Christ who has lived in a slum tenement and worked in the poverty program in East New York, Brooklyn, since 1966, says, ". . . most of the preachers are standing up in the pulpit answering questions that nobody is asking. Nobody in this day gives a damn whether the Son is of one substance with the Father . . . Those thought categories are foreign to us. There are some principles in the New Testament, however, there are some things that Jesus is talking about that have fantastic relevance. These are the things organized religion historically has avoided."

RACE AND RELIGION

Beneath the virtue of prudence lie several layers of clerical hypocrisy. The faithful are weak. The truth might scandalize them. They might leave the Church. These rationales were utilized by churchmen in the South until the secular government in Washington, D.C., introduced a new legal dimension to race relations.

John F. Kennedy, in fact, embarrassed churchmen, as he did labor leaders, lawyers and businessmen, at a series of unpublicized White House conferences on race in 1960–61. The late President reminded the clerics of their vocation. Federal civil rights legislation, he said, must be supplemented by enlightened private citizens, ". . . and certainly by religious leaders who recognize the conflict between racial bigotry and the Holy Word."*

But until pressured by the force of law or emboldened,

---

* "President Kennedy's Second Message on Civil Rights," 88th Cong., 1st Sess., H. Doc. 124 (June 19, 1963).

for example, by the integration of public schools, Southern bishops prudently excused themselves from condemning some of the most brutal repressions of the human spirit the world has ever known.

In fact, in some respects the Church was an acknowledged accomplice. To this day, the Southern Baptist and the fundamentalist denominations are not quite certain that racial supremacy is morally wrong. Supposedly, this has never been a theoretical problem for Catholic theologians, but implementation is another matter.

In fact, in the 1890's, Archbishop Janssen of New Orleans "regretfully" segregated for the first time the races in his diocese because he wanted to protect Negroes from insults in the predominantly white churches. Like other Southern bishops, Janssen also invited missionary priests to take separate and exclusive care of the colored faithful.

The fact that the foul smell of Jim Crow was in the air all over the region during that decade, and also that the local Negro leadership did not appreciate the Archbishop's thoughtfulness, did not change Janssen's plans. Within a few years, of course, the Catholic portion of the Negro population of New Orleans dropped from about 60 to 20 percent, where it stands today.

Racial discrimination, which is at the core of current prejudice against welfare recipients, is at the same time the least complicated, morally, of social issues and the one Christians have unfailingly avoided. Professor Aaron I. Abell of Notre Dame University published *American Catholicism and Social Action—A Search for Social Justice,** which purports to be a comprehensive study of Catholic involvement in social causes in the United States from 1865 to 1950. Abell's work contains exactly two paragraphs on the race question and nothing on public assistance.

---

* Hanover, Pennsylvania, Hanover Press, 1960.

A SLOW STARTER

American Catholic bishops generally have accepted progressive social changes only when they had no choice. The heroes of Abell's book are atypical laymen like labor leader Philip Murray, whose life and works were consciously influenced by the papal encyclicals, or solitary clerics like Monsignor John A. Ryan, whose 1906 classic, *A Living Wage: Its Ethical and Economic Aspects,* Abell rightly describes as the *Uncle Tom's Cabin* of the minimum-wage movement.

For a short time, even the Knights of Labor, which had a membership almost two-thirds Catholic, enjoyed the backing of powerful churchmen until the order became identified with violent strikes and "radical" causes, including racial solidarity; then the Catholic bishops helped bury what was probably the grandest expression of idealism in American trade unionism.

Is it cynical to believe that the same parochial concerns which gave rise to the separate school system also put the bishops eventually and unequivocally on the side of labor? Was it the gradually dawning impact of *Rerum Novarum,* revitalized by the encyclical of Pope Pius XI in 1931, *Quadragesimo Anno,* or simply that the sons of union members had begun to fill the nation's bishoprics?

For me, the dichotomy of official Church response on labor and race, at least until the Second Vatican Council, was illustrated by the split reaction to my letter to the Brooklyn Chancery office in 1958, in which I complained about two matters. A pastor in Sheepshead Bay had denounced from the pulpit striking newspaper drivers as "dogs"; and the *Brooklyn Tablet,* the official diocesan publication, had scrupulously avoided news and comment of any kind on the school desegregation riot in Little Rock, which was front-page news for two weeks in the secular press.

The pastor profusely apologized for his remarks. The Bishop read my letter "with interest," and it was at least six years before subscribers to the diocesan newspaper were made aware by *Tablet* editors that America did have a race problem.

THE BOROUGH OF CHURCHES

Brooklyn is the most populous borough in the second largest city in the world. The Roman Catholic diocese of Brooklyn, with a constituency of over 1.5 million in the boroughs of Brooklyn and Queens, ranks in size only behind Chicago, Boston, Los Angeles, Newark and New York.

At least 17 percent of Brooklyn's population is nonwhite, but most, including the Catholics among them, are forced to live in only four out of the twenty-three health districts in the borough. Bishop Bryan J. McIntegert (since deceased) issued a strong pastoral letter in the spring of 1966 in support of the open housing bill then pending in Congress. Subsequently, however, the Bishop did nothing to implement his directive.

Ken Daly, a fair-employment expert, headed an ad hoc committee of white and black Catholic laymen, including this writer, which met in 1967 with representatives of the Bishop, at Daly's request, to submit a list of civil rights proposals to the Bishop. The agreed-upon joint submission ranged from a plan for integrating the schools and diocesan construction sites, to the establishment of a full-time human rights office in the diocese to effectuate the various proposals. Nothing happened.

The ad hoc committee then approached the official Diocesan Senate of priests. When told that the proposals would require some study, the committee strategically reduced all of them to this: let the Bishop implement his pastoral letter by purchasing three apartment houses, with federal financing, in Bay Ridge. The Bishop, as landlord, could with impunity move any tenants, of any shade of black, and including welfare recipients, into his buildings and thus integrate a bastion of middle-class white Catholic supremacy in his diocese. What followed? The Senate collectively endorsed the "principle" of open housing.

Joe Mulholland of the Queens College faculty, the keynote speaker at a kickoff meeting of a laymen's association at the Brooklyn War Memorial, after reciting the futile efforts of the committee, said, "It is fitting that we who are concerned about the future of this diocese are meeting tonight in a building dedicated to the dead."

As late as July, 1969, the official position of the Brooklyn diocese on fair employment in church construction was at best quite laissez-faire. Federal law required the diocese to insist on "no discrimination pledges" in construction contracts, but beyond that, said one official, equality at the job sites *was the responsibility of the trade unions.*

Brooklyn is the way it is in large part because of the *Tablet,* which like its secular counterpart, the *Daily News,* not only reveals the worst in New Yorkers but has helped greatly to shape the unpleasant elements in the civic character. The moral chauvinism of the *Tablet* is suggested by the capsule reviews of its drama critic, who once described O'Neill's towering tragedy *Long Day's Journey into Night* as "a sordid tale of a lapsed Catholic family."

Patrick F. Scanlan, managing editor of the *Tablet* until his retirement in 1968, proselytized his reactionary views with the implicit approval of his Bishop among over 100,000 readers during the past three decades. Scanlan clearly was a member of the Catholic Old Guard. Even those enlightened clerics who deplored his crudities did not suggest that Scanlan was a rebel.

In Scanlan's Christmas column of December 21, 1967, he expressed his fervent wish that the spiritual observance of the feast would blot out pacifist picketing, the burning of draft cards and those "theologians or pseudo-theologians who confuse the people with strange pronouncements." Instead, said editor Scanlan, "Christmas Day will be devoted to the Christ Child."

In fairness to the *Tablet,* during the past year the paper's coverage has tended to cancel out the bigotry of the bulk of its readers. This is not to say that the *Tablet* has become humane, but simply more honest.

Moreover, on purely parochial questions, such as removal of the restriction on sectarian school aid in the New York State Constitution, the *Tablet* (echoing the stand of the New York bishops) showed it had not lost sight of the old values.

THE SECULAR CITY

Catholic parochialism in the large cities is particularly tragic because Italian Catholics, Poles and Slovaks constitute the bulk of the blue-collar class threatened by black aspirations. In a city like New York, white craftsmen overwhelmingly concerned about affluence in this life and "real" happiness in the next, along with their spiritual leaders, are alienated by the attempts of Mayor John Lindsay to improve the quality of life in the city and to give some hope to its black and Puerto Rican residents. The cry of "crime in the streets" encompasses a host of unpleasant happenings which *possibly* might disturb the comfort of the Italian plumber. It also gives him an excuse to say to hell with the city, even if he continues to live there, just at a time when urban life desperately needs devotees.

The martyred pastor Dietrich Bonhoeffer argued against any conflict between Christians and their temporal existence.

His American disciple, Dr. Harvey Cox, described his own
major work, *The Secular City,* as "a celebration of the liberties [of the secular city] and an invitation to its discipline."
The popularity of the book extended, of course, beyond those
theologically oriented. Dr. Cox wears a beard, served time in
a Southern jail for his civil rights activities, and is still young
enough to be emulated by idealistic collegians.

Cox also projected as one of his secular urban heroes the
late President John F. Kennedy. His linking of the Kennedy
style and substance to the needs of our times had a sure-fire
appeal for a generation disillusioned by official ineptitude
and expressions of good will. Said Dr. Cox, the technopoli-
tan man, like Kennedy, is pragmatic to the point of being a
kind of modern ascetic.

The Secular City also appeared at a time when many between the ages of twenty and forty *wanted* to believe in the
worth of the cities. Long-distance commuting, the antiseptic
quality of life in the suburbs, the availability of good brownstones at reasonable prices in racially integrated areas, and
disgust with fathers and older brothers who returned from
wars of liberation only to run from the sight of dark faces
in their old neighborhoods—these are among the interrelated
reasons for the phenomenon of inner-city migrations by
whites who made up in quality what they lacked in numbers.
For the most part, the new arrivals have been more tolerant
of people, more appreciative of the arts and less enamored of
false middle-class values than many of the residents they
replaced.

Nevertheless, despite the broad appeal of the secular-city
ideology, the Bonhoeffer-Cox statements were intended primarily for Christian readers. It is among those few who tend
to see social issues from a Christian perspective that the new
urban theology will have its most pervasive and enduring
effects.

What are these effects? At the present writing, almost

every large city in the nation has a handful of religious working in ghetto areas at activities that would have been forbidden by their bishops and made front-page news less than
three years ago. These religious frequently wear secular
dress, keep strange hours, socialize with drug addicts, and
sometimes use and hear language indecorous even for policemen. Some live in tenements; some have been arrested for
disorderly conduct, i.e., civil disobedience. The members of
the inner-city apostolate, if so it may be described, uniformly possess and apply advanced notions on the liturgy
and share a common disregard for mindless authority.

Nuns in quasi-civilian dress drift in and out of this ghetto
ministry teaching school or tending the sick. On occasion
they also get arrested wearing picket signs and sometimes can
be seen at cocktail parties maintaining their convent poise
over a Manhattan cocktail.

Most, but not all, of the clerics are only slightly older than
the college students who listened to Tom Hayden declare
war on middle-class America at the SDS Port Huron conference in 1960. The way-out religious include Protestants
and Catholics, but the homogeneous nature of Roman
Catholicism and the highly structured and authoritarian
backdrop against which they work single out the rebel priests
as one of the real phenomena of this decade.

A NEW BREED OF RADICAL

In Brooklyn, the contrast between accepted past practice
and conduct vaguely acquiesced in today is particularly
startling.

Perhaps because of the conservative reputation the diocese has acquired, Church officials tolerate highly irregular
pastoral activities in Brownsville, Fort Greene, Bushwick,
Bedford-Stuyvesant and East New York. On the one hand,

the Chancery office could not cope with the adverse publicity that would follow the mass resignation of sixteen or so priests in protest of repressive measures. But at the same time, no way yet has been found to bridge the great gulf between the young militants and the clerical bureaucrats who reflect the prejudices of Brooklyn's lay Catholics.

So it would appear that Brooklyn by accident has raised a generation of radical priests who refuse to quit their ministry. They remain to annoy their bishop with their tactics and to reproach him by their example with the silent accusation that he has lost his own vocation to cater to the poor.

Like the worker-priests of France, their ghetto counterparts in Brooklyn are radicals only partly by design. In matters within their special expertise, such as worship and confessional guidance, they tend to de-emphasize symbolism in favor of community and to stretch canon law in order to achieve humane results. But in political and economic matters, while desirous of dramatic changes in the status quo, they usually lack a sound ideological battle plan. Like most of the Students for a Democratic Society, the Roman-collar militants are anxious to cure society's ills, but they do not know precisely how to proceed because they also are alienated from the sources of power.

Ten or eleven young radical priests, most of them looking to relieve their frustrations, played a galvanizing role in the formation and early operations of the nonsectarian Christians and Jews United for Social Action (CUSA). The sometimes too visible participation of the priests at CUSA protest rallies and marches caused some anticlerical observers to conclude that this was the same old paternalism; but CUSA eventually became one of the more militant community action groups in the city. For a time, even diocesan officials liked to suggest that CUSA was a Catholic-front group, but not any more.

In fact, the antipoverty programs officially sponsored by the Church proved to be such models of (at least) surface efficiency that one suspects that CUSA's critics of two years ago would be grateful if churchmen *did* control CUSA's affairs.

Today, the five CUSA storefronts in East New York, Brownsville and Bedford-Stuyvesant function primarily as welfare rights organizations under the umbrella of the Brooklyn Welfare Action Council, itself an affiliate of the City-Wide Coordinating Committee of Welfare Groups and of George Wiley's National Welfare Rights Organization based in Washington. BWAC and the storefronts, however, still receive some of their financing, with no strings attached, from the Brooklyn diocese. For a time the diocese, through its Social Action Department headed by Father Robert Kennedy, paid the salaries of welfare organizers Rhoda Linton, an ex-Methodist missionary, and Ellen Murphy, a CUSA Baptist from Brownsville. In its formative months, BWAC also held its meetings and mimeographed its calls to action at Kennedy's offices in downtown Brooklyn.

In September, 1966, Father Jack Powis, who has appeared on television to advocate the end of the parochial school system, was arrested with Reverend Milton Galamison, Mrs. Thelma Hamilton, Vinnie Negron, Reverend Bob Nichols of the East Harlem Protestant Parish and other members of a People's Board of Education for refusing to permit the official board to conduct its business. Later, Powis, a member of the Ocean Hill-Brownsville Governing Board, played a major role in the community's confrontation with the United Federation of Teachers.

Fathers Regan, Matty and Equale are familiar faces to the guards at welfare headquarters and at City Hall. Matty and Equale also worked for a few months as laborers in factories. Fathers John Hyland and Bill Duncan, who were arrested with two VISTA workers and several recipients at a Brooklyn welfare center in January of 1968, became students of racial dynamics and experts on welfare problems and client organizing. Duncan lives in a Bedford-Stuyvesant apartment that has become an offbeat scene for local black nationalists.

Over a five-week period the two men visited the major urban ghettoes of the North and South as well as the Mississippi Delta. On their return, they reported that there seemed to be more action among the Brooklyn clergy than elsewhere. However, Duncan and Hyland also made a formal presentation to the Chancery office of blueprints for social change which among other things urged the diocese to finance training of black leaders for community service. Their report, along with similar documents, has since been gathering dust.

LEAVEN OR ABERRATION?

Charles P. Gillet, a graduate of Union Theological Seminary, wrote a report based on a summer internship with the City-Wide Coordinating Committee (entitled "The Church and the Welfare Crisis in New York City") which indicates that except for those in Brooklyn, very few local churchmen are involved in welfare activities. Moreover, the Brooklyn ghetto priests represent only a tiny portion of the clergy complement of the diocese. The question then arises whether the isolated pockets of clerical militancy in Brooklyn and elsewhere argue a sharp change of direction for the organized Church. The answer at this time would appear to be no.

To begin with, Protestant theologian Professor Graham Taylor, who was active in the Workmen's Compensation movement, anticipated Bonhoeffer, Cox, et al., by over fifty years. The Church, Taylor said, was born in the city.

The highest mission of the Church was to build up the community out of itself, and not itself out of the community. Professor Taylor anticipated a great future for the "religious expression in social action" which has never quite materialized, but it is most depressing of all to read of Taylor's enthusiasm about dramatic changes occurring at that time within the Church. Young people, he said, were attracted by a new appreciation within the Church for "beauty and order in human relationships."*

While it is true that the Brooklyn Catholic diocese increased its total outlay for social action from $32,017 in 1966 to about $120,000 for 1967, most of which went to the welfare rights movement, these sums represent less than 1 percent of the total $37 million expended in 1966 by diocesan Catholic Charities, and, according to Father Bill Duncan, only an infinitesimal portion of diocesan revenues.

By stretching the point only slightly, it is evident that the diocesan acquiescence in sit-ins and other protests is quite compatible, if not with the traditional paternalistic approach, at least with the orthodox notion that a priest, wherever situated, must adapt to the mores of his people. If militancy is in the air, we can hear the Bishop saying, then I suppose we must tolerate a certain amount of civil disobedience by our ghetto priests in their pastoral roles.

Furthermore, the Bishop and other religious in Brooklyn can take vicarious satisfaction in the activities of their ghetto confreres without paying the price. They can defend the sincerity of these young men who give witness for the whole crowd without, and this is important, disturbing the order of things outside the welfare ghetto area. Brooklyn has not had the massive confrontations between Negroes and their clerical supporters and comfortable, middle-class white Catholics

* *Religion in Social Action,* New York, Dodd, Mead, 1913.

which tore apart the Church in Milwaukee and in Cicero, Illinois.

Laymen in the Brooklyn diocese, seeing no signs of clerical revolt outside of the ghettoes, are content to dismiss the few militants as further evidence that the Church is big enough to contain numerous aberrations. In short, white Catholics feel that the ghetto priests are neither disturbing nor representative.

Some of the young priests are aware that they are being used by the Chancery office. I know of at least ten workers in ghetto neighborhoods who were among those from Brooklyn who left the priesthood in 1967–69. Their reward for years of service to the Church at token salaries was a chilly farewell. They also left with the bitter knowledge that the fastest way to be dispensed from their vows of celibacy was to marry in a civil ceremony. The frustrations of those that remain stem from the knowledge that they are out of the mainstream of clerical life in Brooklyn, yet dependent upon that milieu to actualize their vocations. I once asked Bill Duncan what answer he gives, on his many trips to Albany with picketing recipients, to a legislator who asks if he represents the Bishop of Brooklyn: "I have to tell him no."

These militant clerics see no middle ground between themselves and the other 95 percent of their fellows who function in the old structured way, many of them conscientious and dedicated, but oblivious to the larger social problems because of the system.

For the most part, the rebel priests are the product of conservative Irish-American homes. Like the upper-middle-class activists on the New Left and unlike the sons of immigrants who helped organize workers in the 30's, they are unable, through no fault of their own, to relate to their parents or to authority, or to the labor unions whose backing probably is essential to achieve meaningful reform.

Several of the Brooklyn priests marched at Selma. Their

enthusiasm over the impact on national opinion created by the sight on TV of clergymen and nuns marching with labor leaders, lawyers and oppressed blacks, has begun to wane. The black radicals who killed the civil rights movement realized before everyone else that Selma changed nothing.

If the ghetto priests are sometimes inadequate, it is because they have difficulty formulating long-range programs which in order to be meaningful for *them* must also include their bishop. Rebuffed by the Chancery, they resign themselves to doing good deeds on a case-by-case basis. But even here, their ambiguous role creates additional problems. The priests are trained in the seminary to be "leaders" in a setting which includes organizing altar boys under the guidance of a benign pastor. But the white ghetto militants must operate, under minimum supervision, as celibates in a world that has a swing all its own. The increased tempo of black militancy has also tended to reduce their effectiveness. By the middle of 1969 Bill Duncan was seriously considering a transfer to a poor white area.

Their almost total involvement in secular affairs also calls for an expertise that few have the time or the patience to acquire. Welfare clients cannot adequately be serviced without a good knowledge of local regulations, which devote four or five pages, for example, to a discussion of circumstances justifying the inclusion of a telephone in the budget. In addition, the day-to-day indignities inherent in welfare administration everywhere cannot be fought on a grand scale without an appreciation of relevant legislative history, politics, unemployment cycles and factory wage scales. Father Harry Browne of Manhattan won the respect of his Strykers' Bay Tenants Association and of author Joseph Lyford (*The Airtight Cage*) by mastering the incredible complexities of the housing laws. Jack Powis of Brownsville, over a two-year period, became an expert on public education law. But these are unusual men.

A PLACE ON THE LEFT

At the same time, I am among those who believe that idealists on Church payrolls can and should be given a role, in a less structured setting, that goes beyond the resolution of immediate, day-to-day problems. The pull of religious service can be translated into a Christian (or Jewish) social dynamic called nonsecular humanism, the sporadic efficacy of which can hardly be denied.

One may disagree, as I do, on pragmatic grounds, with the philosophy of Monsignor Robert Fox, who achieved some fame with his "Summer in the City" program in recent years, featuring art classes, street dramas, block parties, etc. Fox is repelled at the sight of big organizations or strangers "manipulating" the poor. Even the Church, he says, has no right to use its power to "impose" reforms upon the ghetto.

At times Fox sounds like a Northern manufacturer or a Southern school board complaining about "outside" agitators. But Fox does believe in rent strikes, welfare sit-ins, block sweeps, provided the stimulus for these activities emanates from the people themselves. Reforms must derive from a sense that the community is acting in Judeo-Christian concert. Naïve? Perhaps. But Fox's philosophy can be dismissed summarily only by those who have not seen the poor sold out by their best friends.

Lenin characterized religion as the opiate of the masses, but what mysteries was he prepared to substitute? For you and me, a good concert may nourish that portion of our being that hungers for the eternal. For many a poor person, however, an adequate welfare budget is hardly a substitute for the aesthetic joys of Church worship. Episcopal layman William Stringfellow pointed this out to his clerical co-workers in East Harlem, whom he felt were neglecting the liturgy in their daily secular rounds.

There is an old church near the abandoned Brooklyn Navy Yard where whites from all over the borough congregate with Negroes and Puerto Ricans at noon mass every Sunday. Behind the altar an expressionistic mural brightly splashed with several colors depicts Martin Luther King saying "I have a dream," and a black Christ lying at the foot of the cross. A star attraction is the angular young showman with a Van Dyke beard, Grayson Brown. Accompanied by Marie Lee on the guitar, Grayson leads an audience that represents several levels of sophistication in a rousing medley that includes black songs of rebellion, "The Battle Hymn of the Republic" and Bob Dylan's "Blowing in the Wind." The Anglicized Bantu lament "Kumbaya" often serves as the Communion hymn.

Grayson directs an integrated girls' choir at the midnight services each Christmas. The red robes, the rocking to and fro and the non-Roman clapping of the hands caused one middle-aged white visitor in 1968 to remark, "My God, it's gospel singing!"

A typical sermon by one of the three-man team of Fathers Tom Mannion, Gerry Gannon and Tom McCabe that operated the parish in 1968–69 might extol the positive aspects of Black Power, or suggest how diocesan funds could be utilized to achieve open housing. The special parish announcements included an appeal one winter from Cesar Chavez not to buy California table grapes. One hears regular reports on sales at the OEO-funded cooperative food store, and all are asked to remember in their prayers those who have fallen and died in Vietnam "on both sides."

One of the lectors, Jimmy Hill, attends a Catholic college that tolerates fraternities that deny him membership. In the evenings Hill moderates parish youth activities in a converted brownstone near the church that combines a psychedelic décor with a huge photograph of Malcolm X glowering over the dance floor.

After mass, buns and coffee and conversation are available in the rectory. The sociability, the guitar mass and the sermons combine in equal proportions to account for the singular popularity of Saint Ann's Church as a "relevant" place of Sunday worship. But the object that sticks in the recollection of one visitor is the phrase "Celebrate Life" across the pop-art poster that decorates the front side of the altar. The one hymn that insists on being remembered concludes with the words, "Yes, you will know we are Christians by our love."

A FADING PROMISE

Time is running out on the Christian churches in America. Too much has happened during the past five years to permit the various hierarchies to continue doing business in the same old way. The escalation in Vietnam followed hard upon the murder of John F. Kennedy to usher in a violent, lawless period in our history that will not end until much that is good and bad in our society is destroyed.

Poets and intellectuals, alienated as always, pulled out of the organized religions in this and every other age and nation. But today the American churches face more widespread defections. Those blue-collar bigots who no longer see the financially depressed parochial schools and membership in the Knights of Columbus as status symbols are themselves products of this cynical period. Even these will come to despise spiritual leaders who talk about open housing in tones that cannot be heard. The timid concessions made to progress in recent years by the Catholic bishops show clearly that they are both frightened and uncertain as to how far they can or should go. The forced resignation of the youthful Bishop James Shannon of St. Paul because of his stand on birth control and the chilly reception that greeted James

Forman's Black Manifesto show that a reactionary time may
be upon us.

As for the radical clerics, the quandary of the sectarian
wing of the New Left is not caused especially by disillusion-
ment at the gap in high places between rhetoric and performance. Seminarians are pleasantly indoctrinated to joke at the
fallibility of bishops. It is, instead, a problem both of vocation and belief. If social ills cannot be fought by priests who
are acting not only by themselves for their black or Spanish
constituents, but also as agents of the most potent organization in New York City, then what does it gain to play an
ambiguous role while in the service of a Church hierarchy
which is at best, like most of the lay membership, cool toward
proposals for remedying social injustice?

Albert Camus wondered what kind of a God would tolerate the murder of children. It is customary for believers to
reply, on Camus' terms, that life would truly be absurd if
there were no God; but this response does not take account
of the root conundrum that as human beings the only glim-
mer of God's justice comes from the actions of those who
purport to speak in His name.

Stephen Rose spoke about all creeds when he wrote:

> . . . the priority is not on supplementary structures that will
> enable the "far out" clergy to experiment on the edges of the
> religious institution. I do not propose an occasional "Christian
> coffee house" here, a maverick ministry to the poor there, or
> a series of *ad hoc* activities carried out without the knowledge
> or consent of most church members. Such an approach only
> shields us from the depths of the Protestant sickness. The
> first persons to see this should be the *avant garde* within the
> churches. Of all people, they should realize that such scatter-
> shot renewal is, at best, partial and at worst a concession on
> the part of the status quo, anxious to please the prophets in
> order to keep them confined to the periphery.*

* *The Grass Roots Church*, New York, Holt, Rinehart & Winston,
1966, p. 5.

In other words, if the Church is to play a meaningful role in the secular city, it must act as an entire community.

"Where the moral duty is simple but difficult," Reinhold Niebuhr says, "the religious impulse is required to furnish the necessary dynamic for its fulfillment." No one seriously disputes the *right* of a Negro to buy a home in a white neighborhood. No relatively sophisticated white denies that economic exploitation and the refusal of decent job opportunities contribute heavily to family breakup and the size of the welfare rolls. These are fairly uncomplicated moral issues and are so recognized, on the theoretical level, by Church leaders.

Is it too cynical to suggest that churchmen *want* to believe that the bulk of reliefers are moral delinquents, because to admit to economic causes would betray the startling contrast between Christian rhetoric and reality, between the comfortable circumstances of the great mass of believers and the innocents on the AFDC rolls? The same churchmen who are acutely aware of the high cost of construction labor are inexcusably oblivious to wage scales paid in the most expensive city in the world to factory workers. In 1969, I took a young Colombian to a sectarian employment referral agency. The only jobs the dispatcher ever had available, he told us, paid the federal minimum wage of $1.60 per hour, i.e., the starting salary she also would have received in a clothing factory in rural Tennessee.

Prudence also tends to magnify the problems of implementation to the extent that the social scorecard of organized religion on these issues lacks even near-misses. Like labor leaders, most of our Men of God have been content to make Olympian, self-aggrandizing pronouncements. But a pastoral letter on open housing is not the same thing as the purchase by a Church landlord of an apartment house in a white neighborhood. Double discrimination against Negro welfare recipients easily coexists with vague sermons on loving one's brother.

The present Church structure perpetuates the compromises deemed necessary to maintain that imposing edifice. Union officials, contractors and monsignori from the Chancery office are permitted to talk like good Christians as they celebrate over a rye and water a new construction contract while white men elsewhere continue to build the new parish schools and black men work for $70 per week in Brooklyn's sweatshops.

Integrating a neighborhood, insisting on the presence of dark faces at a church construction site, loaning money to ghetto businesses, demanding a humane welfare administration, are measures which conceivably might shake the foundations of a church. But out of the ruins will rise a less ostentatious, higher-quality structure that will have more meaning for those who choose to remain and also a greater impact on the surrounding community.

The only alternative in this turbulent age is for the Church to continue substantially as before as a kind of sociological artifact, helpless to rebut the more sophisticated charge that the moral pretensions of Christianity are a monstrous lie.

FOUR

THE
UNIONS

CHAPTER NINE

SOCIAL SECURITY IS
THE ANSWER?

*Poverty was our original enemy from the day the
first trade union was established; it will remain the
enemy until it is exterminated from American
life.*

—*George Meany, President, AFL-CIO*

LIKE POLITICIANS EVERYWHERE, trade union officials
know the advantages of empty rhetoric, but the gap
between declarations and performance by professional labor egalitarians is particularly evident in the welfare
sector. The indifference to progressive reforms of public
assistance administration on the part of all significant elements of the American labor movement may be attributed
generally to the conservative orientation of our unionists

toward the role of government in industrial affairs. The traditional Anglo-American disdain for poor persons forced to depend on public aid, of course, has also prejudiced both the leadership and rank-and-file members of all ethnic and racial groups, and at all economic levels.

These attitudes, and the contradictions they present, are reflected in the exaggerated importance placed by labor since the passage of the Social Security Act in 1935 on Old Age, Survivors and Disability Insurance as the major vehicle for maintaining adequate income levels among workers no longer in the labor market and their families.*

In fact, Leo Perlis, the national director of the Department of Community Services for the AFL-CIO, has attributed the low level of public understanding of Aid to Families with Dependent Children and other relief programs in part to the "social insurance orientation of a segment of the labor movement which has all too often looked upon public assistance as a lesser evil—lesser, that is, than hunger and starvation."

The segment that Perlis refers to is a euphemism encom-

---

* OASDI, popularly known as "Social Security," is, along with Unemployment Insurance and Workmen's Compensation, a form of comprehensive "social insurance," i.e., a benefits system financed at least in part by the individual and/or his employer. Since social insurance relates to employment, in this country and in England, it pays "earned" benefits as contrasted with welfare "handouts" from general tax revenues to individuals qualifying on the basis of a "means test."

In 1969 employees contributed (involuntarily) through payroll tax deductions 4.0 percent of their earnings (up to $7,800 per annum) plus .80 percent for Medicare, for a total of $4.80 on a weekly salary of $100, which will increase to $5.20 in 1971–72. These contributions are matched by employers, almost all of whom in the United States are subject to the legislation.

OASDI benefits are paid according to a complicated formula which though not exactly proportionate to earnings pays much higher benefits to workers with large incomes who probably need the benefits less than chronically low-income workers unable to accumulate savings. These last receive OASDI benefits too low to avoid recourse to public assistance (as with any other income, OASDI is deducted from the welfare grant), while the tax on marginal workers imposes a disproportionate hardship during the years of employment.

passing all labor unions in this country, whether AFL or CIO in origin and of all political complexions. Labor's disdain for public assistance cuts across ideological lines. The formula for a "national crusade" urged upon the Federation by Walter Reuther in 1967 included remedies for every conceivable malaise afflicting the movement, but made no specific reference to welfare. As late as 1960, Emil Mazey, secretary-treasurer of the UAW, in an article in the AFL-CIO monthly, *American Federationist,* vigorously advocated health care for OASDI beneficiaries to be provided exclusively through the Social Security system. "Public assistance," said Mazey, "or any other types of free medical care are generally repugnant to most self-respecting Americans, whatever their ages . . ."

While it is true that the Democratic leadership under Presidents Truman, Kennedy and Johnson has instituted periodic and sometimes, as in 1961 (with Aid to Dependent Children of Unemployed Fathers), substantial changes in the public assistance titles, these reforms were due to pressure, not from labor lobbyists or interested politicians, but from "advisory councils" of responsible citizens appointed by the White House and from social work professionals and economists.

Over three hundred persons appeared to testify or submit position papers at hearings held by the President's Advisory Council on Public Welfare which concluded in June, 1966, with the most sweeping proposals for reform of the system ever advanced by an official body. Only four persons represented organizations affiliated with the AFL-CIO. None of these were from New York City, the nation's welfare capital.

The fifteenth issue of the *Encyclopedia on Social Work* published in 1965 discusses labor's involvement in various charitable programs and related legislative efforts but makes no reference to public assistance. A review of back issues since 1960 of the AFL-CIO's *American Federationist* uncovered almost nothing about public assistance except for occasional reprints of speeches by Perlis and annual statements on the subject from the Federation's Executive Council.

The 1964 statement which followed President Johnson's State of the Union message "Waging War on Poverty" vaguely recommended "special aids" for those unable to sustain themselves and demanded that benefit levels and coverage of state social insurance and welfare programs "be brought up to date." The 1965 statement does make a number of specific recommendations for abolition of residency requirements and some other restrictions on eligibility. The statement also urges the affiliates to lobby for reform in state legislatures and to educate the public on the importance of public assistance. In 1967, the Federation's hierarchy, reportedly goaded by Walter Reuther's criticisms —"The movement is irrelevant, inert, etc."—lobbied valiantly to defeat the retrogressive measures advanced by the House Ways and Means Committee. The Executive Council also urged a multibillion-dollar solution to the nation's urban crisis, including a "complete restructuring" of public welfare administration.

However, I have been unable to find in any of the literature or published policy statements general or specific comments about the AFDC-U program. Readers are not advised that the families of thousands of unemployed members are entitled to these benefits and should apply. Likewise, the availability of welfare supplementation in cities like New York that combine relatively high cash assistance with low median incomes for factory workers evidently is a *verboten* topic in labor circles.

AN AMERICAN PHENOMENON

Labor's preoccupation with earned benefits pegged in some way to past employment relates to our predilection for the "deserving" poor. On this side of the Atlantic the Darwinian concept of survival of the fittest, the frontier spirit and the numerical dominance of craftsmen in the labor movement combined to cast the proud, two-fisted male artisan as the exclusive prototype of the American worker.

Labor's repugnance for public assistance also has its roots in a history of mutual antagonism between trade unions and social work agencies. In the United States, philanthropists who dominated the private agencies were often notorious union busters, and still are. Claude Ramsey, the enlightened President of the Mississippi AFL-CIO, has complained publicly that on civil rights issues he finds himself in an uneasy alliance with "responsible" management types who either want to use racial integration to defeat organizing efforts or are as paternalistic to their workers as to the objects of their philanthropies.

Only since World War II have the organized charities made a serious effort to include union officials in their boards of directors. The social work professionals, however, who until recent years barred the legal profession from their councils and evidently communicated only with God, seem to have written off the unions entirely as instruments of reform.

Moreover, unlike their British cousins, American unionists, except for a three- or four-year period during the 30's, have never had to cope with a membership driven by want to the brink of revolution. While the number of Americans on the relief rolls had soared to 8 million by 1938, the peak of the Depression, by 1941 the number had declined to 5.5 million, and to 3.5 million by 1945.* The American experience has tended to confirm the predictions of the classical economists that in a free market the *incidence* of poverty will gradually decline. The Census Bureau of the United States Department of Commerce reported that in 1966 15 percent of the population lived below the "bare survival" poverty level of $3,200 for a four-person family as opposed to 18 percent in 1964 and 22 percent in 1959.

But because only 15 percent of Americans live below the poverty line and because they are aged or Negro or Puerto Rican and scattered in tiny pockets across the country, they have not aroused the sympathy of either the voting public or of most of those unionists who have led the hard core of their membership into prosperous times.

President George Meany and his associates still cling to a Populist rhetoric which links their members with all "workers of the [free] world," but our trade unionism is a uniquely American institution. It was born and flourished in a Jeffersonian mold which embodies both libertarian Democratic principles and a fundamental, though sometimes qualified, abhorrence of state regulation of commerce. Today, the American labor movement paradoxically remains more faithful to the free-enterprise tradition than some of our major corporations.

In the 20's, American unionists were cool even toward the early unemployment insurance proposals advanced by Senator Robert LaFollette of Wisconsin. It is ironic, considering labor's current enthusiasm for Old Age, Survivors and Disability Insurance, that as late as 1931, the national leadership of the American Federation of Labor was openly

---

* The June, 1969, total for cash assistance recipients, 10.2 million (47 recipients per 1,000 population), represents a startling 10 percent increase over 1968 but does not come close to the 1938 relief total as a percentage of the U.S. population. (*Public Assistance Statistics,* June, 1969, HEW, *supra* p. 1 and Table 15.)

opposed to a federal social insurance program. According to the published recollections of the late Edwin Witte, one of the architects of the 1935 legislation, labor was hardly instrumental in its passage. The five union representatives appointed by President Roosevelt to the Advisory Council on Economic Security, unlike the employer members, infrequently attended Council meetings. Spokesmen for organized labor took little part in the congressional hearings on the bill; while the Federation did endorse the Social Security Act in its final form, Witte had a "strong feeling" that labor's positions were influenced by political considerations unrelated to the merits of the legislation.

Undoubtedly, the labor leaders were influenced by their developing liaison with the Democrats. According to political scientist J. David Greenstone,* ideology played no part in the partisan alliance which continues to this day; the vicious anti-unionism of bourgeois employers, most of them Republicans, drove labor into the Democratic camp. Greenstone also makes the cogent observation that labor pursued its self-interests by attempting to broaden the base and to elect the candidates of the party most sympathetic to trade union objectives. A perennial key consideration in the alliance has been increased Social Security benefits, legislation at least as beneficial to the political heirs of FDR as to union members.

The Democrats, with the encouragement of their union allies, seem to view any proposals for radical changes in the existing OASDI system as an attack upon their spiritual inheritance from the New Deal. Social Security was the creature of President Roosevelt, who boasted that while governor of New York he introduced the "cradle to the grave" concept with a contributory social insurance scheme.

New Deal-oriented intellectuals like Arthur Altmeyer,

* *Labor in American Politics,* New York, Alfred A. Knopf, 1969.

one of the first chairmen of the Social Security Board, though concerned about public assistance reforms, have been equally if not more insistent that the Social Security structure not be tampered with.

The welfare researcher who has been raised to believe that liberal Democrats and organized labor are usually on the side of the angels may be confused to read that the Republican leadership, including the late Senator Robert Taft, consistently has been in favor of abandoning OASDI and substituting a system of flat pensions predicated, roughly, on need. Professor Milton Friedman, Barry Goldwater's economic adviser in the 1964 campaign, has denounced OASDI financing as irrational and immoral because it establishes benefits in terms of past productive effort rather than need.

The reactionary Carl Curtis of Nebraska once suggested a "Double Decker" approach, rejected out of hand by the AFL-CIO, that would combine public assistance and pensions in one program. Curtis' proposal, which in principle resembled the current Canadian formula, would have established a universal minimum monthly retirement benefit of forty-five dollars. (It would be unfair, however, to press the ideological point too far. Friedman et al. do not specify the sum in hard dollars they would advocate for the guaranteed minimum-income level sufficient to maintain human dignity among the poor. Moreover, in the spring of 1969 New York Republicans led by the liberal Nelson Rockefeller enacted some of the most repressive and degrading— to the clients—welfare measures in our history.) In 1967, party leaders and AFL-CIO lobbyists did oppose strenuously the "freeze" on Aid to Families with Dependent Children and other repressive welfare amendments, but it is a historical fact that the Johnson Administration finally acquiesced in the cuts and that the AFDC "reforms," included as usual in the same package with Old Age, Survivors and Disability Insurance, were enacted into law while Social Security benefits were increased 12.5 percent across the board. The percentage increase had the effect, of course, of aiding most the workers least in need of higher benefits.*

Philosophically, the emphasis on earned benefits is consistent with organized labor's bread-and-butter image of itself as the collective bargaining agent of the employed worker. Labor views OASDI as the fulfillment of its obligation to retired members. But Social Security conceivably will never be adequate to do more than add a small measure of comfort to the lives of those beneficiaries whose lifetime earnings have produced savings sufficient to sustain them and their dependents. Low-income workers, who suffer most from the payroll tax, probably will find their modest OASDI payments buried in a welfare budget. Since the "security" aspect of OASDI appears to be minimal at best, labor's corresponding lack of interest in long-range cash assistance programs has only one ultimate explanation.

The New York Moreland Commission might have been referring to the attitudes of organized labor when it reported in 1963 that "full acceptance of public welfare becomes a kind of criticism of our economic system." The spirits of Andrew Carnegie and the men who died in the Homestead strike must be crying together in the dust at the sight of

---

* In late 1969 several Democratic congressmen denounced the Nixon welfare proposal calling essentially for a basic floor of income for all Americans, as legislation that would aid the hard-core poor at the expense of elderly OASDI recipients. While contributors to the tax reserves from general revenues might diminish the "integrity" of the Social Security system, at least a greater proportion of the needy would be aided by funds deriving from the progressive income tax rather than from a payroll tax imposed on employers and employees.

House Democrats, who have much to lose, especially those from the big cities, were also noticeably cool toward President Nixon's recommendation that OASDI be made nonpartisan by automatically linking future increases in benefits to rises in the cost of living.

George Meany and Company alone on the barricades defending the American Way of Life.

THE ENGLISH EXPERIENCE

W. J. Cash in his 1941 classic, *The Mind of the South,* said that the power structure of that region always made room at the top for potential revolutionaries who proceed to make political capital out of their humble origins. To this day the most serious obstacle to collective representation in the South is the refusal of white workers to regard themselves as a disadvantaged and exploited minority.

Daniel P. Moynihan, a reformer, has tempered his criticism of current public welfare laws and practices with the curious reminder that those European nations which take better care of their poor also restrict class mobility. This is true. But it is no comfort to a black child who must live like an animal on handouts under the Aid to Families with Dependent Children program to be told that in theory there are no insurmountable obstacles to his becoming an attorney.

In the last analysis, however, the impact of American labor's middle-class attitudes toward welfare can best be gauged by observing the positive role of British labor in the reform of public assistance. The day-to-day concern evidenced by British unions throughout this century for the welfare of all the indigent, whether within or without the work structure, the result of a deeply ingrained class consciousness, stands in sharp contrast to the American experience.

The enclosure by the state in the fifteenth century of arable lands for sheep raising sometimes resulted in evicting whole village populations. This disruption of the natural order also had the effect of instilling in English laborers, whether on the farms or in towns, a firm conviction that the state, if all else failed, owed them a living, from the Poor Rates, if necessary.

The proliferation during the eighteenth and nineteenth centuries of Settlement and Removal Laws contained obnoxious features which were transposed intact to American soil. But for adult workers with large families the laws also reflected the beginnings of the *parens patriae* concept which reached fruition in the current universal assistance programs. If the worker struck out for strange parts in search of employment and failed to find it, he faced the awful indignity of being transported back, with his wife and children, like a common criminal. But at the same time Settlement, with its concomitant obligation on communities to care for their own in times of need, became a right recognized by those who controlled the English economy. Poor relief was the price the landowners and the new industrial class had to pay for their monopolies.

The Poor Law Reform Act of 1834 attempted to destroy this notion. Since poverty, from the dreary viewpoint of the Edwardian reformers, could not be attributed to basic defects in the economy, relief monies were not to be used to provide indigent artisans with the tools of their trade. Interference with the free play of market forces had produced a dissolute working class along with other evils and thus was anathema in the sight of God. The anti-union, churchgoing philanthropists who ruled England in 1834 evidently saw no inconsistency in their attempts to dignify the poor by making them beg for relief and by forcing the workers among them to depend upon handouts in the form of wages wisely distributed by the captains of industry.

The major effect, however, of the Reform Act of 1834 was to develop a solidarity among English workers that has persisted to the present day. The seemingly disparate interests of the weavers, farm laborers, journeymen, shoemakers and mechanics coalesced in the face of Poor Law innovations which treated the entire lower segment of the British population as a *class* to be regulated.

E. P. Thompson, author of a definitive history of the English working class,* gives much of the credit for propagating the new attitudes to the radical journalist William Cobbett. The lands of the medieval Church, said the journalist (with some historical truth), had been held in trust for the poor. The descendants of the feudal poor, as a class, still had a claim on those lands, since confiscated by the state. This claim, Cobbett believed, had been implicitly recognized by successive governments since the Elizabethan era through the distribution of Poor Law benefits. From this premise, Cobbett argued that the community had an obligation to succor the needy and the helpless, not out of charitable motivations, but as a matter of *right*. Cobbett viewed the Reform Act as a massive assault upon his rights theories. In the last year of his life he urged the masses to resist the new Poor Law with violence.

The development of a welfare rights concept in England was also aided by economic conditions. By 1900, all segments of English society had come to accept old-age assistance pensions and the costs of burial for most workers as chronic and necessary charges upon the Poor Rates. In that year one-third of the population of London lived below the prevailing poverty line. Dr. Eveline Burns has written that the late nineteenth and early twentieth centuries changed radically the economic and social world in which the Poor Law functioned; the staggering unemployment lists during 1920 to 1938 also refuted forever the early Victorian concept that employment cycles exactly corresponded to labor supply and demand.

Nevertheless, the active participation of British unions in reform of the Poor Law, as their special concern, had a last-

* *The Making of the English Working Class,* New York, Vintage, 1963.

ing impact on the *type* of Social Security made available by the government.

George Lansbury, one of the Labour representatives elected to the Board of Guardians of the Poplar (Welfare) Union in London in 1894, in an emotional speech, perhaps expressed labor's humanistic view of the subject which persisted through several evolutions in welfare administration into the current universal assistance program. Said Lansbury, "From the first moment [of his election] I determined to fight for one policy only and that was decent treatment for the poor outside the workhouse and hang the rates! [i.e., special taxes for poor relief] . . . My view of life places money, property and privilege on a much lower scale than human life . . . and so when I stood as a Guardian I took as my policy that no widow or orphan, no sick, infirm or aged person should lack proper provision of the needs of life, and able-bodied people should get work or maintenance."

Whereas in the United States unemployment insurance is a minor aspect of income maintenance measures, in Great Britain this was the point at which expansion of the security programs began. Labor accepted a limited insurance concept for unemployment benefits but also pushed for acceptance of a "separate status" for security purposes for the worker who once held a job in a covered occupation but had exhausted his insurance benefits rights. Like Cobbett, modern labor theoreticians insisted that a worker's unemployment (or earnings inadequate to support him) was the fault of society.

In 1942, Ivor Thomas, a Labour representative in Parliament, argued that those unable to work were entitled to "remuneration" to enable them to maintain reasonable standards of comfort and self-respect as an "inalienable right not subject to any test of means or needs." In November of the same year, the Beveridge Report, which had as its basic premise a guaranteed national minimum income, projected England into a new era of comprehensive social security under one integrated program. (Health benefits were to be provided separately.)

Because the Report implicitly rejected the American notion that care of the nonemployed should be measured first by the extent to which individuals had participated in the labor market, basic budgets under the new program were to make allowance for "inefficiency in purchasing and also for the certainty that [recipients] will in fact spend some of it on things not absolutely necessary." Since the British wage system, like the American, is predicated on the product of a man's labor and gives no consideration to the size of his family, allowances for extra dependents were deemed necessary for inclusion in the guaranteed income levels.

Michael Harrington has lamented the fact that European welfare programs have taken some of the militancy out of the union movement across the Atlantic. But that is another problem. The British unions and perhaps also their allies in France and West Germany are to be commended for maintaining a working-class solidarity that brought about truly humane welfare programs for all the poor and not-so-poor alike. The American system, with its OASDI base that is now so attractive to our trade unionists, might well have been devised by dedicated actuaries employed by a fraternal organization of salesmen.

A CONFUSION OF LABELS

While even its most vigorous proponents concede that OASDI has never been completely wage related, the correlation is still close enough to justify a characterization of Social Security as a unique combination of "insurance" and "investment" features. Even though workers who have made small contributions receive a larger relative return from the system than those who pay the maximum, essentially the potential benefits are *purchased* by a worker out of his earnings. New York City's Human Resources Administrator Mitchell Ginsberg has complained that adherence by Congress to the modified insurance principle has effectively blocked efforts to transfer Old Age Assistance recipients out of public assistance and onto the OASDI rolls.

Without financing out of the general tax revenues it is doubtful if the OASDI reserves could safely absorb the 2 million aged on the public assistance rolls and certainly not the 4.8 million AFDC children and their parents who are the prime focus of concern in the War on Poverty. Accordingly, it was a naïve and futile gesture for several international unions to urge their members to pressure their congressmen in 1967 for a 50 percent increase in Social Security benefits. Even the most sympathetic representatives are hamstrung by the system itself.

In fact, "liberalizations" of the Social Security Act, supported vigorously by labor and the Democrats, have had reactionary effects. Expanded OASDI coverage has increased the number of OASDI recipients aged sixty-five and over from 2.8 million in 1950 to over 16 million in 1968, while the Old Age Assistance caseload correspondingly declined from about the same figure as OASDI in 1950 to slightly over 2 million in 1968. The 800,000 recipients lost to OAA had been supported out of general revenues financed by a progressive income tax, but now they and other erstwhile reliefers receive benefits out of the nonprogressive payroll tax reserves, to which low-income workers contribute sums highly disproportionate to their earnings, and to which some of our wealthiest citizens contribute nothing.

Without the aid of Social Security, labor organizations might be hard pressed to wring contributions from employers that would pay the same cash benefits under an industrial pension plan. Public assistance, however, does nothing for the prestige of a bargaining agent; the union leaders cannot take credit for average increases in benefits predicated on need, and the knowledge that union members employed full-time are on relief is foolishly deemed (by the leadership) a slur on the efficiency of the union's representation.

Much of the battle in Congress over the Medicare legislation (i.e., health insurance under the Social Security system) in 1965 focused on the so-called "means test" that labor projected as its principal objection to expanded health coverage for the aged under the existing Kerr-Mills formula. Prior to the 1965 amendments, the unions saw Kerr-Mills as a mere extension of the obnoxious public assistance programs, largely because it was then available only to the destitute.

Labor wanted its people to receive health care as a matter of *right*. In practical terms, this meant that no degrading affidavit of need, associated in the public mind with welfare, should be required as a prerequisite to receipt of benefits. Labor threw its entire arsenal of weapons into battle with the American Medical Association and its allies in Congress and deserves much of the credit for passage of the legislation. Richard Harris' in-depth account of the legislative maneuverings* showed that the unionists knew how the game is played. At one point, said Harris, when it appeared that Senator Russell Long might destroy the Administration's bill with rival legislation of his own, a Louisiana labor leader forced Long to yield by blocking in the state legislature a bill intended to benefit the Senator's private financial interests.

But what did labor accomplish? Medicare unquestionably is a social advance more liberal in its coverage than OASDI, but since it is tied into the Social Security system it suffers from some of the inequities and inconsistencies inherent in that scheme. Whereas the OASDI structure was merely the *excuse* for originally including in Medicare coverage the

---

* *A Sacred Trust,* New York, New American Library, 1966.

aged not eligible for OASDI, the 1967 amendments rein-
forced the "insurance-investment" principle by refusing to
include recipients of Social Security disability benefits of all
ages. While Medicare automatically covers any person at-
taining age sixty-five who is eligible for OASDI or monthly
railroad retirement benefits, the plan provides for only one
hundred days of post-hospital care; moreover for each of the
last eighty days the patient must pay five dollars.

In other words, Medicare does not adequately serve the
aged afflicted with drawn-out terminal illnesses and who
possess modest savings. Because it is Social Security, it does
not and never will contemplate in its scope the working
father with three children, a wife and an income of $5,000
a year. Said the House-Senate Joint Conference Report on
Medicare, "In starting a new program such as hospital insurance, it seems desirable to the Committee that the program should be *completely* in actuarial balance." (My
emphasis.) In fact, insofar as trade union rhetoric tends to
suggest that expansion of Medicare ultimately will solve the
nation's health needs, promulgation of the insurance concept
dilutes the political emphasis on more basic solutions.

What happens to the needy sick not covered by Social
Security or who have exhausted their Medicare allowances?
If they are doubly fortunate to be in a high-wage industry,
they probably will also be protected by an adequate union-
negotiated health plan. But many plans provide no more
benefits than Medicare, and the person who lacks funds and
who needs medical attention must go on the public dole. He
becomes a welfare recipient. He must undergo a means test
and other indignities.

Even from the ideological stance of organized labor, the
"right" of the worker to receive Social Security fades into
the more dubious entitlements under public assistance. Leon
Keyserling has estimated that as of the end of 1966 from 40
to 60 percent of OASDI beneficiaries were living below

Keyserling's poverty level of $5,000 a year for a four-person family. In 1967, 58,000 of the total (about 2 million) Old Age Assistance recipients in the United States also received OASDI benefits. Recent sharp increases in the cost of living indicate the current number of OASDI recipients on relief is rapidly rising.*

But the irony is that if there ever was a fundamental difference in law between the two types of benefits, the distinction has faded since 1935. The periodic expansions of OASDI have had the effect of weakening its "contractual-statutory entitlement" base while reinforcing the social considerations inherent in the entire Social Security Act.

Even if it were true that few union members ever have the need to appear at welfare centers, the fact remains that organized labor, instead of seriously seeking to change public assistance administration, has accepted its underlying Poor Law rationale and used welfare as a horrible example in order to procure medical benefits for workers in a more humane, though illogical, fashion.

The United States may never make health benefits available to all of its citizens regardless of income, not to speak of a universal assistance program including family allowances. But something less than this might prove adequate. Recent reports from England indicate that elements in the Labour Party now believe the "no-means test" approach is both unnecessary and unwise. A "system of selective social services and benefits" geared to income and determined in an impersonal, nonhumiliating way by the tax collecting machinery has been endorsed by the former and present ministers for Social Security Planning in the Labour Cabinet.

In the meantime, however, on this side of the Atlantic, labor's insistence on elevating OASDI at the expense of

---

* In July–December 1968, a startling 68 percent of new OAA recipients nationwide (39,700 out of 57,700) had OASDI income. (National Center for Social Statistics, Report A-5, July 12, 1968, HEW, Table 5.)

public assistance has helped perpetuate the welfare stigma. The "means test" is a red herring. It is not degrading in itself but only as applied in current welfare administration and in the package of indignities suffered by welfare clients. Every citizen exposes his personal finances via a means test when he files his income-tax return or when he applies for a bank loan.

No one believes that income affidavits are necessarily degrading, even when public benefits are involved. Because a bank loan, unlike cash assistance, may constitute an "enrichment" in some cases by permitting the purchase of a new automobile, our mores permit the applicant to walk boldly into the bank. Because the prospective tenant and the project authorities both view public housing accommodations as highly desirable and not easily available in the big cities, no one considers that the requisite affidavits and inquiries into income and character degrade the applicant. We require only the ADC mother, who has no other choice, to wear the beggar's robes.

MEDICAID

Ironically, the "Medicaid" provisions, Title XIX of the 1965 amendments to the Social Security Act, passed into law almost unnoticed in the furor over Medicare. When first enacted this extension of the existing Kerr-Mills legislation contained a means test for medical assistance for the needy that could accommodate almost anyone's ego. The statute contained a built-in "rights" concept not found in the cash assistance titles by generally prohibiting the states from recovering the cost of assistance. The Act commanded the participating states to provide for "all health needs" pursuant to "a flexible income test" which, according to the Conference Committee, "takes into account medical expenses and

does not provide rigid income standards which arbitrarily
deny assistance to people with large medical bills."

New York State took advantage of the liberal intent of
the legislation to exempt a person's "homestead" along with
certain other possessions in computations of need. New York
also pegged eligibility at income levels of $3,000 per annum
or less plus $500 for each dependent up to a maximum in-
come of $9,000 per family. This included a significant por-
tion of New York's low-income population. Alarmed at New
York's generosity, Congress reduced the level of federal
matching funds in 1967 and in the spring of 1969 Albany
Republicans, in an economy mood, reduced eligibility
almost to the welfare level. New York labor unions, with one
or two honorable exceptions, did nothing to save the state
program.

When viable, the Medicaid program dragged labor feet-
first into the field of public assistance. In New York State
few unionists in low-income industries could ignore it without being charged with callous indifference toward their
members. Because of its public assistance character, administered in New York City jointly by the health and welfare
departments, a massive educational campaign was required
by public and private agencies, and some local unions, to
overcome the welfare stigma. The number of Medicaid
recipients on the rolls in New York City slowly reached
750,000 by the end of 1967.

The availability of free medical assistance, under welfare
auspices, to that portion of the stable, blue-collar work
force, the least economically secure and therefore most paranoiac about "welfare" as symbolic of the evils of our times,
could have acted as a leaven in changing public attitudes
toward the welfare poor. The young apprentice plumber
has reason to believe that his union card is like money in the
bank; but right now his annual earnings do not exceed
$7,000 and he has a wife and four young children to support.

He shares title with his mortgagee to a $20,000 house in a suburban development.

The young plumber's income suffices, with strict economies, to pay his normal expenses; but the periodic medical bills are unpredictable and sometimes staggering. He pictures himself with middle-class righteousness as being oppressed, despite his industry and thrift, by the System. It is virtually impossible for this man to discuss rationally the question of discrimination by his union against Negroes. There are many thousands of union members like him.

For a time it was respectable to seek Medicaid benefits. It was also difficult to see how business agents in future years, if the program had continued at its original eligibility levels, could have avoided accompanying their members to the welfare centers and to state hearings to complain about the denial of both medical and cash assistance benefits. The involuntary confrontation of some labor leaders with poverty in their own house could have brought the entire movement into the War on Poverty.

Instead, Medicaid died a fast death and there is every reason to believe that New York labor unions rejoiced at the event.

Social Security, the standard to which American labor has rallied since 1935, has become the symbol of labor's evolution into a middle-class movement. Social Security is an extra benefit for those journeymen plumbers and carpenters who could adequately live out their retirement span without such aid; it is the cream for their Irish coffee. But as a device for keeping dark-skinned factory workers and their families off the welfare rolls, Social Security certainly is not the answer.

TEN

UNION MEMBERS ON WELFARE?

. . . the challenge we faced in the past from the conservative bloc is simply nothing compared to what we might have to face in the near future from the civil rights organizations and their allies . . . The alliance between civil rights and the war on poverty poses all kinds of new challenges to principles and values of trade unionism.

—*Peter T. Schoemann, President, Plumbers and Pipefitters International Union**

U NION LEADERS IN New York, a labor town that contains about 8 percent of the nation's welfare recipients, justify their noninvolvement in welfare with the insane pretense that few if any of their members are or

* David Jones, *The New York Times,* June 18, 1967, p. 32.

should be on public assistance. The leaders also refuse to believe that the dependency of the black or Spanish-speaking AFDC mother derives from the economic state of the man who fathered her children. Faced with a scandalous disparity in earnings between members from minority groups and increasingly affluent white craftsmen, respectable unionism in New York City has also managed to avoid a class struggle in its own house by consigning a large portion of the male working poor to the jurisdiction of the racket unions.

By comparing published statistics relating to earnings by occupation, with welfare eligibility levels and estimates of gross union membership, a strong argument can be made that:

(1) a significant percentage of the labor force, including organized elements, *must* have recourse, on a recurring basis, to cash and medical assistance benefits; and

(2) an equally significant number of welfare recipients *must* be union members now, or have held cards during much of their working lives, or will become members upon reaching maturity.

THE WORKING POOR

Leon Keyserling, who uses $5,000 per year for a four-person family as a "deprivation" floor, attributes the poverty of 60 percent of the citizens living beneath that level to work-related conditions. Forty percent of the poverty in the United States, says Keyserling, derives from full-time or part-time unemployment; during a year when unemployment averages 4 percent, perhaps 12 percent of the labor force is out of work for periods averaging about three months within the same year. Another 20 percent of Americans are poor because of substandard wages paid to the family breadwinners when they are employed. In 1965, the United States

Bureau of the Census estimated that one-fourth of about 7 million families living on annual incomes of less than $3,130 were headed by a person who worked full-time.

Qualitatively and in the surrounding social context, Keyserling's figure is realistic. Television, for example, may be a luxury by monastic standards but is a necessity for the AFDC mother who has five or six children to train, control and entertain. A level of affluence that may induce a glow of well-being among Indians on a reservation will not suffice for this purpose among Negro tenants in an urban slum.

Keyserling's poverty level coincides with the point at which both the poor and the affluent consider that actual deprivation ceases to be a reality, and plan their lives accordingly. A nationwide Gallup Poll made in 1967 confirmed that an impressive majority of Americans *believed* that $101 per week was necessary to support a four-person family.

A study made in the summer of 1964 in Southern California by Professors Stone and Schlamp of 600 representative ADC-U families (with unemployed breadwinners) and 600 families not on welfare but with equivalent incomes and profiles, concluded that in terms of basic needs most low-income workers hover close to the assistance level. The earnings of the group that had never received welfare aid ($3,682 per annum) was only 19 percent higher than the average earnings income ($3,099) of chronic reliefers when employed. (The researchers were also advised by the study group that union membership was the fourth most important aid in finding jobs.)

Columbia sociologist Barbara Rubin, Father John Mulhern and Luz Maria Martinez of the Young Christian Workers in Williamsburg determined that in 1967 there were literally thousands of factory workers, mostly Negro and Puerto Rican, in South and Central Brooklyn who

earned between $1.50 and $1.75 per hour. In one sample of
one hundred nonwelfare breadwinners—all Puerto Ricans
selected at random—Miss Rubin estimated, on the basis of
total income and family size, that over half of the group was
eligible for supplementary assistance. Twenty Brooklyn employers were represented in the sample and fifteen unions,
eight of them affiliated with the AFL-CIO.

The New York City Department of Social Services (formerly the Welfare Department) estimated in 1967 that $2.00
per hour for a forty-hour week was required to keep a four-
person family off the relief rolls. The same year Human Resources Administrator Mitchell Ginsberg stated publicly that
there are nearly as many eligible families off New York's
relief rolls as receive assistance. Studies based on the 1960
census for New York City by Professors Richard Cloward
and Frances Piven of the Columbia University School of
Social Work concluded that about 716,000 persons unrelated or in families appeared to be subsisting in 1960 on incomes at or below the welfare level.

Aided during 1967–69 by sharp increases in the city's
cost of living that have virtually wiped out wage gains among
marginal workers, the City-Wide Coordinating Committee of
Welfare Rights Groups has made good use in its organizational and educational campaigns of the Ginsberg-
Cloward-Piven findings, with the result that New York City's
Home Relief (husband-wife-children) program that provides
locally financed supplementary assistance to low-income
families with a steadily employed breadwinner increased
75.8 percent in 1967–68 as compared with 53.3 percent
in the Aid to Families with Dependent Children category.
While the AFDC caseload (657,089 recipients) is considerably larger than HR (92,352) and therefore more controversial, the HR total is no pittance and, perhaps more
important, points to a considerable number of workingmen

who do not appear in the AFDC figures but whose economic
circumstances precipitated their abandonment of the AFDC
women and children.

POOR UNION MEMBERS

During 1966–67, almost 900,000 employees out of 3.7
million in New York City's nonagricultural establishments
had gross cash hourly earnings of less than $2.25. During
the same period, unofficial figures from government sources
confirmed the obvious—that New York is overwhelmingly
a union town. Units of the New York City Central Labor
Council (AFL-CIO) have about 1.4 million members, and
the Teamsters at least 70,000 cardholders in the metropolitan area.

When the largely unorganized, yet moderately well-paid
nonprofessional employees of banks, insurance companies
and universities are omitted from the total, it is apparent that
only a minority of low-wage shops in New York have avoided
the unions. More specifically, 34,500 employees in the
unionized hotels had average gross weekly earnings in June,
1967, of $83.52, an increase of less than $3.00 over 1966,
for an average work week of thirty-six hours. A nonunion
apparel shop in this city, if it exists, is a quaint anachron-
ism, yet 238,200 workers in that industry earned $90.74
(a $4.50 increase over 1966) for a thirty-four-and-a-half-
hour week. Over 31,000 workers in a category called "miscellaneous fabricated textile products" actually averaged
$77.90 in June, 1967.

As late as the winter of 1969, I relied upon one of my
union contacts to find a factory job for a bright young native
of Colombia, who at the time had been three years in this
country. Much to my chagrin, Maria started at $1.64
per hour (four cents above the federal minimum wage) and

six months later was earning only $1.67. The official explanation was that she was a good worker but slow. In other words, in this case even from the viewpoint of the collective bargaining agent, earnings were geared strictly to production, with no regard for a decent living wage level.

Nationally, a poll made for the Federation by John F. Kraft, Inc., showed that a startling 22 percent of AFL-CIO families in 1967 earned less than $5,000 a year.

There are also those currently outside the work force—the dependent mothers, their children and the aged—who have been or will become union members for portions of their lives. Can the movement rightfully ignore them?

It is difficult to overlook the fact that a welfare child, if he does not die young or become a professional criminal in the big cities, will become a blue-collar (union) worker, but in recent years only a handful of influential unionists have conceded any responsibility for the training and job placement of poor children. I know of no one in the movement who agrees that AFDC mothers, many of whom will enter the work force in their middle or late thirties when their youngest child is in high school, deserve some recompense *right now* for their future contributions to the Social Security tax reserves and union treasuries.

Perhaps most pathetic are the 58,000 Old Age Assistance recipients who left the employment rolls with Social Security benefits too low to sustain them. They probably sang the labor songs, walked the picket lines and dutifully hit the bricks on occasion, trusting in the good faith of the union leadership. These same people, because of their own improvidence, terminal illnesses, a lifetime of low wages, large families, or combinations of all four causes, find themselves in their declining years consigned to the clumsy mercies of public welfare administration. The officials of their unions are not likely to come visiting.

But while neglect of nonworking mothers, infants, and

old people is at least consistent for a union movement that
in its maturity is almost more in love with free enterprise than
the employers with which it bargains, it is patent hypocrisy,
for example, for New York's unionists to accept monthly
dues from members who are or should be on welfare while
pretending that reform of public assistance is the sole responsibility of Mayor John Lindsay and the social workers.

The standard defense to this charge contains an admission
of additional guilt. A research specialist with the City Central Labor Council once told me, "We don't have any members on welfare; talk to the independent unions." The labor
entrepreneurs organize where the respectable unions refuse
to go; they make most, but not all, of the AFL-CIO unions
look good by comparison.

GO ON TO ORGANIZE

In that special place in heaven reserved for hell-raising
organizers who are framed on murder charges and die before a firing squad cursing the employer class, the spirit of
Joe Hill must be groaning at the sight of some of his successors.

It is doubtful that Bennie the Bug ever heard of Joe Hill,
and Bennie's style, flamboyant as it is, does not exactly correspond to the Populist approach of the Swedish immigrant
who wanted his remains taken "the hell out of" Utah. But
Bennie, in the eyes of the law and the employers he deals
with and the 3,000 or so Negro and Puerto Rican workers he
purports to represent, despite occasional falls from grace,
is a bona-fide representative of cheap labor in New York
City.

In recent years, Bennie and others like him in the metropolitan area have aggressively sought out workers in industries beyond the traditional jurisdictions where wages close

to the federal minimum generally suggest marginal profits or disreputable operations, exploitation, or a combination of all three. In the category described by the New York State Department of Labor as "miscellaneous manufacturing industries" (toys, costume jewelry, pens and pencils), 72,300 employees in 1967 earned an average weekly wage of $89.93.

The respectable unions, who have reputations to maintain and, perhaps, parent organizations to answer to, hesitate to undertake such ventures because the risks entailed are disproportionate to the gains (new members and their dues) to be achieved. A responsible union cannot call any organizing strike without being prepared to furnish a certain amount of subsistence to needy participants. In areas cultivated by the racket unions, the honest AFL-CIO, Teamster, Mine Worker, or United Electrical Union organizer must also hope that the employer is not a front or tax dodge for Cosa Nostra money.

Most of the leaders of the one hundred and fifty-odd independent unions unaffiliated with a national organization in New York City's industries (not to be confused with the seventy representing government employees) have no reputations to maintain and no apparent scruples. Some of these men undoubtedly see themselves as simply being in the business of supplying labor; some of them, perhaps, outclass many of their respectable counterparts in both diligence and honesty. As a group, however, they are rightly known as parasites feeding upon the misery of the working poor. A reputation of this kind in the indelicate world of labor-management relations is not easily acquired.

Unlike the respectable unions which use names identifying the ultimate origin of the organization in a particular craft (the Teamsters) or industry (Mine Workers), the racket groups use vague, generic titles that are difficult to remember and deliberately designed to confuse. The words

"Amalgamated," "Production," "Warehouse," "Service" appear in various combinations with suspicious regularity among the titles of such organizations, with nothing more specific to identify them than a local number.

The entrepreneurs function along several lines. On occasion, because they have encountered an honest employer or a relatively sophisticated work force, the independents might conduct a legitimate operation. For the most part, however, these men provide unscrupulous businessmen with a union that they can happily live with. The bargain includes a labor contract legally sufficient to satisfy the meager requirements of the National Labor Relations Board and which serves to keep legitimate unions away from the employer's door. Most workers in these shops seldom see their contract or enjoy its benefits, but dues are checked off and huge sums of pension monies are at the disposal of union-management "trustees."

At the time of the dissolution of the employer's business, the only "workers" on the payroll may be relatives of the union officials who under the terms of most pension fund agreements are lawfully entitled to divide the corpus of the fund.

Numerous studies have shown that only a tiny percentage of workers in medium- to low-wage industries of all kinds ever receive retirement benefits under union pension plans. A Brooklyn worker-priest, Anthony Equale, spent two months in a racket shop in 1968. "It's amazing," he told me, "there are almost no old-timers in the place. Nobody seems to survive the two-month waiting period before you join the union."

My innocence in these matters was rudely shattered seven or eight years ago at an NLRB hearing which concerned an attempt by a unit of the Clothing Workers to raid a laundry reputedly owned by an underworld figure. I was attempting unsuccessfully to show that a supervisor was lying when she made what I regarded as an incredible statement that representatives of the incumbent (racket) union had not appeared in the vicinity of the laundry during the week before the NLRB election. I ended the cross-examination when the attorney for the independent assured me, "You evidently don't know how this union operates."

At the same hearing, the nephew of the reputed owner walked into the room at a crucial point, smiled, shook hands all around and sat down. After that, every employee-witness, including one who had told an NLRB investigator his life had been threatened before the vote, could remember nothing except his own name.

Judge Irving Saypol of the New York County Supreme Court had this to say about the professional career of Bennie the Bug in a bizarre civil proceeding in which Bennie attempted to attack his own agreement to hold a general election under the supervision of the Court: "He is a twice-convicted and punished criminal for a robbery in the second degree and illegal traffic in narcotics . . ." The judge described Bennie's organization as "a labor union more in name than in fact under the domination of its principal factotum, Ben ——— . . . [who] has a ten-year contract as 'General Manager' . . . the union is his creature which operates in an unlimited field in any kind of work, labor or activity, skilled and unskilled, employed in this [New York metropolitan area] vicinity." The judge also found that Bennie's membership, 1,500 at that time, paid between $6,000 and $8,000 per month into the union's treasury. The constitution had never been submitted to the membership for ratification.

A note of injudicious horror appears in the language of the decision as Judge Saypol relates that a former president of Bennie's union had been a thirty-dollar-a-week messenger for the union when installed as president by the general manager. The man's successor, a part-time sales clerk, became president after meeting Bennie at a hotel. On the witness stand, Bennie candidly admitted that he removed the incumbent from office when she refused to return the keys to his apartment. "She has done nothing but make trouble for me ever since."

Bennie's comic activities conceal a shrewd and ruthless business sense. It is no joke that the livelihood and future welfare of thousands of helpless workers have been awarded by default by the New York labor establishment to the jurisdiction of men who, at best, cannot be said to aspire to any heights of trade union excellence from which they can be accused of falling. On the state level, the official statistics show that while the AFL-CIO added 314 locals of government employees between 1961 and 1964, the Federation also lost 177 locals in industry. "Independent affiliated" groups (e.g., the Teamsters) lost five, but the "independent unaffiliated" category gained three local unions. Despite occasional legal difficulties, Bennie has doubled his membership since Judge Saypol's decision and, at this writing, is himself still in business.

One "amalgamated" local with headquarters in a Brooklyn slum neighborhood collected over $60,000 in dues and assessments from 1,000 members during 1963, the year before its top two officers went to jail. A group in another borough, headed by a notorious ex-convict, reported over $200,000 in dues from about 5,000 in 1965–66. The most prosperous independent of them all, expelled originally from the AFL-CIO on charges of corruption, in an average year represents a shifting mass of over 20,000 workers in Brooklyn alone. Its pension fund had over $1 million in reserves at the end of 1966.

Official spokesmen for the urban AFL-CIO Councils periodically denounce the racket unions and the laws which permit them to prosper. Leaders of affiliated locals are not so outspoken, perhaps because self-righteousness toward fellow unionists is not one of their hypocrisies. They are probably more honest than the public relations men who, despite their strident remarks, are well aware that strong unions have never relied upon, or been deterred by, legal sanctions to achieve their goals.

Those independents actively organizing among New York's sweatshops could be annihilated if respectable unionism launched a massive campaign to enroll the low-income worker. The reason labor has not done so (except of course for Cesar Chavez and his campesinos and for some AFL-CIO locals active in the laundry and hospital industries) is due only in part to the initial high cost and disproportionate return on the organizing investment. Labor also has rejected the working poor because to make common cause with them might open the door to a more equitable distribution of the gravy presently available almost exclusively to the craftsmen who dominate labor's affairs.

THE RICH GET RICHER

White unionists have been one of the mainstays of an economic system which has produced an almost uninterrupted history of progressive affluence for the bulk of their members and near-poverty-level incomes with some welfare supplementation for the remainder.

The survey conducted for the AFL-CIO in 1967 by John F. Kraft, Inc., among a representative sampling of members across the country effectively confirmed labor's bourgeois identification; while the fact that 22 percent of the members earn below $5,000 per annum is substantial enough to warrant greater involvement of labor unions in the welfare sector, the estimate by Kraft that 46 percent of Federation workingmen earn between $7,500 and

$15,000 per year, as opposed to 32 percent in the $5,000–
$7,000 category, furnishes one good reason why Federation
activity tends to neglect the poor man.

The relatively affluent plurality who earn above $7,500
per year also possess greater job protection, based on
seniority, as well as most of the union leadership positions,
and, consequently, a voice in union policies that may be
out of all proportion to their numbers. (In fact, the survey
showed that almost 50 percent of the national membership
was under forty years of age.) Though the survey does not
say so, the higher earners also belong to locals that require
higher dues from members, a per-capita portion of which
goes to the International Union and to other parent groups.
Many of these locals to this day deliberately exclude nonwhites. Accordingly, the influential voice of the well-to-do
brothers that is heard in top labor circles comes on cool,
calm, conservative and quite content with the status quo.

The status quo, however, does not include modest salary
increases. In 1967, when more than 25 percent of New
York City workers earned less than $100 per week, 111,-
000 Contract Construction employees in this area averaged
about $200 ($5.47 per hour) for a thirty-five-hour week,
or a gain of about $9.00 over 1966. In the summer of 1969,
the New York Building Trades struck for, and most of them
achieved, increases of about $29 per week.

In other words, the unskilled or semiskilled factory machine operator who earned $80 in 1965 probably has about
$100 per week today, but the plumber or electrician who
averaged $150 in 1965 now brings home about $250.

The collective bargaining agreement negotiated by the
International Ladies Garment Workers' Union for a three-
year period ending in June, 1970, provides total increases
(wages and fringe benefits) for 27,000 employees of 15
percent. This has the effect of giving net take-home pay
increases each year of the contract of about eight cents

per hour to 21,000 ILG workers in the $2.14 bracket, a sum easily absorbed by the rapidly accelerating cost-of-living index.

Since the portion of total income applied to food purchases rises only slightly with increased earnings, the Puerto Rican and black stitcher in the ILG treads water while electricians and carpenters are able to save enough of their earnings to buy a summer place in the Catskills or along the Jersey shore.

Even within the ILG itself, the new contract perpetuates a disparity in earnings between the new ethnic groups and the older Jewish and Italian workers in dress and outerwear manufacturing, who also enjoyed the percentage increase. For them, the 15 percent computed on an average hourly earnings base of about $2.80 represents actual gains of forty-two cents.

The same bargaining strength that produces disproportionate gains for the high earners in the AFL-CIO also translates into political power in a country that places material success near the top of its value system.

What is more discouraging, however, than the lies uttered in self-defense by the unionists involved is the failure of elected officials and honest unionists to cry "foul." I have heard decent men in labor circles defend "father and son" hiring practices on democratic grounds; since the businessman has the right to will his corporate assets to his son, the craftsman should have the right to bequeath his major asset, his job, to *his* son. The existence of the New York State Commission on Human Rights is a political asset to Albany Republicans and a bureaucratic insult to black and Spanish-speaking teen-agers denied decent job opportunities. After many years of almost total inactivity in the employment sector, SCHR with much fanfare in 1969 chose to crack down on that critical industry—the legitimate Broadway theaters.

A news article by David Jones in *The New York Times*
on June 18, 1967, ingenuously headlined "U.S. Aides Will
Discuss Bias with Officials of Building Trades," quoted
then Secretary of Labor Willard Wirtz as commending the
trades for their sincerity in helping to solve the "problem."
The same article reported that President Peter T. Schoemann of the Plumbers and Pipefitters did not foresee a
meeting of the minds between the unions and government
agencies "happening very soon, like next Monday or the
Monday after that."

On the other hand, those who wonder at the continuing
popularity of the late Senator Robert F. Kennedy among
Negroes, young and old, should know that when C. J. Hag-
gerty, head of the AFL-CIO Building Trades Department,
told a Senate committee that the Federation's four-year
program to eradicate racial discrimination in the trades had
been "ninety-nine percent successful," only Kennedy challenged him.

Powerful as they are, however, the crafts are not the
whole of the American labor movement. Social concern
may still be found in large quantities among CIO unionists,
but even these fail to respond meaningfully to the War on
Poverty or to welfare reform because they have accepted
the free-enterprise notions impressed on the movement by
the crafts. Even labor radicals secretly despise the welfare
poor for being helpless.

A WELFARE RIGHTS–LABOR COALITION?

In June, 1969, Victor Gotbaum, a young and progressive leader of many of New York's public employees, denounced President Harry Van Arsdale of the City's Central
Labor Council for taking no position on the welfare cut-

backs enacted into law by Albany Republicans. Yet only a couple of months earlier Gotbaum himself was noticeably cool toward a welfare rights–labor coalition proposed by me.

About ten union officials attended a meeting one spring afternoon at New York University School of Law. (Gotbaum declined to attend but sent a delegate.) George Wiley, wearing a dashiki, and Hulbert James, in overalls, of the National Welfare Rights Organization, were also present. All of the unionists, by their own admission, were outsiders in terms of influence within the New York labor movement. They had opposed the Vietnam war and the teachers' strike; they had supported the radical dove Paul O'Dwyer for senator over Jack Javits, the candidate of the labor establishment. Most of them in the fall of 1969 would support Mayor John Lindsay over Democratic challenger Mario Procaccino, endorsed by Van Arsdale and the Central Labor Council.

I opened the discussion by pointing out several issues of mutual concern: for example, the imposition of a support burden on low-income stepfathers, the lack of child-care facilities and tax deductions for baby-sitting expenses of low-income working mothers. For about an hour or so the left-wing unionists seemed genuinely enthusiastic about a working coalition with NWRO. They confessed their ignorance about repressive welfare practices. They admitted that even the best industrial unions could not negotiate a contract satisfying the income needs of the bachelor and the man with five dependents. The officials were embarrassed to hear that Hulbert James wrote to four hundred local unions in New York State seeking endorsements of welfare reform legislation and received replies from only two. Wiley was particularly impressive with his pragmatic nonideological pitch for a joinder along traditional union lines of welfare–labor organizations with unrelated but compatible constituencies.

Then New York's labor radicals began to back away: the membership must first be educated to the idea. Cheating by

welfare recipients cannot be ignored. A five-man committee
was appointed to explore further the coalition possibility.
Reluctant to issue a joint statement supporting reform
measures and attacking the punitive welfare legislation then
pending in Albany, each unionist said he would issue his
own statement. The least politically vulnerable labor leader
present—an officer of a large militant CIO unit in the New
York area that had maintained good relations with Van
Arsdale et al.—said he would conduct an experiment with
one of his low-income locals whereby those eligible for welfare supplementation would be sought out and bussed under
union auspices to the appropriate welfare centers.

What followed? The "experiment" never got off the
ground. The committee met one time. Only Nick Kisburg of
the Teamsters and Ed Perlmutter of the Social Service Employees Union (the welfare caseworkers) made their presence felt in Albany. The welfare rights–labor coalition was
only an idle dream.

ELEVEN

SOLIDARITY FOREVER

In days to come organized labor will increase its importance in the destinies of Negroes. Negroes pressed into proliferating service occupations— traditionally unorganized and with low wages and long hours—need union protection, and the union movement needs their membership to maintain its relative strength in the whole society. On this new frontier Negroes well may become the pioneers that they were in the early organizing days of the thirties.

—*Martin Luther King**

IS IT NECESSARY in a critique of this kind to draw up an exhaustive balance sheet to call labor to account? Sensitive labor leaders, with some justification, like to point out that only the misdeeds of unionists make news-

* *The New York Times Magazine,* June 11, 1967.

paper headlines. The public, it seems, is titillated by news of union aggression against the commonweal while the day-to-day accomplishments of the movement in furthering the material welfare and human dignity of the membership are so stuffed with economic data as to make dull reading.

Carping criticisms from the New Left, we are told, overlook labor's many contributions to social progress. The garment industry was a jungle before David Dubinsky became its master. Enlightened labor-management relations in the men's suit and coat industry produced fifty years of higher and higher wages and no strikes. Housing cooperatives, medical centers, unpublicized integration in the Southern shops . . .

The accusation of nit-picking is easily answered by simply pointing to the universal low state of esteem in which the movement is held in circles usually sympathetic to labor's goals. Walter Reuther, prior to the UAW-Teamsters alliance in 1969, in one of his extraordinary series of public statements attacking the Federation for its "sense of complacency and adherence to the status quo," expressed his union's concern for the need of the Federation "to develop stronger ties with labor's historic and essential allies in the liberal intellectual and academic community and among America's young people."

Though Reuther did not say so, it is indeed a phenomenon of our times that a highly idealistic, sometimes naïve generation of college graduates, many of them from union homes, dismiss out of hand the role of labor as an instrument of social reform.

Until his tragic death, Senator Robert Kennedy's wide-ranging compassion had made him a hero among a conglomerate of students, blacks and young white workers. Kennedy's apparent unwillingness to accept all of the dogmas of the Demo-labor coalition also gained him numerous enemies in labor circles. However, the youthful idealism evident in his book *The Enemy Within* suggests that Robert Kennedy's distaste for Jimmy Hoffa et al. stemmed not from a patrician outlook but rather from a sincere view that such men are killers of the workingman's dream. But among unionists, as elsewhere, the senator was probably judged best by the friends he made, and here these included Walter Reuther and the United Automobile Workers.

Claude Ramsey, the president of the Mississippi AFL-CIO, in an August, 1965, report on his troubles with militant rights groups, plaintively remarked, "some of [their] criticism is directed at the so-called Liberal Establishment of which the AFL-CIO is a part and which they [the Mississippi Freedom Democratic party and others] seem to hate as much as anything else."

Labor, as a bulwark of the liberal establishment, like the churches in recent years, has had to live with the indifferent comment of black and white radicals of "too little, too late." These say that what gestures the establishment now makes are designed to maintain its liberal image at the cost of impeding true progress. Labor, like the churches, has not yet been able to articulate an adequate reply.

Until two or three years ago, the Federation's Department of Social Security did not encompass public assistance matters within its jurisdiction. Since 1960, labor's day-to-day involvement, such as it is, with welfare administration has been entrusted to the Community Services Committee of the AFL-CIO and its dedicated director, Leo Perlis, whose many public statements have helped enormously to place the Federation at least *officially* behind the cause of welfare reform.

But the fact of assigning responsibility to a specialized unit—in this case, incidentally, much of the financing of Perlis' organization comes from nonlabor sources—instead of to the main body politic suggests that welfare, in the view of labor leaders, is an esoteric, remotely relevant topic or, at best, tangential to the principal thrust of the movement. At the same time, public relations advantages at almost no cost accrue to the Federation from Perlis' activities.

The National Federation of Public Assistance Employees contains units, as in Chicago, affiliated with the AFL-CIO as well as the independent Social Service Employees Union in New York City, which as a matter of practice and principle place welfare reform alongside economic gains for the members on the bargaining table. But these unionists also represent caseworkers sophisticated enough to appreciate the need for reform by the time they pick up their membership cards. Though atypical, the reform activities of the welfare unions help to excuse the noninvolvement of the rest of organized labor in the problems of the hard-core poor.

It must have come as a shock to those labor leaders who savor the social impact of their speeches to read the results of a poll conducted in 1967 for the Amalgamated Lithographers of America among a broad spectrum of college students. Fifty-five percent of the students said that "statements made by most labor leaders had no relevancy to youth's problems."

Significantly, the preoccupation of the young activists as a group is for the elevation of the very poor. In the eyes of many of the new breed of organizer working in the ghettoes, the apparent refusal of labor to identify with welfare recipients is a major symptom of the philosophical dry rot which coats the movement today. Their distaste for unions stems from a double discovery early in the game that (1) no business agents appear at the welfare centers and at the community action storefronts; and (2) too often labor's representatives emerge as an element of the local power structure intent on maintaining the status quo.

"It is bad enough," says one white VISTA worker in Bedford-Stuyvesant, "that you go to housing court with rent strikers and you find out that some church or the judge's

nephew is your slumlord; but when you find out that a
local school board can't get a progressive program going
because of opposition from the United Federation of Teachers
and you want to try to find a job for a black kid who's
getting out on parole and five or six craft unions don't even
return your phone calls—you say to yourself, 'Where the
hell do you turn if you want to help people with three strikes
against them?' "

No matter how well labor's national performance might
rate on an objective management-type efficiency and progress
scale, it is important both to the cause of human dignity for
the poor and to the health of the labor movement that the
next generation of movers and shakers now believes that
unionism is irrelevant to the needs of the times.

But is that the end of the story? White critics of the labor
movement usually are astonished to find that black leaders
are not as sanguine as whites are about labor's failings. The
Reverend Martin Luther King's hopes for a better future for
working Negroes seemed to rest on combined pragmatic
and idealistic grounds. Blacks need labor, he said; and union
leaders, whether they realize it or not, need American blacks.
To King, the white unionist was soul brother to the black
worker just as William Faulkner cast the dark man in the
role of Absalom to the reluctant white South.

The civil rights leader died for his convictions during the
Memphis garbage strike in 1968. Whatever the future holds,
King's optimistic Christian-Marxist concept of a brotherhood of workers is not entirely lacking in historical justification.

POWER TO THE PEOPLE

This country once before witnessed a short-lived liaison
of Southern black and white workers in the 1890's. The
Populist political movement in varying degrees in every state

except South Carolina encouraged blacks to make common cause with exploited whites. It is particularly poignant in view of Georgia's now-tarnished promise to recall that in 1891 Tom Watson, the Populist party leader of that state, wrote for the benefit of Negro and white farmers, "You are kept apart that you may be separately fleeced of your earnings. You are made to hate each other because upon that hatred is rested the keystone of the arch of financial despotism which enslaves you both. You are deceived and blinded that you may not see how race antagonism perpetrates a monetary system which beggars both."

Watson insisted on integrated meetings and once summoned hundreds of armed white Populists to protect a Negro associate who hid from a lynch mob in Watson's home. The Alabama People's party platform of 1892 called for protection of the legal rights of the colored race and "through the means of kindness, fair treatment and just regard for [Negroes] a better understanding and more satisfactory condition may exist between the races." The brilliant and eclectic Ignatius Donnelly of Minnesota, in a preamble to the platform of the national organization in 1892, said, "We propose to wipe the Mason and Dixon Line out of our geography, to wipe the color line out of politics . . . to take the robber class from the throat of industry."

Though most historians today agree that racial equality was not a primary goal of the Populists, and many, with a notable exception in C. Vann Woodward, tend to denigrate the movement as a primitive upheaval with anti-Semitic overtones, there is no question that the demise of the Populist party in the late 1890's indefinitely postponed all hope of an economic and social awakening in the South. Populist leaders who, we may assume, were fighting not only the prevailing mores but their own prejudices as well generally made peace with the status quo. Watson became an embittered white supremacist.

Watson attributed the party's decline to the hypocrisy of the "nice people" of the South, the Bourbons who controlled Southern Democratic politics then as they do today. Watson's Northern ally, Ignatius Donnelly, made the same accusation in *Doctor Huguet,* a fantasy dealing with the race problem.

The forebears of the civic and business leaders who today bitterly resist the advent of labor unions in Southern communities, at the turn of the century ostensibly wished the Negro well but used race as a club to keep poor blacks and whites in their appointed places. Significantly, Booker T. Washington, the intimate of philanthropists and national political leaders, whose policy of gradualism, more than any other element, made the Southern disenfranchisement movement and the advent of Jim Crow legislation in the 1890's tolerable to the Christian conscience, also urged his fellow blacks to shun all labor unions because they were destructive of private initiative. Dr. King pointed out that middle-class white prejudices toward unionism have been accepted by affluent Negroes.

In the light of what Southern gentlemen have done to the Negro in the name of progress, the late A. J. Liebling's somewhat sympathetic treatment of the Populist Long dynasty in *Earl of Louisiana* is more than understandable. Racism did not become a real political factor in modern Louisiana until 1960 when the New Orleans daily *Times-Picayune* and other respectables teamed with white supremacists to replace Earl Long as governor with cowboy singer Jimmie Davis.

As managing editor of the *Atlanta Constitution,* Henry W. Grady achieved a fame which has endured to this day with his editorials and lectures, particularly a speech entitled "New South" delivered in New York City in 1886 on the theme of national unity. Grady also wrote in the 80's that the corruptible vote of the Negro constituted a menace to Anglo-

Saxon civilization. In North Carolina the Populists for a time achieved astounding political victories by running on the same ticket with Republicans. But men like Josephus Daniels, the crusading editor of the *Raleigh News and Observer* and later Secretary of the Navy in President Woodrow Wilson's Cabinet, beat fusion to an early death by yelling "nigger."

In fairness to Josephus Daniels, however, it should be said that he aided the North Carolina trade unions in their crusade against child labor. So profitable and entrenched was this vicious system that in 1900, 75 percent of the textile spinners in that state were fourteen years or younger. As of this writing, North Carolina has acquired an enviable reputation among the Southern states for its success in attracting Northern industry with the threefold inducement of no unions, low wages and tranquility in race relations. It is no coincidence that North Carolina, with the lowest ratio of unionization in the country (approximately one member out of sixteen nonagricultural workers), competes with Mississippi for the lowest rate of average hourly earnings. The Tarheel state had the dubious distinction in 1962 (when ex-Governor Luther Hodges served as Secretary of Commerce in the Kennedy Cabinet) of containing the highest percentage of black families in the South earning less than $3,000 per year (approximately 83 percent).

Labor unions, of course, are not capable of solving the massive employment problems facing this generation, but, however cynically in some cases, unions do hold themselves out to be brotherhoods, existing for the primary purpose of uniting workers in a common front against their employers. Unions do push up wage scales, and the automaters, who are anxious to replace workers with machines and who with impunity can ignore the unorganized voices of protest, at least must listen to their collective indignation.

THE POPULIST REVIVAL

On the other hand, this proletarian movement has raised up quiet heroes whose efforts at educating Southern whites toward acceptance of racial integration have made the pronouncements of Catholic bishops, for one example, seem diffident. Murray Kempton has written of the "lonely" men who rise up at union meetings to denounce corrupt administrations. Often enough, it is the same lonely men who have risen above the biases of family and friends, infused only God knows when and how with their own private sense of injustice, to demand full brotherhood for nonwhites.

The story is told of the late Philip Murray that he spoke with such passion on the subject of racial equality at a segregated union meeting that his audience was moved to cut the rope which stretched down the center aisle separating whites and Negroes. (Murray, the first president of the CIO, but no bureaucrat, embarked on a union career the night he punched a braker boss for cheating on the count of Murray's output of coal.) In Atlanta in 1949, local Steelworkers' officials with no little effort were able to persuade strikers to reject an economic offer from their employer that would have provided lower pension benefits for black employees. The strike ended when the employer agreed to the same pension plan for all.

In the summer of 1963, a few months before the assassination of President Kennedy, and at a time when the "goddamned Kennedys" was an epithet that greeted the traveler in every airport limousine in the South, I heard Victor Bussie, president of the Louisiana AFL-CIO, tell a union convention in Baton Rouge that God, and not the federal government, had made the races equal.

Claude Ramsey, Bussie's counterpart in Mississippi and

the moderate target of New Left agitation in that state, issued his Report on the Delta Farm Strike in August, 1965. The Report recites Ramsey's version of the dispute between him and the Delta Ministry and the Freedom Democratic party over whether the Delta laborers could be organized from a trade union point of view (Ramsey said no); but the Report is notable in that Ramsey, the spokesman for a predominantly white AFL-CIO in the most bigoted state in the Union, was willing to go on record as supporting the case of the black workers, whose wages and working conditions, he said, "are among the worst existing anywhere in the nation." Ramsey also offered to provide money to the strikers through channels acceptable to him; more important, from the standpoint of publicly identifying labor with the despised minority, Ramsey offered to send a professional union organizer into the Delta situation.

In a bellwether Democratic congressional primary election held in South Carolina on March 23, 1965, a union lawyer who championed civil rights, Medicare and most other aspects of the Social Security program lost to the regular party candidate by less than 2,000 votes out of approximately 13,000 cast. The liberal candidate had the support of the labor groups and Negroes and, presumably, would have won if the flood of new registrations anticipated in the district as a result of President Johnson's voting bill had preceded the election. In 1969 the Populist Henry Howell of Norfolk came surprisingly close to being elected governor of Virginia.

In Tennessee, a state which has had its share of racial conflict and where Confederate memorials abound, the voters chose the neo-Populist Congressman Ross Bass, who voted for the Civil Rights Bill, to fill the unexpired term of the late Senator Estes Kefauver. Bass had the enthusiastic support both of Tennessee Negroes and most of the state's union officials, who worked closely with Democratic politicians and civil rights leaders to bring Negroes to the polls for Bass. The opposition daily, *Knoxville Journal,* noted that Bass' plurality in the primaries corresponded closely to the size of the state's Democratic black registration, but this statistic evidently did not deter a majority of Tennessee whites from helping to elect Bass as well as President Johnson on November 3. Bass lost his seat to Governor Frank Clement in 1966 only because Clement wooed enough Memphis blacks away from Bass by appointing a black man to the judiciary.

Publications distributed to all affiliates in the South by the Clothing Workers, Steelworkers and the UAW in 1964 explicitly endorsed the Civil Rights Bill. Ku Klux Klansmen kidnapped and beat an official of the Woodworkers' Union for cooperating in the desegregation of a Laurel, Mississippi, factory. Incidentally, the Klan, which attracts a gas-station owner, small merchant, middle-income farmer membership is almost as hostile to labor organizers as to Negroes. Cross burnings have not been an infrequent occurrence on the eve of NLRB elections.

During the fall of 1964 the AFL-CIO conducted numerous seminars in the Southern states to educate employers and local unions to acceptance of the Equal Employment Opportunities Act and made lateral assaults on segregation by implicitly assuming that prejudice was abhorrent to all of the members. The fruits of this quiet process will be more evident in future years when the full impact of the Civil Rights Bill will be felt in the South and in the long run will be more meaningful than all the heralded token breakthroughs in the Northern craft unions. A white labor organizer in Tennessee told me recently that integration was so widespread in his state that the organizer's children would never be able to regard blacks as an inferior race.

I cite these occurrences, which are admittedly out of the context of a general history of passive hostility by white

unionists toward blacks, simply to show that the seeds of
change have been present in the South at least since the
late 30's when the CIO began organizing whites and Negroes
in the mass-production industries.

The racial situation in Southern unions today seems to
confirm Dr. King's prediction that the South holds more
long-range promise for truly integrated living than the North.
Southern workers converted to unionism lack the cynicism
of union members in the big cities. Northerners usually are
forced to accept a union shop as a condition of employment.
The price organized labor sometimes pays for this enormous
advantage is to be linked in the minds of the discontented
with Big Government, Big Business, etc. Southern members,
on the other hand, seem to view unionism, like religion, as an
important aspect of their lives and, democratically, as the
sum of its component parts. These workers in large numbers
have readily accepted the human rights package that usually
arrives, in muted tones, with a membership card in an industrial union. Certainly, pragmatic considerations are important. In garment shops organized by the Clothing
Workers in Alabama and Tennessee, skilled cutters and
spreaders (males) receive increases ranging from $1.50 to
$2.50 per hour with the first union contract. At an Urban
League dinner in New Orleans in 1963 I was introduced to
a Teamster's business agent who enjoyed the usual benefits
(a salary of $22,000 per year at that time plus expenses),
prestige and power of that office. But he was a black man and
I asked him how he managed to survive in the Deep South.
"We get a driver four dollars an hour and he don't care
who rides with him in the cab."

Since the passage of the Civil Rights Bill in 1964, the
unions have been in a better position to reconcile working-
class whites to the New Order. Southern employers, who
almost without exception during organizing campaigns used
to shout from the plant gates to the workers of the surround-

ing communities the news of the union's theoretical commitment to racial equality, have decided it is better for business to comply, at least in token fashion, with the Act.

As a consequence, the Clothing Workers in 1965–66, to the astonishment of labor organizers everywhere, were able to win elections among over 1,000 employees in a chain of factories in Southern Alabama. The first election was held shortly after the March from Selma to Montgomery but apparently had no impact on the election because the employer previously had advised his people without equivocation that he intended to comply with the Fair Employment provisions of the Act.

During the negotiations, led by the union's idealistic vice-president, Charlie English, white workers in the National Guard told lurid tales about what supposedly went on at Selma but were quick to acknowledge their fraternity with the sixty-odd black employees, almost all of whom had joined the union. At one point when negotiations reached a temporary impasse, Ed Blair of Nashville, the union's Southern director, delivered a fiery speech attacking the employer in the best Populist style from a platform on the dirt floor of a huge cattle shed before a delighted audience of whites and blacks.

THE NEGRO RESPONSE

One rarely encounters this kind of labor solidarity and esprit de corps in the Northern shops where workers—white, Negro and "others"—have come to view their union as little more than the instrument for adding to their take-home pay. The potential for labor's rejuvenation, however, especially among the minorities, lies beneath the jaded façade of business unionism. Young men like Thurman Harris and Allan Brooks of the CUSA organization in Brownsville, who have every reason to be embittered toward the forces that regulate blue-collar affluence, continue to regard unionism as a good thing, and far more relevant to their lives than organized religion.

It was a sad commentary on the failure of union leadership in the ghettoes that newspaper accounts of the summer riots of 1967 contained almost no references to organized labor except to point out that few of the low-income rioters belonged to the craft unions.

It must baffle European unionists to hear that American labor's involvement in the War on Poverty had been minimal or nonexistent as of the summer of 1969, five years after the war began. According to the Office of Economic Opportunity, organized labor made its first formal liaison with an antipoverty corporation in 1967, in Middlesex County (New Brunswick), New Jersey. There a determined group of poverty officials, some of them former unionists, had procured the cooperation of labor in projects relating to job training and rehabilitation of disabled workers. Welfare recipients, however, were not part of the bargain and, significantly perhaps, the union representing the lowest-paid factory workers in the area refused to join the team. The most dramatic benefit actually accrued to labor when the Middlesex organization successfully persuaded disenchanted Puerto Rican and black members of an electrical workers' local to terminate a wildcat strike. Since 1967 I have heard of no other formal ongoing ties between labor and the antipoverty corporations.

In 1967, the New York City Teamsters guaranteed jobs for 660 men to be trained by the city as truck drivers. District 65, and other AFL-CIO units around the country, have contracted with the OEO to develop on-the-job programs for the training of unemployed welfare recipients to fill semiskilled factory positions. But these efforts are isolated and seem to have decelerated during the past two years. In the job lines that lead to the highest earnings, the crafts have not acknowledged that the War on Poverty has been declared.

"Project RESCU," an OEO program that provided federal funds to New York City to train about three hundred Negro and Puerto Rican youths as carpenters, electricians and plumbers for emergency repair work on slum buildings, never got off the ground because union representatives refused to commit themselves to give cards to the trainees. The only labor representative to attend the many negotiating sessions between city officials and the community action groups came from the Buildings Inspectors Union. It was his sole mission to see that the rights of the inspectors were not violated while the city grappled with poverty.

At a time when even the most obtuse liberal politician pays lip service to the need for "maximum feasible participation of the poor" in programs aimed at their advancement, many unions still have not bothered to hire Negroes to help organize colored shops, perhaps because, as Dave Dubinsky used to say, organizers belong to union management and the management is white.

In the Newark area, the scene of the first of the 1967 riots, with the possible exception of the Teamsters and the Auto Workers, white men not only have ultimate control of the locals but overwhelmingly dominate the day-to-day organizing and servicing of factories in the only major city in the country with a majority black population. For all practical purposes, these men project the image of a new breed of absentee labor landlord who collects monthly dues in return for an extra nickel an hour every other year and for assurances that plant discipline will be subject to "not always impartial" arbitration. Newark also competes closely with the Deep South in humiliations imposed on black and Spanish-speaking male workers in need of welfare assistance.

The New York columnist Murray Kempton astutely pointed out that the riot in Plainfield, New Jersey, had both ethnic and class overtones. The town's black population is divided between a large, relatively prosperous middle class

who habitually send two of their number to the City Council,
and the very poor who hate Negroes who wear suits almost as
much as the white policeman they shot and kicked to death.

For several years now it has been fashionable for white
liberals to deplore Black Power spokesmen preaching class
warfare with heavy doses of racial hate. Violence is one
thing, and if the police and district attorneys are able to sustain their indictments, the Black Panthers, among others,
may become a totally discredited organization. But the
strengthening of the black male ego, even at the expense of
white sensibilities, is a major accomplishment of the
Panthers. Moreover, Eldridge Cleaver et al., while retaining
their militancy, have rejected the separatism of Stokely Car-
michael and have sought alliances with white radicals.

But since the militants do advocate a class war on behalf
of an exploited people too easily isolated, physically and
emotionally, from other Americans, one ought to be pessi-
mistic about a drive for power on behalf of ghetto workers
that does not seek to coalesce with the better elements of
organized labor. It is one thing to despair of a radical future
for labor but quite another to exult in that despair to the
extent of failing to publicly harass and embarrass the movement with minority-group demands.

Walter Reuther, having urged his compatriots to include
the working poor in a massive organizing "crusade" which
also will seek to form "community unions" of welfare recipients, broke with the Federation and joined forces for social
action with the largest and probably most successful and
racially integrated union in the country, the Teamsters. It is
too early to say whether the labor coalition will have meaningful results.

The New Left, the Far Left and Eldridge Cleaver, if they
truly love the poor, may find themselves obliged to accept
Reuther's challenge or offer, whatever it is, not in order to

test his sincerity, because that is irrelevant, but because it
may be their best hope.

Groups of welfare recipients organized under the National
Welfare Rights Organization (NWRO) for day-to-day servicing of clients' grievances and agitation for long-range reforms, exist now in most of the large Northern cities, and
have done much to uplift the morale and economic status of
members on the welfare rolls. But they suffer from a lack of
resources, organizing talent and real power to coerce the
establishment; perhaps most important, since the public symbol of the clients' group is the AFDC mother, what they need
most in the wings is a strong Male Presence. The regular
appearance of professional union organizers at the edge of
clients' picket lines would do more to change the attitudes
of welfare administrators and legislators than ten Moreland
Commissions.

Bill Tate, a black organizer for a militant leftist union
(District 65, Retail, Wholesale Department Store Union)
which represents workers in most of New York City's big
department stores, once addressed a CUSA rally in a Baptist
church in Brownsville, Brooklyn. At one point Tate shouted
to an awed group of male teen-agers in the audience, most
of them from AFDC homes, that they should hang out on
street corners and hurl ash cans into store windows if they
wanted to be bums the rest of their lives, but not if they
wanted to beat the white man at his own game.

Saul Alinsky, the self-styled "last of the white [ghetto]
organizers," demonstrated effectively during the Woodlawn
Organization's battle with the University of Chicago and
other ghetto landlords, that aggrieved residents of poverty
areas require traditional, sometimes brutal, union tactics to
win redress. Moral suasion in the form of protest picketing,
or appeals to reason, says Alinsky, will not move most slumlords, but a fierce-looking, all-black demonstration at his

suburban home brings the bitterness of the ghetto home to roost.

Proponents of right-to-work legislation in Oklahoma in 1963 unsuccessfully sought black support with the argument that the law would open job opportunities hitherto closed to them by discriminatory unions. Black leaders rejected the proposal as a ruse to destroy unions and as advanced by employers eager to pay white and black workers wages as low as possible. In 1963–64 the Congress of Racial Equality helped to organize a necktie company in Los Angeles; the NAACP and the Clothing Workers jointly protested unfair labor practices by a Newark glove manufacturer; and the Reverend Dr. Martin Luther King's Southern Christian Leadership Conference aided a strike sponsored by the Chemical Workers Union in Atlanta.

King, of course, was assassinated during the 1968 strike by Memphis sanitation men whose grievances were so profound that white labor leaders across the country pledged their support. Dr. King's successor, Reverend Ralph Abernathy, later led Charleston hospital workers to victory in their fight for union recognition. The encouragement of New York's labor unions for the predominately black Charleston strikers might have been more enthusiastic if the 1968 teachers' strike in Ocean Hill–Brownsville, Brooklyn, had not reminded organized labor of the growing conflict between black aspirations and the advantages enjoyed by white workers.

In late 1965, during an arbitration in a Clothing Workers plant near Nashville, I had the opportunity to witness at first hand the heartening response of black workers to labor solidarity in the South. Two attractive and intelligent young black women recently hired by the employer, a Northern liberal who had a history of pinning the integration label on the union when it appeared at his other shops in Tennessee, testified on behalf of the union that the employer had planted them among a group of slow, white male pressers in order to justify discharging the men. Though the women stood to lose the padded earnings falsely credited to them by the company, as well as all hope of advancement, to the employer's astonishment, they defiantly told the hearing officer that since the white workers had received them well, they were not going to fink for the boss.

After the hearing, someone suggested to Buster Smith, the local union official, that they take their star witnesses to lunch at a good restaurant. "That," he replied, "is the least we should do."

LA RAZA

The thunderous reception, by off-Broadway standards, that greeted "El Teatro Campesino" at its first New York City appearance in 1967 was persuasive evidence that sophisticated liberals are only too eager to back trade unionism in its prime manifestations.

Despite only two or three days advance notice of the opening on July 20, the box office at the host theater in the West Village had to turn away several hundred persons prepared to contribute three dollars apiece to the strike fund of the Delano grape pickers for the privilege of viewing folk drama at its best. Unscheduled performances were held later before capacity audiences at St. Mark's-in-the-Bouwerie.

Except for two "Anglos," the actors in the company are Mexican-Americans from the vineyards who are compensated at the same rate (five dollars per week) as the strikers for whose benefit the group is touring the country. They sing, in English and Spanish, songs of social protest including the labor classic "We Shall Not Be Moved," interspersed with serio-comic skits dramatizing the action in Southern California. Between scenes, a commentator wearing a som-

brero and a Pancho Villa mustache recites the history of the
strike (by 1967 three major growers had signed contracts
and contract negotiations had begun with several others) to
remind his audience that "El Teatro Campesino" is not all
fun and games.

This depiction of a class struggle contains one element
that was missing from the protest plays of the 30's. It is true
that the grower and the labor contractor belong in the catalogue of traditional enemies of the common man. The di-
visive "scab" also appears in his usual role, kissing the
boss's ass. But at one point a campesino bearing a placard
which reads LA RAZA aligns himself with the figure of a
nun representing the churches and with a white man in a
steel helmet who declares that he is the "Spirit of the
American Labor Movement."

It is the mystical concept of La Raza, so important to the
current success of the grape pickers and so relevant to labor
organizing efforts among today's poor, to which the audience in the Village responded most heartily in July, 1967.
La Raza includes elements of class consciousness, pride of
race, outrage at injustices suffered and a sense that this particular family of workers, by collective action, ultimately
will triumph.

Like the early Black Power militants, some of the
workers have periodically attempted to identify La Raza
exclusively with Mexican-American separatism, but these
efforts have been beaten back by their leader, Cesar Chavez,
who on one occasion early in the struggle prevented a vote
on a proposal to ban Filipinos from membership in the
United Farm Workers' Organizing Committee. "Vote,"
Chavez told his campesinos, "if you like, but as for me, I will
go organize for the Filipinos" (who then had a union of their
own but later merged with the UFWOC).

La Raza, under the guidance of Cesar Chavez, is the
leaven in a winning formula that does not exclude Filipinos,

Okies or blacks in its sweep or, on evidence of articles and photographs in the workers' newspaper *El Malcriado,* from union leadership positions either.

La Raza, therefore, in essence differs not at all from the more optimistic version of the Black Power concept; when a black militant tells mothers in his audiences to "love your black babies," he does so because the Negro's failure to take pride in himself feeds the apathy which hangs heavy over the racial ghettoes of the big cities and the colored sections of our small towns to the delight of bigots everywhere. The Brooklyn chapter of CORE denies active membership even to the Caucasian spouses of their leaders not because they hate their wives, but simply because all of them have concluded, rightly, that white faces tend to dilute the psychological impact of slum delegations visiting the Man Downtown.

The Christian hope of black and white overcoming together has come to be viewed by the new militants as a three-way handicap: it suggests that (1) whites may still be *leading* their oppressed brothers along paths of progressive moderation; (2) whites are offering consolation by temporary, almost patronizing, participation in black misery; and/or (3) in particular instances, if neither of these impressions is valid, the powers-that-be will think so anyway and respond accordingly. The Black Panthers, if they survive, have introduced a more realistic emphasis to the integrated struggle aimed at economic discrimination against poor blacks and whites.

Like the campesinos of Cesar Chavez, the black activists have no use for soul brothers who have sold out to the white man by becoming brutal policemen, two-bit line foremen at $2.50 an hour or professionals who serve as window dressing for ambitious public officials, churchmen and labor leaders. *El Malcriado,* for its part, has added a new dimension to the civil rights movement with a delightful cartoon entitled "La

Dolce Vita en el Norte," which depicts the difficulties entailed in organizing poor farm workers above the Mason-
Dixon line.

Consequently, organized labor, which has brought La
Raza into its house, has plenty of room for Black Power.
Labor leaders know all about it. By and large, like politicians, they have concurred in the democratic, anticolonial
American notion that, all things being equal or almost equal,
a workers' representative should come from the same ethnic
stock as his people. The most gifted and enlightened WASP
will not arouse a meeting of Polish steelworkers in the same
positive way as one of their own who has won their respect
and admiration, nor will the average employer believe otherwise. Furthermore, no honest unionist will deny that in a
strike situation the leadership summons up emotions that go
far beyond the sometimes thin hopes of substantial monetary
gains, and the most important appeal is to something like
La Raza.

It is only with respect to blacks and Puerto Ricans in the
big cities that many labor leaders, the respectable ones as
well as the other kind, have violated their own rules. Then,
like Uncle Tom's benign master, they wonder why the plan-
tation workers bite the hand that feeds them.

A COMMON CAUSE

"El Teatro Campesino" opened in New York during the
six-week stoppage by welfare caseworkers, and the company
demonstrated its affection for the strikers by offering the
caseworkers tickets at fifty cents apiece. The gesture proved
all the more admirable in the light of the drama that subsequently emanated from the cheaper seats. The strikers,
members of the independent Social Service Employees Union
(SSEU) that had been denied the support of the New York

City Central Labor Council, booed all complimentary references to the AFL-CIO in the skits and clearly did not have
the heart to applaud attacks by the campesinos on their
enemy in California, the Teamsters' Union. (SSEU has since
affiliated with an AFL-CIO unit and UFWOC has made
peace with the Teamsters.)

A vice-president of a rival union of municipal employees
in the Federation, whose members had crossed the SSEU
picket lines, was literally driven from his seat. At the inter-
mission, an SSEU official deemed it prudent to publicly
apologize to Harry Van Arsdale, president of the City Central Labor Council, for jeers directed by the strikers more
at his office than at his person.

Whatever the merits of the strike—any stoppage by public
employees has deplorable aspects—it was a reflection on the
bad health of organized labor in the world's largest city that
its leaders evidently had no qualms about abandoning the
caseworkers to the vengeance of the citizenry. Except for
Joe Curran's union, which provided some money and the
use of the National Maritime Union hiring hall for SSEU
meetings, only the Teamsters, which also reportedly sought
their affiliation and mediated on their behalf with the Lindsay
Administration, offered substantial help to the welfare caseworkers. It was as if labor's chieftains had decided that the
poverty stigma of their clients had rubbed off on the SSEU
members.

Undoubtedly, there were some valid considerations for a
hands-off attitude. But New York City labor previously had
supported breach-of-contract stoppages, and Van Arsdale in
1968 incredibly threatened a citywide stoppage of AFL-
CIO unions if the city's Board of Education did not capitu-
late to the United Federation of Teachers in their unlawful
strike against the black, white and Puerto Rican children of
New York. The welfare strike, on pragmatic grounds, also
may have been doomed to failure from the very beginning;

but it is noteworthy that the SSEU, which alleged bad faith on the part of the city's negotiators, struck only over non-economic demands, some of which (e.g., reduction of the maximum caseload and de-emphasis on investigations of recipients), if implemented, would have benefited worker and client alike. The city resisted what could have been real reforms of welfare administration with dubious legalisms against fact-finding by third parties (now mandated by New York's Taylor Law) and with the old employer saw of management prerogatives.

The SSEU leadership, to its credit, is one of the handful of labor groups in the country which seeks to use its public relations offices and bargaining power in the cause of welfare reform. The SSEU also publishes a biweekly news sheet which advises clients' organizations of new administrative policies and clarifies existing policy for the benefit of recipients. The belligerent tone of the publication is set by the opening paragraph which usually prefaces the good and bad news with the remark, "The Commissioner's office has not yet announced . . . but these are the facts."

Many of the more than 4,000 predominantly young case-workers (the turnover is enormous) who struck in 1967 were New Left radicals and other idealists, complete with beards, sandals, bare feet and flowers, who saw public assistance employment as a good way to know and to help the poor. Many others, however, shared the traditional, inbred case-worker scorn for the recipients, and the SSEU leadership walks a tightrope between elections assuring membership meetings that their primary concern is to satisfy the needs of caseworkers without alienating the clients' groups that have backed the SSEU.

The city administration was able to break the strike because the lot of the caseworker is hopelessly intertwined with the opprobrium that is heaped on the recipients. In fact, be-

cause the entire system is so self-defeating, a strike by caseworkers paradoxically saves the city money on workers'
salaries with little attendant losses due to fraud or mistaken
overpayments. At the same time, the clients on regular budget
allowances have no complaint because their checks arrive
regularly without investigations and other harassment.

Instead of their fellow unionists, the striking caseworkers
found their support among organizations of the welfare poor.
Not all of the clients' groups trusted the union's sincerity in
promoting the clients' interests, and others simply despised
trade unionism. However, CUSA and several smaller groups
either adopted the attitude that "we are using them and they
are using us" or actually believed that the strike was on their
behalf too. These clients' groups publicly backed all of the
strikers' demands and supported the strike activities, in their
own way, by attempting to protect recipients in need of
emergency allowances and who were caught in the cross fire
and left waiting for hours for service from welfare personnel.

The CUSA Brooklyn group, accompanied by three white
priests, sat-in for two days at welfare headquarters in Manhattan until city officials agreed to a Saturday night negotiating session which resolved clients' demands, some of which
had also been the subject of the SSEU negotiations. Another
group at a Brooklyn church fasted for welfare peace.

CUSA personnel from Brownsville, East New York and
Bedford-Stuyvesant took daily "combat" positions at almost
every one of the welfare centers in downtown Brooklyn. With
buses provided by the SSEU, they toured the borough's ghettoes, including Williamsburg, where CUSA has no storefront,
to bring to the appropriate centers emergency cases and
needy, eligible persons not on relief who were afraid to apply
while the strike was on. CUSA activists, some of them vet-
erans of the last welfare strike in 1966, also stalked the
corridors of the centers demanding service for their people

from hostile supervisors as well as from workers who had been directed to aid the union cause from within by stalling the intake proceedings.

In sharp contrast to the almost total victory won by white teachers in 1968, the welfare strike ended with a face-saving agreement that future disputes would be submitted to non-binding and unpublicized mediation (but not fact-finding) and punishment of a mild sort would be levied on twenty-nine activists charged with various strike offenses.

But even though the strike could be described as a failure from the trade union standpoint, there is no question that the strike, at least in Brooklyn, achieved a new rapport between worker and client. The welfare recipients acquired a sense of dignity and a greater appreciation of their own power. The caseworkers, for their part, if they were unsympathetic before, came to respect the erstwhile welfare "types" who were willing to walk with them in the hot sun and the rain.

Allan Brooks and Bernice McLean of CUSA spoke on behalf of the city's recipients at a giant pep rally held during the strike at Manhattan Center. Mrs. McLean, a dynamic young woman who bore the first of her four children in Birmingham, Alabama, at the age of fifteen, articulated the dimensions of the new alliance when to a standing ovation she told the audience, "What the city is doing to you, they is doing to me and everybody else on welfare. We are in this thing together."

WHAT MIGHT HAVE BEEN

It will always be a cause for deep regret among those who see a future for the poor with organized labor that James Hoffa in 1965 rejected the shrewd invitation of Martin Luther King to join with the civil rights movement in a massive economic assault on racial injustice in Alabama.

The occasion was the murder of Mrs. Viola Liuzzo, the wife of a Detroit Teamsters' official, during the Selma-to-Montgomery march. Dr. King asked the Teamsters to boycott trucking in and out of Alabama. Harry Bridges, president of the West Coast International Longshore and Warehouse Union (unaffiliated), pledged the powerful support of his organization to the boycott; his members actually refused to unload one ship out of Mobile and let another pass only because it was at sea when the murder occurred. Significantly, Harold Gibbons, a Teamsters Vice-President, regarded by many unionists as an excellent progressive choice to succeed Hoffa, was present at the ILWU meeting before Bridges announced the boycott.

Apparently after some deliberation, Hoffa did not pledge Teamsters' support. He attended Mrs. Liuzzo's requiem mass in Detroit, along with Roy Wilkins and Bob Moses, of the Student Non-Violent Coordinating Committee, and the Teamsters and other unions gave money in her memory to the King organization and to SNCC. Hoffa certainly would have had the backing of his entire membership. Viola Liuzzo was killed helping blacks, but she was also a Teamster's wife, one of their own. There were legal problems, of course, but even a one-day stoppage, or the declared threat of a statewide boycott of one of the most bigoted states in the nation by the most powerful labor organization in the country, regarded in some civil rights quarters as among the most progressive on race relations, would have shaken the South's white-supremacy structure. Perhaps more important, it would have represented a dramatic psychological commitment that would have helped change the face of organized labor.

FIVE

COMMUNITY CONTROL

TWELVE

POOR BROWNSVILLE

I N NORTH CENTRAL BROOKLYN lies a community with a colorful but turbulent recent Jewish past that is now both the joy and despair of the War on Poverty. Brownsville may never join its neighbor Bedford-Stuyvesant, or Harlem, Selma or Watts, as one of the "glamor" areas of the struggle for racial equality; but social historians will find in tantalizing quantity in poor Brownsville today all of the dynamics and frustrations of the populist urban revolt that has characterized the civil rights movement since the passage of the Economic Opportunity Act in 1964.

The antipoverty programs in Brownsville have produced enlightened black leadership of the caliber of Major Owens and Thelma Hamilton, the Puerto Rican Vinnie Negron, strong welfare rights groups, and a local school governing board that in 1968 successfully challenged a predominantly white labor union, the United Federation of Teachers, for the right to control the education of Brownsville's children.

The area in recent years has seen the kind of rehabilitation of individuals dreamed of by social workers. Its social and economic problems suggest, however, that the face of Brownsville will not be improved until the entire city suffers and emerges from a holocaust.

In 1970, six years after the War on Poverty began, Brownsville remains a festering slum. Drug addiction, crimes of violence and infant mortality rates are among the highest in the country. The average per-capita income hovers close to the welfare benefits level. Absentee landlords, drunken building superintendents, corrupt building inspectors, resentful policemen and garbage collectors service Brownsville's residents.

HOME SWEET HOME

Housing conditions are incredibly bad. Unlike Harlem and Bedford-Stuyvesant, where solid, still-gracious old brownstones, formerly occupied by affluent whites, give character to whole blocks and neighborhoods, Brownsville today is a community depressed by an urban renewal scheme announced several years before actual demolition was to begin.

A visitor approaching the area by car from downtown Brooklyn along Eastern Parkway in June, 1969, veered sharply to the left at St. John's Place and was welcomed to Brownsville by the corpse of a rusted panel truck lying across the entrance to an abandoned Sinclair gas station.

Continuing along the Parkway to Atlantic Avenue, the visitor passed a deserted synagogue and at least fifteen frame houses in various states of disrepair or ruin. If he turned south on St. John's Place, he saw on one corner of East New York Avenue and Strauss Street a functioning movie house with numerous broken letters in its marquee and a police dog guarding its box office. On the other corner, giving grim testi-

mony to civic failure, stood two five-story tenements vacated
by tenants shortly after a rent strike two and one-half years
earlier. Pressured by the strike, the owners decide to forsake
their relatively small equities in the property rather than
undertake costly repairs. Some of the windows and doors
were sealed with sheet metal; others lay open to the elements
and to the youthful drug addicts who had stolen most of the
plumbing fixtures in the buildings.

At the time of the rent strike, the Strauss Street tenements
had twins around the corner on Herzl Street. Though these
were in better shape, the city chose only Herzl Street for
demolition in the spring of 1968. It may have been coinci-
dental that the buildings were torn down shortly after CBS
televised a documentary on housing conditions in Brownsville and that the film was entitled "A Visit to Herzl Street."

City Hall formalized (and quietly announced) in 1964 a
massive urban renewal program for Brownsville that was to
replace most of the tenements north and south of Pitkin
Avenue with high-rise housing projects. But the advent of
Mayor John Lindsay, who wanted to reorganize and con-
solidate the municipal housing agencies, followed hard upon
the escalation of the Vietnam war and the increased federal
financial neglect of the cities.

Consequently, demolition of the gutted residences that
pockmark the area did not begin, even in token fashion,
as of the fall of 1969. Renewal still seems a long way off
and some community groups have continued to discuss, in
romantic and vague terms, the possibility of forming "seed
money"* corporations to sponsor, with federal assistance,
housing "rehabilitation" efforts, as if Brownsville's decay
could be equated to a few rundown streets on the West Side
of Manhattan.

* This expression refers to the relatively small sums of money required to be raised by the private sponsors under the various housing
programs as a good-faith showing intended to "seed" the enterprise.

At the same time, the knowledge since 1964 that whole neighborhoods eventually would be replaced deterred countless landlords, including the merely prudent as well as the unscrupulous, from making needed repairs on their buildings. More often than not, rent strikes and code enforcement activities persuaded titleholders and mortgagees with marginal financial interests in slum tenements simply to abandon their property.

In this housing limbo, Brownsville became a welfare dumping ground. Even in the adjacent black ghetto of Bedford-Stuyvesant, the Welfare Department has difficulty finding accommodations for black recipients. In Brownsville, however, landlords with no future in the community exchanged their prejudices for exorbitant rentals willingly authorized by welfare officials. The budget of one of the tenants on Strauss Street, before the evacuation, included $160 for monthly rent of a six-room apartment in a building the horrors of which were suggested by the urine-stained vestibule, complete with pimps, the broken front-door lock, the alcoholic janitor and rats that roamed the halls even in daylight.

DISMAL ISOLATION

The location of Brownsville accounts for much of its present condition. The community lies far enough away from Manhattan to make for an unpleasantly long trip on public transportation. Ancient elevated trains still loop around the outer edges of the area. But never in its career did Brownsville know the quasi-suburban joys of nearby Flatbush, a middle-class Jewish community in the heart of Brooklyn that is a composite of little villages separated by farmland and connected by trolley lines in the 1880's. Instead, Brownsville, a mass of open land around 1900, developed within the next two decades into an urban enclave of cheap frame houses and old-law tenements with bathtubs in the halls. Working-class Jews, many of them employed in Brooklyn's factory belt that runs along the East River to Queens, moved to Brownsville from the Lower East Side of Manhattan. Murder, Incorporated, flourished there in the 1930's. Abe Reles, a local hoodlum turned police informer, mysteriously fell from a window in the Half Moon Hotel in Coney Island. Gang leader Louis (Lepke) Buchalter died in the electric chair.

Author Alfred Kazin has recorded that period in his haunting memoir, *A Walker in the City.** In Kazin's time, as today, Manhattan was "New York" and every neighborhood between Brownsville and "New York" was the "City." In 1951, with Brownsville's ethnic solidarity beginning to disintegrate, Kazin wrote that even the few black newcomers became infected with "the damp sadness of the place."

Though I was born and raised in Brooklyn, Brownsville was so alien to my own experience that I never had occasion to visit the community until 1965. During basic training in Virginia in 1952, we regarded burly Arnie Fleischman, a Brownsville boy, as an exotic plant. On a Friday night Arnie would play poker in the barracks with colored soldiers until about 10:00 P.M. when, with tears in his eyes, he would watch the fights televised out of the Eastern Parkway Arena in Brownsville.

The Jewish population began to flee Brownsville en masse during the 1950's as the black ghetto located in Bedford-Stuyvesant, swollen with migrants from the South, began to push its borders further along and across Eastern Parkway. Many Orthodox Jews, taunted by black and Puerto Rican teen-agers, left hurriedly. Poignant symbols of their presence remain today. The Good Shepherd Center, at Sutter and

* New York, Harcourt, Brace, 1951.

Hopkinson Avenues, a yeshiva only four years ago, has menorah candles engraved in the stained-glass door of its chapel.

NEVER A DULL DAY

The Eastern Parkway Arena now caters to parish bingo parties and organized crime moved to greener pastures. But violence found a permanent home in Brownsville. During the first ten months of 1967, its 73rd precinct reported the highest total of crimes, including twenty-five murders, in Brooklyn. If anything, the situation worsened in 1968 and 1969.

"Look up and down this [Pitkin] Avenue," a merchant told a reporter for *The New York Times* in March, 1968, "and you'll see more gates than you will see in any prison in the U.S.A." (The caption on the news story read "Brownsville: Frightened People Who Live in Decaying Buildings.") But neither gates nor the army of squad cars and the random police spot check of passing vehicles prevent crazed drug addicts from twisting the gates open with crowbars wide enough for a man to reach through a broken glass window.

Police activity increases twice a month on welfare check days. Recipients usually wait in their vestibules until the mailman arrives, but purses are snatched later. Tensions between the community and the Police and Welfare Departments are further aggravated by the number of fraudulent reports which help to inflate a crime rate that is already high.

On the other hand, one gets the impression that the enormity of the problem permits the police to pick and choose their priorities. In my own predominantly white neighborhood of Park Slope, about five miles and a ten-minute auto ride from Brownsville, the local precinct responds swiftly whether we complain about fights among teen-agers or the explosion of firecrackers. Not in Brownsville. One Sunday morning at Strauss Street some teen-agers threw a brick into the window of the storefront operated by Christians and Jews United For Social Action (CUSA) and made off with some file cabinets. The patrolman who arrived on the scene laughed when I asked him if an investigation would follow. "Listen," he said. "Two hours ago I caught three kids tossing a typewriter into an ashcan. I let them go because I didn't want to go downtown to court, and what the hell is a stolen typewriter around here anyway?"

Brownsville's isolation and its chaotic circumstances also create a climate conducive to police misconduct. The reports of brutality may be exaggerated, but responsible citizens, who can cite specific instances, say it is the cause of the evident hatred for white, and perhaps especially black, policemen in Brownsville.

At the CUSA storefront one night I heard a very popular black community relations patrolman engage in this frank dialogue with a group of welfare recipients:

If you think the cops in this precinct are bad, you should've seen the precinct in Queens where I spent five years. We got some fine men here.

I think myself you policemen are not tough enough on the young hoodlums who live in this community.

Well, you welfare mothers don't lay the law down to your kids. How do you expect the police to keep them in line?

It's your responsibility, that's why! It's not our fault they's no daddy around to beat their behinds. Besides, my big quarrel with the cops is that a bunch of teen-agers are killin' themselves under my window and you people don't show up until it's all over.

Missus, have some sense. I'm a cop and I've got a gun, but if I'm walking alone at night and I see a gang lined up down the block—you don't think I'm gonna break up that fight by myself, do you?

The CUSA ladies applauded the guest speaker and thanked him for coming.

To an outsider, Brownsville looks like a garrison state. Its indigents choose to remain close to home, even when invited by antipoverty groups to leave Brownsville with their children for a weekend in the country. They are afraid of returning to sacked apartments. The tapes of many interviews I conducted are closely punctuated by the howling of police and fire sirens. Mrs. Thelma Hamilton, the education chairman of the Brownsville Community Corporation, lives in a new and fairly comfortable development on Christopher Avenue, but it is a nightmare to sit on her thirteenth-floor balcony. During one half hour in August, 1968, we watched these events:

(1) Two small children conversing while leaning precariously out of windows on separate floors of another building several hundred feet above the street;

(2) two foot patrolmen chasing a teen-ager;

(3) five black children taunting and throwing stones at a stooped, elderly white man; and

(4) two automobiles colliding at the corner.

IT'S NOT THE SAME HOT DOG

The new focus of the civil rights movement is on economic exploitation—low wages, the denial of job opportunities and decent housing, over-priced consumer goods—rather than segregation, and Brownsville has more than its share. But by comparison with attempts to remedy consumer practices and sweatshop factory conditions, the war on housing has been a howling success.

Brownsville, along with other poor communities in New York, provides labor for marginal industries that pay less than $2.00 per hour in the most expensive city in the world.

The young men of Brownsville, some of them with families, who are not college-bound and are denied admission to the crafts, tend to make their way into seasonal, semiskilled employment at wages of $70 or $80 per week in plastics, costume jewelry, leather goods and toys and doll factories in Brooklyn where, in most cases, they are required to pay dues to labor organizations owned by white gangsters.

Consumer fraud exists in Brownsville in large quantities, but it is extremely difficult to prove. Periodic raids on retail stores by agents of the Bureau of Weights and Measures, assisted by local activists, uncover only the more blatant varieties of fraud.

Welfare recipients know that grocery store prices rise for a few days after the checks arrive. In other parts of the city, the Sabrette frankfurter served with gobs of sauerkraut out of a traveling steam table is a godsend to shoppers and football players on a cool fall day. But in Brownsville, the odors that rise from under the striped umbrella do not intoxicate. You will be lucky if your frank is hot and tastes of meat. Until late 1966 a delicatessen at Strauss and Pitkin did a thriving business in tiny hot dogs, buried in kraut, onions and relish, for only one dime; but three of these, I believe, did not equal the protein content or the taste of just one of Nathan's Famous hot dogs in Coney Island.

But the slum merchant will add that he also cashes welfare checks and extends credit to recipients at no extra charge. The hot-dog vendor can prove he does not attract the same crowds as the peddler in Greenwich Village. Besides, "I got held up last week!" Some merchants must charge more, and give less, in order to pay higher premiums on burglary and fire insurance or, if you will, to maintain a profit level adequate to induce them to remain. At what point does the honest slum merchant become an exploiter?

The crime rate, police brutality, the complexity of legal relationships between consumer and merchant, and between tenant and landlord, together with the traditional absence of free legal counsel physically located in the community (introduced in token fashion in the fall of 1968), encourage Brownsville's poor to drop out of the larger society.

To them the Law means City Hall, the police and the penal statutes. Redress in the civil courts is an alien concept to them. "What the hell good is it," said community leader Vinnie Negron, referring to the neighborhood legal services program, "if the lawyers can't handle criminal cases?"*

Criminal defendants are regarded with more than a little compassion. The black educator Herman Ferguson, out on bail pending appeal of his conviction of conspiring to assassinate Roy Wilkins, ran as a candidate in 1968 for United States senator on the Freedom and Peace party ticket. Admittedly, Ferguson had become a cause célèbre among the young black radicals. Moreover, many of the ministers and civic leaders who invited him to address their people probably were impressed with Ferguson's almost mystical ability to instill race pride in black children. But it is also fair to say that deep in their hearts, more than a few of these decent men and women did not care whether Herman Ferguson was guilty or innocent.

At the same time, the white press exaggerates the extent of Ferguson's influence among blacks. At a rally for community control of the schools held during the 1968 teachers' strike, Ferguson was permitted to speak at the insistence of a few militants. According to *The New York Times* story the next day, Ferguson's speech dominated the entire proceedings. But it was apparent to some spectators that while the bulk of the audience listened quietly but dreamily to Ferguson, they sat up for Reverend Milton Galamison, a

---

* Negron, Thelma Hamilton and Joe Francois, president of the Brownsville community corporation preoccupied with the teachers' strike, discovered to their chagrin that a black policeman on leave of absence had been hired to head the new OEO legal services office. "Not only is he a cop, but we have yet to meet him."

black militant appointed to the city's Board of Education by
Mayor Lindsay.

RELATING TO THE OUTSIDE WORLD

Federal funds made available under the Economic Opportunity Act began to flow into Brownsville in early 1966 and
continued unabated into 1970 but at the same level and for
programs suggested in part by Congress. After an unsuccessful experiment in establishing community progress centers
to serve paired poverty areas, the city settled on a formula
whereby community corporations were created to supervise
and to funnel cash into neighborhood projects. The New
York City Council Against Poverty, composed of unsalaried
representatives of the poor, the public at large and city agencies, sits at the peak of the antipoverty bureaucracy assisted
by full-time personnel on city payrolls in the Community
Development Agency of the Human Resources Administration, which also encompasses the activities of the Welfare
Department.

Dominant civic organizations, like the Brownsville Community Council (BCC), became the new quasi-municipal
legal entities. The Council hired Major Owens as its first
executive director. Owens, an activist-intellectual, holds a
master's degree in library science. He ran unsuccessfully for
City Council in 1965 as an independent and directed the
first massive rent strike in New York while chairman of the
Brooklyn Congress of Racial Equality. The Brownsville appointment, however, took Owens out of a relatively obscure
job as a branch librarian. Within two years his accomplishments as executive director of the BCC program had gained
him citywide and some national attention; in the spring of
1968, Owens succeeded George Nicolau, who resigned the
$32,000-a-year post as commissioner of the Community

Development Agency because of congressional "hostility" to the plight of the poor.

In his Brownsville post Major Owens directed the activities of about 250 employees, most of them nonprofessionals and many of them hired off the welfare rolls. A black man whose puritan regard for efficiency and programmed operations sometimes clashes with the "soul" culture of the ghetto, Owens incurred the enmity of sluggards on the payroll as well as young radicals whose gospel is black separatism at any price.

Despite bitter opposition, Owens retained a white man as his second in command. Owens also managed, in other ways, to win out in the internecine warfare because he could demonstrate that his programs, built on anger rather than hate and aimed at specific, attainable objectives, made sense.

While executive director of the BCC, Owens was the only local antipoverty official in the city to press for free legal services under the Economic Opportunity Act. In February, 1967, he took a delegation from Brownsville in a snowstorm to picket the midtown headquarters of the Association of the Bar of the City of New York. The demonstration helped loosen the resistance of Bar officials to community control which had delayed the advent of the citywide legal program.

Later that same year, Major Owens sent the largest contingent from the metropolitan area by bus to Washington to lobby for more funds for the War on Poverty.

Though more cynical, I believe, about organized labor than are Michael Harrington and Bayard Rustin, Major Owens also believes in consensus politics. He valued highly the pragmatic Christian militancy of Martin Luther King, who was martyred in Owens' home city of Memphis. During his term with the BCC Owens attempted to form a working liaison with the representatives of welfare caseworkers, the Social Service Employees' Union, to fight exploitation in

Brooklyn's factories. These efforts never got off the ground, however, because the SSEU, like the United Electrical Workers, another liberal-to-radical labor union interested in organizing the blue-collar poor, was itself alienated from the AFL-CIO power centers.

Owens' efforts as executive director were greatly aided by the political backing of Mrs. Thelma Hamilton, the *grande dame* and education chairman of BCC, who is ideologically very close to Major Owens. Mrs. Hamilton, a former recipient herself, heads a powerful coalition of blacks and Puerto Ricans, including most of the welfare rights militants. With solid Puerto Rican support, she defeated the incumbent to become president of the BCC in 1966. The following year her slate, headed by Joe Francois, a black man, and composed of black, Spanish and white candidates proportionate in number to the ethnic makeup of Brownsville, defeated an all-black ticket. A victory by the separatists in that election would have driven the Puerto Ricans and whites out of the Brownsville Community Council.

Another major figure to emerge out of the early antipoverty campaigns in Central Brooklyn was Frank Espada, a thirtyish white of Spanish descent. When the War on Poverty began, Espada, a tall, thin, intense activist who, in another age, could have passed for a teacher-guerrilla in the employ of Fidel Castro or Emiliano Zapata, was working for a contractor and donating much of his free time to an organization called East New York Action, in a desolate neighborhood adjacent to Brownsville, located in a middle- to low-income community known as East New York. He later became deputy commissioner of CDA and then an official of the Urban Coalition, a private organization dominated by urbanologists who feel that the quasi-public antipoverty structure cannot make a meaningful dent in poverty.

I met Espada for the first time on a bleak winter night in 1965 at his East New York storefront. Jim Davitt, another volunteer lawyer with the newly formed CUSA action group in Brownsville, and I visited Espada to learn about anti-poverty programs and funding. Though federal financing was in sight, no monies were yet available, and his group relied on the services of unpaid volunteers and financial con-tributions from the community to pay the rent and the elec-tric and phone bills.

I doubt if any one of the four or five people present that evening had a prevision of the clumsy size of the bureaucratic whirlwind about to descend upon the poor communities in New York, but the mood was hopeful. I recall that Espada intrigued us with one of his case histories. Black tenants in a three-story house near the East New York Action storefront had successfully struck their landlord and were using their rent money to buy fuel oil and to make necessary repairs.

Espada was also quite knowledgeable, even in those days, about welfare. He may be one of a mere handful of political activists of the past three decades, along with Thelma Hamil-ton and Major Owens, to insist publicly that low wages, large families and racial discrimination combine to place good citizens on the relief rolls.

One of these, Agropino Bonillo, a $65-per-week short-order cook who depended on Home Relief to help support his wife and ten children, was kicked to death by Browns-ville teen-agers in April, 1966, near the dreary railway terminus that separates East New York from its neighboring community. The philanthropist Frederick Richmond, who established a memorial fund for the Bonillo family, remarked at the time that no other event had made him more conscious of his own advantages. Frank Espada, with the help of local clergymen and the community organizations, organized a massive candlelight procession through the streets to the place of the murder. Nonwhites marched with Puerto Ricans. Speakers at the demonstration denounced the intolerable conditions which made the killing possible.

Though at first he restricted his operations to East New York and Brownsville, Espada is credited with the formation in 1966 of the City-Wide Coordinating Committee of Welfare Rights Groups ("City-Wide"). To many of his listeners, the concept of effectively uniting welfare clients along trade union lines appeared hopelessly visionary, but Espada argued a forceful case for a client organization on strictly pragmatic grounds.

Welfare apathy, he said, could be dissipated by uniting recipients in a common front against their "employer," the Welfare Department. Unlike a tenants' union, which experience had shown foundered as soon as warm weather mooted the heat problem, a welfare rights group would be nourished by complaints that do not end when the biweekly check arrives. Paradoxically, argued Espada, by demanding more benefits for welfare recipients *as a matter of right,* i.e., to which they are entitled because they satisfy the statutory qualification of need, a welfare league would in the long run help reduce the city's welfare costs.

With the legal assistance of Edward Sparer, and waving copies of the militant writings of Richard Cloward and Frances Piven* of the Columbia School of Social Work, Frank Espada spoke at countless meetings in storefronts and tenements all over the city in what must have been one of the most successful organizing campaigns ever in this classless country among alienated poor people.

"City-Wide" eventually became a major force in the National Welfare Rights Organization under the sophisticated but militant leadership of a black former Cornell professor, George Wiley, who has been arrested at sit-ins almost as often as he meets with influential politicians, labor leaders and philanthropists. It is a tribute to Wiley's powers of persuasion that in 1969 the New York Assembly's Demo-

---

* See "A Strategy to End Poverty," *The Nation,* May 2, 1966; and "Finessing the Poor," *The Nation,* October 7, 1968.

cratic Minority Leader Stanley Steingut became converted to the welfare rights cause and that Senator Frank Church and Congressman Jonathan Bingham, among other elected officials, suffered through a welfare diet in a week-long experiment proposed by Wiley. But the NWRO leader may have scored the most dramatic public relations coup of his career when he persuaded the influential food critic of *The New York Times,* Craig Claiborne, to go on the diet at his East Hampton home in the summer of 1969 and then to write one of the most biting critiques of the welfare system to appear in print.

The momentum generated by the protest demonstrations of 1966-67 by antipoverty groups continues. But except for the welfare rights movement, the status quo manifests itself in *causes* like school decentralization, rather than in ongoing organizational activities. Whereas other community action groups folded or disappeared into the antipoverty structure, most of the rights groups survived to become definable components of George Wiley's group to be reckoned with on the poverty scene. My own organization, Christians and Jews United for Social Action, began in Brownsville as an activist association with broad interests, but in time found its permanent identity as a loose coalition of CUSA storefronts in Brownsville, East New York and Bedford-Stuyvesant.

Whether or not one agrees with their methods or is impressed with their material gains, in terms of self-help and rehabilitation the New York City welfare rights activists must be included among the more successful elements of the War on Poverty. This form of community action testifies to the strength of the human spirit which may still create, out of the gutted buildings and garbage, a black and Spanish version of the "Brunzvil" immortalized with affection by Alfred Kazin.

CHAPTER
THIRTEEN

THIS LITTLE LIGHT
OF MINE

I'm gonna let it shine,
All over Brow-ow-nsville;
I'm gonna let it shine.

CHRISTIANS AND JEWS United for Social Action
(CUSA), a private, nonsectarian self-help organization, emerged on the Brownsville scene on a bitterly
cold Sunday in January, 1966, in a rash of anti-establishment
publicity. The modest material successes and enormous
failures of CUSA suggest, in miniature, that the worth of
the War on Poverty can best be described in terms of its
positive impact on the attitudes of its participants.

For the most part, the rallies and picket lines only chipped
away at the visible peak of New York's iceberg of economic

discrimination, but on an individual level the whites, Negroes and Puerto Ricans involved in the CUSA experience, in getting to know the other half, acquired a humbling knowledge of themselves.

White lawyers, myself included, who were thrown for the first time into close frequent contact with ghetto residents in a common cause that was also alien to their ordinary activities, discovered the dormant racism they had inherited. They also had the unique opportunity to view the kind of poverty which, if attributed at all to human failure, had to be laid on the doorstep of their own kin and class.

As for the indigenous who, in time, came to dominate numerically and to control the CUSA branches in Brownsville, East New York and Bedford-Stuyvesant, association with whites in a militant but democratic endeavor not focused awkwardly on racial prejudice alone permitted and encouraged them to retain a healthy anger toward the white establishment without the destructive urge for strict racial separatism. Organizations like CUSA probably helped foster a tolerant climate in Brownsville in which young white teachers crossed the picket lines in 1968 to prevent, despite the best efforts of the teachers' union leadership, a War Between the Races in New York City.

Vinnie Negron came to one of the early CUSA meetings held in a brownstone in the middle-class Park Slope section of Brooklyn. We invited him as an authentic voice of the ghetto to counsel the assembled white lawyers, priests, housewives and a smattering of black professionals on how we could best help poor people on a part-time basis. At the time Vinnie was twenty-four years old; he had a wife and four children and, among other roles, despite his heavy Spanish accent, was president of a predominantly black block association on Legion Street.

Negron, of course, spoke of voluntary legal and other services to the poverty community but, surprisingly, he stressed most the notions of contact and communications. A black lawyer's wife present at the meeting objected that in Brownsville we would be regarded as well-off liberals getting our kicks out of patronizing poor people. Negron said "no."

"Ordinarily you drive in your cars along Eastern Parkway to the Kennedy Airport. You pass Brownsville and you see the rotting buildings and you say, 'Only slobs could live here.' We look at your big fast cars and we say, 'Those people care only about themselves.'

"But after you spend some time with us and do some good and talk to people and listen to them, too, you can believe we will say rich white people are not so bad after all. And you will find out that many good people live in those dumps in Brownsville."

And so it began. In December, 1965, the group raised among themselves enough funds to rent a storefront on Legion Street for $85 per month and agreed to hold all future meetings in Brownsville. An assignment roster was prepared; some members would represent CUSA at meetings of the Brownsville Community Council and other civic groups. Three priests agreed to report on racial attitudes at diocesan construction sites. The lawyer members said they would serve as house counsel to three or four block associations including Vinnie Negron's.

I vividly recall my first session in the basement of Vinnie's apartment house. Though the lights were dim, Negron sat behind a kitchen table, wearing dark glasses. About fifteen adults, almost all of them black, and about four impassive children sat on folding chairs. An attractive black woman took notes. Two men, smelling of whiskey, wandered in and out.

This night the main order of business concerned a duty squad of tenants who would take turns each morning measuring the conscientious performance of the sweeper sent out by the Sanitation Department. Vinnie opened the meeting by apologizing for the sparse attendance of Puerto Ricans. "I tell you the truth, my own kind needs a kick in the pants!" After explaining the legal niceties and the practical implications of rent strike legislation to an animated audience, I walked out into that god-awful neighborhood marveling at the vitality of the human spirit.

In early 1966 CUSA moved to a more central location at 1823 Strauss Street and acquired a slumlord. Thelma Hamilton, assisted by Margie Freeman, who had recently left a convent in Bedford-Stuyvesant, manned the storefront. Mrs. Hamilton, a long-time activist in the Brownsville schools, served both city and community while on the payroll of Acting Commissioner of Labor James J. McFadden as a neighborhood liaison to the department's job-training program.

An arctic blast struck the city in January, 1966. Residents of 1823 Strauss and adjacent tenements on East New York Avenue and Herzl Street complained to Thelma Hamilton and Margie Freeman about lack of heat. The managing agent, located a few doors away on Strauss Street, threatened to evict CUSA if we caused him trouble. Instead, the two women deluged the Buildings Department with phone calls that brought inspectors and temporary emergency services until they discovered how serious the problem was; for years our landlord had been diverting huge sums of money from the rent rolls that should have paid for fuel oil and a new burner for the Strauss–East New York–Herzl complex of buildings. We found that welfare department personnel had closed their eyes to the physical and social horrors visited upon ADC children in those buildings and had acquiesced in the exorbitant rentals being charged, most of which we discovered later violated the rent-control law.

One Sunday night, during a blizzard, tenants and CUSA personnel arrived for a strategy meeting at the storefront to find one of the plate-glass windows broken by a brick and snow piled on the floor. The crowd was eager to blame the landlord. (Teen-agers, however, actually did the damage that day and on two later occasions.) Ray Williams, a black lawyer from the neighborhood and a vice-president of CUSA, mounted a desk to declare war on all landlords. A crowd of young priests appeared out of nowhere, frustrated by their inability as individuals to seriously change life in Brownsville but eager to mount the barricades in a collective attack on poverty. Somebody phoned City Hall and the Lindsay Administration obligingly dispatched buses to take our tenants from their frozen apartments to the heated armory on Bedford Avenue where the Salvation Army waited with blankets, donuts and hot chocolate.

HERE COME THE POLITICIANS

The broken window touched off a rent strike. Williams and Cosimo Di Tucci appeared in court on behalf of tenants who had been served with notices of dispossession. Jim Davitt counseled tenants on Saturdays. Law students checked records at the County Clerk's office for the names and addresses of the true owners of buildings. Neil Prior and other lawyers supervised the collection of rent strike petitions and requests for rent deductions. A printer contributed glued stickers that read "We Are on Rent Strike—CUSA" (in red) and "Members of the Brownsville Tenants' Association" (in blue).

About 200 persons marched on a frosty Saturday night in February under the CUSA banner. Riding in a sound truck behind the police escort, Vinnie Negron, in staccato Spanish, and Grayson Brown, in cool English, took turns exhorting tenants to come join a March of the People. "This," said Major Owens, as he saw the crowd assembled for the rally at Good Shepherd Center, "is beautiful!"

Another demonstration in March set out from Strauss Street across Eastern Parkway to Ocean Hill and returned for a rally at a black Protestant church on Stone Avenue. The house publication of the Retail Wholesale Department Store Union assigned Miriam Levinsohn to photograph the rally.

On a stormy Sunday CUSA descended by bus and car on the Antioch Baptist Church in Bedford-Stuyvesant for a celebration by National CORE honoring James Farmer. Bewildered at first by the motley collection of white, Spanish and black adults and screaming children surrounded by a somewhat perturbed middle-class Negro congregation, Farmer rose to the occasion to applaud the Revolt of the Poor People of Brownsville. The populists roared; the TV cameras traveled over a sea of rain-streaked picket signs that praised Farmer on one side and denounced slumlords on the other.

Until the novelty wore off, CUSA adopted the Saul Alinsky technique of picketing the enemy at his home or office. Ida Posner, an old-time resident of Brownsville, led an interracial delegation to predominantly Jewish Manhattan Beach to picket a landlord who happened to be Jewish, with signs referring to "Christians United for Social Action" (the original name of CUSA). The man's neighbors came out to say they did not like him either. On the way home, Mrs. Posner said, "Now that I'm in this thing, you've got to change the proper name of CUSA. It's embarrassing!" "Jews" was added to the official title at the next meeting, but the organization continued to use the code name CUSA which by then had acquired an abbreviated identity of its own. Jews, including Ida and six to eight law students at various times, stayed active in CUSA. After graduation in 1968, Bob Jaffe returned to teach in Brownsville during the teachers' strike. He, Ida, other young teachers and older residents prominent in Brownsville antipoverty work helped refute the charges of anti-Semitism circulated against the Ocean Hill-Brownsville leadership by the UFT.

Almost every night for a month the storefront at Strauss Street featured pep rallies in English and Spanish attended by tenants, reporters, city officials and activists from other communities looking for the sparks that had ignited this populist bonfire. A stream of white students and their teachers poured in and out of the store each Saturday until the local teen-agers complained with much justification that they were tired of being gawked at. A more formal educational session took place one afternoon in February when a graduate class in social welfare administration from New York University walked past the urine-stained hallways, the pimps and the drunken janitor at 1823 Strauss to a CUSA workshop in the $160-per-month apartment of welfare recipient Frances Brownell in a building since condemned as unfit for human habitation.

Ray Williams argued with a boy friend of one of the students who wanted to know why Mrs. Brownell felt no obligation to patch the broken plaster. "Sure," the visitor said, "all you people want to do is complain about the landlord; you've got no sense of responsibility!" Teen-agers Pat Dickinson and Aida Ramirez told the class that young girls are not necessarily safe among their own kind in Brownsville; Pat's younger sister had been accosted an hour earlier by a pervert in their hallway on Herzl Street. CUSA Vice-President Thurman Harris described what growing up in a slum ghetto does to the self-confidence of a young man looking for a job.

That winter, thanks to the indomitable Bob Samuels of the Brooklyn page of the (now defunct) *World Telegram* and other reporters, the rest of the city discovered that on nights when thermometers dropped to twelve degrees above zero, whole clusters of buildings in Brownsville were completely without heat. Reporters who interviewed the evacuees the night of the blizzard were aghast at the picture which emerged of wholesale pocketing by managing agents, with the passive acquiescence of the title owners and mortgagees, of that portion of rent monies intended for the purchase of fuel oil.

Publications as diverse as the Communist *Worker*, the reactionary *Brooklyn Tablet* and Harlem's *Amsterdam News* covered the CUSA activities. The newspaper season was otherwise dull. The direct action evoked romantic memories of the workers' class struggle of the 30's. Unlike the striking teachers in 1968, landlords constituted an unsympathetic element in the New York establishment, and for a while Bob Samuels, who became a familiar figure at demonstrations as well as at addicts' group therapy sessions on Legion Street, was able to persuade his skeptical editors that white readers would not feel threatened by militant doings in the ghetto.

These were some of the headlines: "[Parks Commissioner] Hoving Shocked by Brownsville"; "[City Council President] O'Connor Promises Action on Brownsville Slums"; "Up-Lift Cum Realism in a Brooklyn Slum"; "[Buildings Commissioner] Moerdler's Impulsive Visit to Brownsville"; "CUSA: A Cot, an Apostolate and a Cold, Four-Room Flat"; "Non-Violent Protest in Local Ghetto Area"; "CUSA: A Fight Versus Housing Ills."

Until OEO funds arrived in the summer of 1966, CUSA survived on contributions. A column by John Leo in the *National Catholic Reporter* raised over $4,000. Most of the individual donations were small, but a retired judge in California sent $20 checks for about six months straight and a professor at the University of Minnesota twice endorsed over to CUSA his monthly salary checks.

CIO unions—NMU, UAW, Clothing Workers, District 65, RWDSU—contributed about $2,000 to the cause. Articles about CUSA appeared in at least two union newspapers. Organizers spoke at CUSA rallies. Tentative arrangements were made for an ongoing organizing venture with District 65 whereby CUSA activists would plant themselves in target shops to sign up members for the union and to invite them to evening organizational meetings held under CUSA auspices. It seemed for a time that we were in the vanguard of a new populist movement that would place the alienated poor on center stage with elements of organized labor, however reluctantly, championing their cause.

Then, as suddenly as it all started, the excitement died away. Warm weather arrived. The heat problem disappeared. Tenants lost interest in organizing and being organized. Though CUSA survived, it never regained the momentum of those days, and when I see Thelma Hamilton, she is likely to say, nostalgically, "Whatever happened to CUSA?"

FIGHTING A WAR WITH SLINGSHOTS

Unlike other small activist groups in New York City that sprouted into being in 1966 and later died from lack of leadership, goals or financial nourishment, CUSA survived into 1970, but barely.

All elements of the antipoverty structure, heavily dependent on OEO for funding, suffered from the recurring harassment of the federal agency by Congress which forced Sargeant Shriver's agents to come begging each spring with budgets covering tens of thousands of ongoing programs across the country. Each year Congress slashed the request for appropriations, sometimes down to the previous level; this, in effect, forced most existing programs to retrench, or by insisting on reallocations of budgets, members of the House and Senate arbitrarily imposed their collective will on highly complicated and volatile schema for fighting poverty.

By the time President Nixon had appointed Congressman

Donald Rumsfeld in 1969 to replace Shriver, Congress already had indicated its displeasure with community action in favor of more traditional programs for rehabilitation such as job training. As a consequence, idealistic men and women —including lawyers in the Washington OEO office as well as storefront welfare aides—suffered on many occasions, in addition to the usual rigors and frustrations, the insult of being forced to wonder where their next meal would come from. Program directors who had to borrow interim funds from local banks had no choice but to deduct the interest payments from Congress' largesse, when the funds allocated to the poor finally arrived. Disconnected telephones and dark storefronts lit by candles became, in New York, symbols of the War on Poverty. When the bills went unpaid, the utility companies did not, of course, blame Congress, but the feckless poor.

Monies to finance the city's Headstart programs in the summer of 1966 did not travel from Washington to the Council Against Poverty to Brownsville and other communities until the middle of July. By that time, licensed teachers who had signed on for the summer got tired of waiting and took other jobs. Staff positions for Headstart and other programs snarled in red tape were filled by ex-welfare recipients, for example, at extravagant salaries, because qualified personnel were not always available.

Mario Procaccino, the comptroller (or top city fiscal officer) during those years, may have been accused unjustly of, at best, indifference to the need for speedy delivery of the antipoverty checks. But Procaccino later showed himself quite eager to pay wages to striking teachers; this and his negative attitude toward the War on Poverty and block aspirations, generally, helped enormously to win him the Democratic nomination for mayor in 1969 (but not the mayoralty in November).

During 1966 and 1967, CUSA underwent profound internal crises. After Thelma Hamilton took full-time employment with the education unit of the Brownsville Community Council, no strong black leader with wide appeal emerged to replace her as president and day-to-day coordinator of the several CUSA programs. Except for Bernice McLean, Lorraine Hubbard and Verna Serrano, who also serviced welfare clients, CUSA, having achieved a modest fame as action-oriented, found itself with a surfeit of activists and few members willing to master the dreary formalities of devising new programs and applying for funds.

Personality quarrels erupted with even more frequency, it seemed, than in the most volatile of middle-class organizations. At a raucous membership meeting in September, 1966, Bernice McLean won a second chance for the full-time director, a black professional, by reminding the group (about seventy were present), "You don't kill a hog until you leave him in the sun awhile." At the end of the meeting, a group of the staff people listened politely to Father Jim Regan, who counseled patience and tolerance. When Regan had gone, a sedate-looking woman startled me by saying, "I don't care what the priest says. If that son of a bitch don't watch his step, I'm gonna cut him, I swear to God I will!"

After the director finally was ousted a few weeks later, his friend, the Brownsville delegate to the Council Against Poverty, and a political foe of Thelma Hamilton's, held up financing for about six months with charges made to the Council of white Catholic dominance of CUSA. At the time the delegate's children were attending parochial schools. The few whites, most of them radical young priests, still remaining in CUSA were not affected, of course; the delegate succeeded in hurting only the blacks and Puerto Ricans who worked in the storefronts on antipoverty payrolls.

Despite the problems, the organization underwent periodic rejuvenations. Jaded by attendance at too many inconclusive Reform Democrat meetings, the CUSA gatherings reaffirmed my faith in the democratic process. The meetings began late and lasted too long, but grievances were always resolved, a constitution and by-laws adopted and other actions taken, in large part because the membership, especially the blacks and Puerto Ricans, felt that CUSA was far more important than its quarreling component parts.

True social contact between the races—not the polite encounters at communion breakfasts and midtown luncheons that characterized traditional civil rights activities— seemed to occur in CUSA as a matter of course. Young law students who worked in the East New York, Brownsville and Bedford-Stuyvesant storefronts in the summers of 1966 and 1967 appeared en masse at tenement birthday parties on Saturday nights and went with staff members, recipients and "outsiders" on bus trips into the country. Fund-raising parties in Park Slope, where it all began, brought black and Spanish ghetto militants into an unabashed dialogue with white professionals.

The activism continued. Thelma Hamilton, Vinnie Negron and Father Jack Powis were arrested, along with Reverend Milton Galamison, at a sit-in at the Board of Education. Lessie Freeman and Ellen Murphy drew suspended sentences for refusing to leave the welfare commissioner's office. Thurman Harris joined the black caucus in Merriwether Hall during the student demonstrations at Columbia. Allan Brooks, Bernice McLean et al. devoted most of the summer of 1967 bussing emergency cases into the welfare centers in buses provided by the striking Social Service Employees Union.

GETTING TO KNOW THE WELFARE MAN

In September, 1966, several burglaries and the inevitability of another winter forced CUSA to follow the tenants out of the abandoned Strauss Street building. Allan Brooks, Bernice McLean and Verna Serrano set up an elaborate headquarters store, complete with a Xerox machine and air-conditioning unit, at 100 Sutter Avenue, where they remained until the next and most decisive financial crisis took them in the fall of 1967 to the Good Shepherd Center. Refunded for the summer of 1969, the two ladies and a younger newcomer, Mrs. Ann Chandler, opened an adult education center for welfare mothers on Saratoga Avenue on the Ocean Hill side of Eastern Parkway.

An incredible efficiency was evident at the Sutter Avenue operation. I and other lawyers who had attempted, unsuccessfully, during the hectic winter of 1966 to establish clerical procedures at Strauss Street whereby separate case files would be maintained for each building under surveillance or attack, were astonished to find that Bernice McLean, a high school dropout from Birmingham, had established elaborate client files for each welfare recipient who sought assistance at Sutter Avenue. In my prejudice, I had attributed the disorder at Strauss to ghetto mores; on a visit early one Saturday morning to the Sutter store soon after it opened I saw clean, tastefully patterned curtains on the windows and, along with machine-printed signs advertising the National Welfare Rights Movement, Headstart, etc., signs professionally hand-lettered by Mrs. McLean (in English) and by Mrs. Serrano (in Spanish).

These are samples:

ATTENTION: PARENTS!
CAMP APPLICATIONS FOR CHILDREN
AGES 7 TO 10
COME IN AND FILE YOURS
TODAY!

CUSA

REGISTER FOR ADULT CLASSES IN ALL
CUSA OFFICES. CLASSES WILL BE AT
GOOD SHEPHERD CENTER

CUSA

WELFARE RECIPIENTS ARE ENTITLED TO:
1. ONE BLANKET EVERY YEAR
2. MATERNITY CLOTHES

WELFARE MEETING EVERY WEDNESDAY
AT 1 P.M.
REUNION DE WELFARE TODAS LAS
MIERCOLES A LA 1:00 P.M.

CUSA

—NEWS FOR THE WEEK—
Problems

WELFARE ————————————————
HOUSING ————————————————
SCHOOL ——————————————————
RATS, ROACHES ——————————————
LACK OF SUPERINTENDENT —————————

DOES BROWNSVILLE HAVE A
DRUG ADDICTION PROBLEM?
WHAT ARE YOU DOING ABOUT IT?
GROUPS OF ADDICTS MEET DAILY
AT 579 HOPKINSON AVENUE AT A
STOREFRONT RUN BY AN EX-ADDICT.
GROUPS OF RELATIVES MEET ONCE
A WEEK

Mrs. McLean in particular became a lay expert on welfare and acquired a reputation at the Brooklyn centers for

refusing to advance a fraudulent or tenuous claim. In a burst of superconfidence at one point she won the indignant backing of the City-Wide Coordinating Committee of Welfare Groups to take a delegation on the quixotic (and still unfulfilled) mission of "organizing" Westchester County. One of her former clients, relocated in Mount Vernon, had been told by her new caseworker, "Take those [minimum standards] forms back to Brownsville where you got them."

One day in May, 1967, without advance notification, I took my tape recorder to a rights meeting at Sutter Avenue. Bernice McLean presided. Ten or twelve women, three of them Spanish, sat on both sides of a rectangular table. Because a black woman, with a baby in her arms, had come for the first time, much of the meeting was devoted to a discussion of the basic rights of recipients and how CUSA could help poor people to help themselves.

MRS. MCLEAN: "In case some of you don't know, this man here is Mr. Jim Graham. He wants to sit quiet with his machine and hear what we got to say. Let's try to act right smart, now. This lady over here is Missus ————, whom I have been trying to help."

She then proceeded to deliver a concise ten-minute lecture on what welfare was all about. Minimum standards?

"You check those items on the form that you feel you gotta have, but never received, like a snowsuit for the baby and mittens for your other kids. Your worker is supposed to give you those things to bring you up to standard. After that, if you need them, you gotta buy them out of your regular check."

Mrs. McLean explained how she became involved with CUSA. Her caseworker, she said, had told her she was lucky to be on welfare in New York and had no right to complain about anything.

"Then on the street I met Mr. Al Brooks. He told me to come to a CUSA meeting. I went and I read and read the manual. Now I know it by heart and I know a lot about client rights. For example, a new caseworker can come into your house but you don't have to let him in after five o'clock. Make him sit down. Sure, you gotta talk to him and answer his questions, but only about your problems, and he's gotta be polite."

A woman who said she was a diabetic and had no children interrupted Mrs. McLean.

"They are afraid of CUSA all right. You people must have put a bomb under them. One time I went to the Brownsville Center and sat around for an hour until I told the intake woman that the CUSA people where I came from were on their way down to see the director. In two minutes, a supervisor was sweetly asking me, 'What's your problem, lady?' "

MRS. MCLEAN: "Yeah, but don't go down to the centers and say you're from CUSA if you're not gonna work here. We need volunteer ladies . . ."

After the meeting I asked the diabetic if she liked CUSA because it meant extra welfare benefits to her. "No, believe me, that's a small part of it. I'm here every day in this store. I actually miss this place on Sunday when it's closed. Everybody on welfare, you know, feels lonely, but especially someone like me with no man and no kids. Now, I don't feel alone any more!"

That last statement probably sums up the present role of CUSA. The organization became and continues to be a unit of the welfare rights movement combining, in its own special way, socializing with service. CUSA and similar groups serve to champion and pep up the morale of the most impotent, yet most easily organized, class of citizen in America, for whom any material gain or move out of apathy is progress indeed.

LOOKING BACK

The advent of warm weather in 1966 was probably only an excuse for the sharp stop in CUSA's momentum. In retrospect, it was naïve to believe that direct action could make more than a slight dent in the enormous socio-economic problems of a place like Brownsville.

Our massive rent strike did force several slumlords out of business, including our own "managing agent" who also went to court on fifteen separate criminal charges. We (foolishly) persuaded the city to delay condemning the Strauss–East New York–Herzl complex while we negotiated with a third mortgagee in an unsuccessful attempt to persuade him to rehabilitate his property. During the spring and summer of 1966, tenants who might have qualified for $200 or $300 relocation expenses if evicted by the city quietly disappeared on their own from the buildings which soon became ugly tombs.

It is also true that the newspaper publicity miraculously restored "defective" boilers to working order, and some landlords, but not all, in subsequent years might have sought other methods of exploiting tenants who are on welfare; more important, the persistent shout of "no heat—no rent" caused Brownsville to be bracketed with Harlem and Bedford-Stuyvesant as a prime target in the city's War on Poverty. The size of New York's request for OEO funds for the community reflected the impact on the Lindsay Administration of the cumulative horrors of Brownsville. Furthermore, a crash program involving several municipal agencies resulted, *inter alia,* in a posting of 15,000 violations of the Buildings Code, the issuance of five hundred summonses, and vacate orders on eighty buildings. At an all-day "conference against poverty" on June 4, 1966, at Colonel David Marcus J.H.S. 263, Mayor Lindsay assured the community that if we could put a man on the moon we certainly could clean up Brownsville.

However, it is also fair to say that as of this writing the War on Poverty has barely begun and in fact may have come to a slow halt. Mayor Lindsay's political fortunes declined sharply in 1968–69 in large part because he was identified with the turbulence set in motion by the War on Poverty and thus became a victim of the white political reaction that followed. People were regenerated by community action. Yes, the seeds of change have been planted. Poor people have been aroused. Confrontation politics is here to stay. President Nixon's urban adviser, Daniel P. Moynihan, who is sometimes too cerebral about poverty, does not believe, however, that the War on Poverty has achieved even these results. He says the authors of the Economic Opportunity Act could not agree whether community action would rehabilitate through "servicing" the poor or turning them against their masters.

Whatever the intent, leaders of the poor—until such time as they too became bogged down in red tape and utterly dependent for survival on government funds—saw community action as a means of persuading poor people they had nothing to lose by trying to better themselves. The momentum of this awakening will not slow down. In this light, *The New York Times* editors were correct to say, "Looked at as a whole, community action has been a success."*

If this were not so, those four empty buildings between Strauss and Herzl Streets would stand as a colossal monument to human failure. But CUSA's losses, as well as its achievements, parallel those of the War on Poverty. While poor people and their allies have gained a better knowledge of themselves and their potential, the status quo has been threatened but only slightly impaired.

* November 1, 1967.

As the Ocean Hill–Brownsville School Governing Board was to find out in 1968, and thereafter in mid-1969 when the powerful teachers' union was able to block a meaningful school decentralization plan in Albany, the War on Poverty only triggered a tentative assault on gross inequities in New York society. Black militancy, we now know, will be regarded with amusement and perhaps affection until it threatens entrenched vested interests. In the big cities, the privileges that poor people are most likely to endanger are those enjoyed by members of predominantly white trade unions, including school principals entitled by Civil Service pseudomerit examinations to $18,000-per-year jobs.

EPILOGUE

EPILOGUE

DURING THE WRITING of this book two contradictory passions warred with each other and with the better side of me that simply wanted to write an honest critique of some defects in our society. I was afraid at times, for selfish reasons,

(1) that no serious reforms would occur at all, prior to publication, in the nation's remarkably uniform system of welfare administration, or in the attorney-client relationships, the Ministry of God among men or the trade union brotherhoods, so as to require me to leave the reader swathed in unwelcome despair, or

(2) that 1969 might witness advances of such magnitude as to moot the carping comments that thread the thirteen chapters of this work.

I need not have worried. The major institutions dealt with here have not lost their essential characters, shifted their priorities, or opted for meaningful reallocation of resources within the American Establishment.

Welfare administration remains essentially unchanged and isolated from the power centers. President Richard Nixon's reform proposal contains several good features, particularly the provisions for federal financing of day-care centers for children of working mothers and cash allowances for previously ineligible intact families headed by marginal workers. But much depends on Congress' willingness to appropriate the necessary funds; in any event, until the adoption of a more radical form of income distribution and realistic increases in wage levels to correspond with the cost of living in our large cities, the welfare system as we know it today will continue to provide in clumsy, degrading fashion for abandoned mothers and their children.

The Supreme Court declared unconstitutional state welfare residency requirements, but the specter of hordes of indigents migrating into Arizona gave politicians in that state an excuse for reducing benefits payments to ADC recipients. Albany Republicans in 1969 followed the traditional Anglo-American practice of oppressing reliefers for their own good by abolishing special or extra allowances in favor of a more dignified single semimonthly grant—but at a cash level inadequate for survival.

As for the working poor, their lot, on balance, continued to worsen. The $29 per week increases won by the New York building trades in the summer of 1969 tended to confirm the prediction by Thomas O'Hanlon in *Fortune** that by the end of 1969 factory wages in the urban centers would average almost $2 per hour less than the earnings of *laborers* in the construction industry. A Senate subcommittee under Harrison Williams in mid-1969 held hearings on the subject of rapidly increased poverty among America's aged.

Spokesmen for the welfare rights movement in 1968 for the first time agitated for higher minimum-wage levels. The

* "The Stranglehold of the Building Trades," November, 1968.

movement also acquired local chapters in New Bedford, Massachusetts, and Flatbush, Brooklyn, of workers and their families on Home Relief. A letter-carriers' union in New York City, accusing the federal government of being a low-wage employer, pointed to members with large families who were theoretically entitled to welfare supplementation. But for the most part critics on all sides of the welfare spectrum failed to relate the incredible rise in AFDC and Home Relief recipients to sharp increases in the cost of living, maldistributions of blue-collar income, and the savagely low unskilled and semiskilled wage structure in New York and other large cities. Mayor John Lindsay, one of the more candid and iconoclastic of our liberal statesmen, nevertheless exulted in his end-of-the-year Economic Report in the noticeable increase in available jobs (not in manufacturing, however) and the concomitant decline in nonwhite unemployment, without making any reference to the real wages accruing to the fortunate blacks. New Deal politicians, of course, have spouted this optimistic nonsense for three decades.

It is true that the Lindsay Administration, in the person of Commissioner of Commerce and Industry Kenneth Patton, has pioneered in refusing to welcome to New York businesses paying less than $2 per hour. However, the low state of Lindsay's political fortunes* probably precludes any attempt to achieve a consensus among the city's power figures in labor, business, politics, etc., on balancing unemployment against higher factory wages and less welfare supplementation.

No book about welfare and poverty could or should conclude on a truly upbeat note after the assassinations of Martin Luther King, Jr., and Robert Kennedy. These two men, from different worlds but allied on the important rights

---

* Though reelected, the mayor received less than a majority of the votes cast in the three-man race in November, 1969.

issues and both essentially moderate in their demands, evoked more hatred than all the Rap Browns and Eldridge Cleavers combined, simply because King and Kennedy, together or separately, seriously threatened the status quo.

Were they sincere? I once heard a Birmingham lawyer say, "King is in it for the money. Any darkie here will tell you that." Even when praising Robert Kennedy, *The New York Times* editorial writers would make passing reference to his supposed ruthlessness and lust for power. But Dr. King lived ascetically and left a modest estate to his family. All agree that Senator Kennedy's death destroyed Gene McCarthy's chances of becoming President, and it is a matter of record that seven months later black athlete Rafer Johnson retained enough faith in his white friend and political leader to accompany the man's widow to the hospital for the birth of their last child.

Most important, however, to most black Americans and those of Latin origin, King and Kennedy symbolized their hope, however naïve, for a better life. The preacher of nonviolence lobbied for a guaranteed annual income and was killed reminding organized labor that black sanitation men are also members of the family. The Boston Irish Catholic who respected clean unionism and despised the other kind also led the first band of politicians in the nation's history to fight on the floor of the Senate for humane reforms of the public assistance system.

The white middle class, for its part, now wonders which of the black leaders can be trusted; and who, now that Bobby Kennedy is gone, will persuade those sullen young policemen and journeymen lathers who voted for George Wallace, to share the American Dream with black men?

Richard Nixon was elected President without labor support on a platform that included a proposal for national minimum welfare standards (i.e., a guaranteed annual income). Hubert Humphrey, who said little if anything about welfare, had the backing of the AFL-CIO leadership and the older members but not their sons. A Gallup Poll taken in August of 1969 showed a startling disparity in antiblack attitudes among Americans over fifty years of age (70 percent) and those under thirty (46 percent). The poll also found that blue-collar youths were no more reactionary on race than their college-educated contemporaries. The sons of the entrenched lower middle class also would probably be less antagonistic on ideological grounds than their parents or the union leadership to legislation benefiting welfare recipients, *provided* union officials and their Democratic allies were more sanguine about government-financed medical assistance and similar free programs, intended to benefit primarily those workers with incomes too close to the welfare eligibility level. Admittedly, such benefits threaten a bargaining agent's sense of accomplishment, but help considerably to take the sting out of the life of the twenty-five-year-old apprentice welder in Chicago with several children and a marginal income. Instead, the AFL-CIO continues to speak with the voice of President George Meany, the aging but still powerful ex-plumber who denounced the work compulsion features of the Nixon welfare proposal (which exempted mothers of preschool children) while betraying his ignorance of the fact that since 1967 Congress has required such recipients to accept work or training. Insisting on the viability of the labor movement, Meany, when asked by a reporter in August, 1969, what labor should do to make the movement more relevant to today's youth, replied, "Nothing."

IN DEFENSE OF SCABS

The thirty-four-day New York City teachers' strike in the fall of 1968 confirmed Dr. King's prediction that the most complex racial battles would be fought in the large Northern cities. Even at first glance, the dispute appeared to be an exaggerated attempt by a powerful union to protect a kind of job security for its members ("the right not to be transferred from one school to another") against the efforts, however clumsy, of a black and Puerto Rican experimental school district in Brooklyn to provide, through decentralization and community control, a meaningful education for its children. One would have hoped that the realities of the urban crisis might have persuaded the United Federation of Teachers, an otherwise relatively progressive labor organization, to yield some ground. Instead, the union's leadership chose to strike the entire school system over a localized dispute that could not be resolved by the usual labor relations techniques.

In the process the teachers (and supervisors who also struck) imitated, with gusto, the winning pattern set by the New York police in 1966 in defeating a proposed Civilian Review Board. "Mob rule," "vigilantism" and other thinly disguised racial epithets were hurled at Ocean Hill–Brownsville; anti-Semitic utterances by a few individuals were disseminated in UFT literature to inflame the minds of middle-class Jews across the city. Strikes, like wars, even the defensive variety, are messy affairs. Even a teachers' strike cannot, without contradicting itself, be conducted politely. But in this case the UFT tactics resulted in a polarization that aligned all blacks and the indigent Puerto Ricans with college radicals and most thirtyish white liberals against the rest of the city's population. John Lindsay, whose administration has been noticeably responsive to the complaints of the downtrodden, was pilloried by cops, taxicab drivers and housewives as a mayor who "don't care about the [white] workingman." Paul O'Dwyer, perhaps the only radical candidate ever to run on the Democratic ticket for U.S. senator in New York, was defeated by a large margin during the strike by incumbent Jacob Javits; O'Dwyer, a union lawyer who had alienated the AFL-CIO leadership because of his refusal, on account of the Vietnam war, to back Humphrey, also lost the normally Democratic and antiwar Jewish middle-class voter because he, too, was closely identified with black aspirations.

Gross violations of the equal-protection principle occurred during the strike and in its wake. When students boycotted the schools for a couple of days to protest a strike settlement which reimbursed the strikers for lost wages and gave them blanket immunity against punishment, truant officers and principals outrageously charged some pupils with delinquency. *The New York Times* applied a time-honored double standard known only too well to blacks and welfare recipients by drawing moral equations between the refusal of a black and Spanish governing board to guarantee the safe return of striking teachers and the unlawful work stoppage itself which deprived innocent children of thirty-four days of schooling and cost the city hundreds of thousands of dollars.

Moreover, as the strike progressed it became evident that UFT President Albert Shanker was also waging a vanguard action on behalf of the school principals, the entrenched beneficiaries of the Civil Service system who stood to lose considerably more than the teachers from a decentralization scheme that would place higher premiums on actual administrative abilities and community needs and desires than on success on a written exam. Shanker also fronted for Harry Van Arsdale, the president of the New York City Labor Council and one of the most politically powerful men in New York City, who threatened a massive work stoppage by AFL-CIO unions if Ocean Hill did not behave.

Ironically, Van Arsdale has a highly responsible image. He is a certified liberal, who among other good works in recent years placed more blacks into his union's (Local 3, IBEW) apprenticeship ranks than there are black union electricians in the entire United States. But Van Arsdale's religion is trade unionism. Just as racial bias, in his view, soils the House of Labor, job security for his members, whether white or black, is a prime article of Van Arsdale's faith. In this case there was good reason to believe that New York's Mr. Labor backed the UFT not over the thin issue of the nine "illegally" transferred teachers, but to crush even the possibility that the Board of Education would give any real control to black and Spanish communities over school construction and repair contracts for work overwhelmingly performed, even in Van Arsdale's 38,000-member union, by affluent white craftsmen.

While Van Arsdale may be more sincere than most unionists about breaking down racial barriers, he also believes in the right of union officials, including himself, as well as craftsmen, to bequeath their jobs to their sons, thus perpetuating what liberal unionists benignly describe as "ethnic buildup." The extravagant basic hourly rates and the unbelievable twenty-five-hour week that Van Arsdale has negotiated for his men also contributed heavily, according to Thomas O'Hanlon, in *Fortune,* to the current wage-price spiral which hurts the low-income white and black worker even more than welfare recipients whose benefits at least rise in rough tandem with increases in the cost of living.

Furthermore, strikes in the big cities by unionists, whether or not on public payrolls, tend to push more and more white taxpayers to the suburbs; they also directly injure not-so-affluent blacks and Puerto Ricans who, being most dependent on public services for their comfort and survival, suffer most from work stoppages by sanitation men, public school teachers and fuel oil deliverers. In fact, it may be that the plight of the urban poor and the rescue of our creaking cities will be achieved in large part only by drastically curbing union power.

The poor have reason, then, to be wary of friends like Al

Shanker and Harry Van Arsdale. They may be two of the more honorable personalities in the labor movement, but this is not saying a great deal. Michael Harrington and Bayard Rustin, who have a pragmatic regard for consensus politics, lent their enormous prestige to the UFT cause. I, too, am of the opinion that the War on Poverty cannot be won without the cooperation of the unions, but to date the current labor leadership has given almost no indication that reform of the welfare system, equal employment opportunities, realistic factory wages or job training in the ghettoes are vital considerations. The one large exception may be the unique organizing alliance between the two largest and least pretentious unions in the country, the UAW and the Teamsters; their joint $5.5 million attack on poverty, if implemented by professional organizers, should go far toward cleaning up the urban sweatshops and relating the welfare system to the plight of the low-income workingman. But this remains to be seen.

THE CLIENTS WERE WAITING

Not least among the ironies that came out of the New York school strike, despite the extravagant rhetoric on both sides about black separatism, were widespread instances of genuine interracial community relationships, for the most part in integrated areas, never before known in this city. Resistance to the strike and the tangible goal of true decentralization incorporated the hope of black and Spanish parents for advancement in the white society. The white minority that chose to join them—parents and idealistic young teachers, many of them Jews, who crossed the UFT picket lines—could say for the first time they had gotten to know and like black people.

The strike also afforded a good opportunity for a group of

VISTA lawyers to relate to their clients. In conjunction with
a Master of Laws program at New York University's Law
School, twenty-six recent graduates were assigned in September, 1968, as "house counsel" to ghetto organizations. They
also learned more than a little about New York's vested interests. Two of the VISTAs, Fred Weisberg and Jed Eisenstein, sat in a state judge's chambers with me and Mort
Cohen, of the South Brooklyn Legal Services, while the judge,
invoking numerous pieties, charged us with reckless disregard for the public weal for refusing to withdraw litigation
we had started as a result of the strike. The novice attorneys
said they found the conference utterly depressing, because
while Cohen and I spoke of the rights of aggrieved residents
of South Brooklyn and Brownsville, it was apparent that the
judge, in his concern about tranquil community relations,
had only the pro-strike white community in mind.

The strike also gave impetus to the city's neighborhood
legal services program. Mort Cohen and approximately one
hundred other attorneys in about nine local units around the
city which began operations early that summer responded,
with alacrity, to the command of Major Owens and the city's
Council Against Poverty to give priority to opening the
schools. A floodtide of litigation came out of the neighborhood offices that went beyond the plight of the ghetto schools
to rouse some white middle-class communities to fight back.

Suits attacking unlawful payments and agreements against
"reprisals" made by the city to the strikers at the point of a
gun, and suits asserting civil rights violations in the strike
activities of principals and district superintendents, will re-
verberate through the courts for some time to come and,
hopefully, will establish legal principles applicable to similar
urban crises across the country. Fostered for the most part
by lawyers for the poor, the school cases, along with constitutional assaults on zoning and urban renewal plans, rein-
force the theory that the salvation of the big cities is

intertwined with the methods the White Establishment selects to solve the problems of race and poverty.

In the school strike, a powerful union demonstrated its ability to paralyze, with impunity, a vital public service and, more important, to cause the white majority to blame, not the strikers, but Mayor Lindsay, because their children were on the streets. This phenomenon showed clearly that the courts have a peculiar obligation to redress inequities in future urban crises. The law schools also have a special responsibility to advance minority grievances through the courts. The schools have the necessary talent—competent students working under the direction of specialists—the scholarly objectivity and, presumably, immunity from political pressures.

In working closely with neighborhood legal services attorneys, the law schools will utilize a multidimensional opportunity never before available, not only to service society and the poor by channeling just grievances away from riots and into the courts, but also to educate students in the life of the law and thus enhance the image of the law school as relevant to the needs of the times. To the extent that fear of controversy (i.e., alumni pressures) or of diluting the prestige, in traditional terms, of the school through "crass" community involvement causes an urban law school to stand on the sidelines, its true relevance may be symbolized by the faded oil paintings of long-deceased deans and judges that are hung on school walls to suggest a gracious past.

WHERE DID THE PREACHER GO?

It is one of the paradoxes of Christianity in this country and especially, perhaps, among Roman Catholics, that the young believer is instructed in the minutiae of Church ritual and dogmas, then spends the rest of his life waiting in vain for guidance from the pulpit in resolving the tortured and more important moral issues of the day.

Is a citywide strike of 25,000 teachers and principals violative of statute, contract and oath of office to be condoned because a black community said to nine of them, "We don't want you"? How does one balance trade union loyalties and a civil libertarian respect for due process against our history of oppressing blacks? Christians and Jews who sought the answers to these questions looked to the editorial pages of the daily newspapers, to the weekly news magazines, to columnists Murray Kempton and Jimmy Breslin and a (pro-Brownsville) report by the New York Civil Liberties Union. For the most part, churchmen told them nothing.

It is true that few, if any, Church leaders openly supported the strike. Politician-preacher Donald Harrington courageously opposed the UFT. The Catholic Bishop of Brooklyn offered the use of parochial classrooms (an unwelcome gesture, however, to those trying to open the public schools). The diocesan newspaper, *Brooklyn Tablet,* now under a new, more enlightened editorship, finally came down, after the third walkout in two months, on the side of the children and decentralization.

But at the same time, a representative of the Catholic Teachers' Association could write a letter to the *Tablet* urging God's forgiveness for "mob" tactics in Brownsville. Good people all over the city, with clean consciences, could physically prevent children from entering their schools; conservative political candidates with Irish and Italian names were elected to office during the strike on "law and order" platforms that rested on support for an unconscionable as well as an illegal walkout by public employees.

Two nights before Christmas I happened to walk our family pet past the home of one of these civic leaders located on a block that remains almost lily-white by virtue of a "gentlemen's agreement" among its residents. As we passed, the man and his wife had just come to the door to shout the tidings of the holy season to a chorus of children from his parish church who serenaded his home with Christmas carols. Even my dog sneered.

The pragmatic reader may answer that moral guidance from the pulpit at best has porous results; at worst—look at Father Coughlin—it may be a two-edged sword. What about concrete performance by the People of God? It probably is ungracious to belittle the fact that the Catholic diocese of Brooklyn, once the most reactionary in the country, now has a disproportionate number of priests and nuns working in unorthodox ghetto ministries. Dr. George Wiley, director of the National Welfare Rights Organization and a difficult man to please, has praised the community organization approach of Brooklyn Catholic Charities. The diocesan newspaper projects a humane if still somewhat conservative image, and does its best to advance, in addition to the usual parochial concerns, the brotherhood of man.

So what, says Father Bill Duncan, a priest active with the welfare rights movement in Bedford-Stuyvesant. In an article in *Commonweal,* Duncan confirmed what I had suspected all along. The Church in Brooklyn was buying its own peace of soul by furnishing personnel and monies (in token quantities, Father Duncan pointed out) to ghetto missions for use *only in the ghetto* and not for open-housing parades into white neighborhoods. The white Catholic world outside of places like Brownsville, responsible in large part for ghetto misery, must remain undisturbed.

So too must all the secret facts about Church finances. It might embarrass the bishop if his black constituents discovered that the bank safeguarding large diocesan deposits refused to make mortgage loans in changing neighborhoods; or the bishop, like university presidents, might be shocked himself to learn that the handsome return on prudent stock investments of Church monies by highly respectable brokerage firms came out of the blood of black men in Rhodesia or Mississippi.

The Brooklyn Catholic diocese joined with its Manhattan counterpart and several Jewish and Protestant denominations in 1968 to apply their collective and several economic bargaining power to firms discriminating against blacks and Puerto Ricans. Fine, except that the Equal Employment Opportunity Act and black militancy had already persuaded all but the most obtuse bank, insurance company and retail store in the Northeast to hire sufficient dark faces to keep the wolves at bay. Moreover, neither in New York nor anyplace else in the country, no matter what its other accomplishments, has Project Equality yet to tackle the building trades which control over 3 million highly desirable blue-collar jobs in the United States. This lag occurs despite the fact that, after the government, the churches are the nation's largest employer of construction labor. As with school integration, the burden of fighting economic discrimination at its worst is left to vulnerable politicians like Mayor John Lindsay.

The appearance of progress or piecemeal advances in a period of our history that calls for huge chunks may be worse than no progress at all. Black militants believe this, of course, but the same flash of insight seems to have penetrated the twenty-three or so Brooklyn priests, most of them working in the ghetto, who left the priesthood in 1967–68. Most persuasive, perhaps, to the White Establishment is the testimony of those sons and daughters representing a wide range of leftist political ideologies who cannot distinguish benign institutions like the churches, the labor unions and the bar associations from the ancient oppressors of the poor.

INDEX

ABOUT THE AUTHOR

JAMES J. GRAHAM received an A.B. from Ford-
ham University, an L.L.B. from St. John's University
and an L.L.M., in labor law, from New York University.
He is associate professor at the College of Law of the
University of Arizona, where he teaches poverty law
and coordinates clinical activities. He was formerly associate director of the Project in Social Welfare at N.Y.U.,
and has been senior staff attorney of the Center on Social
Welfare Policy and Law at Columbia School of Social
Work. Professor Graham has worked as a union lawyer
and has practiced privately and as a National Labor Relations Board trial lawyer.

James Graham is a founder of CUSA (Christians and
Jews United for Social Action), based in the Brownsville slum in Brooklyn, and was co-counsel in five law-
suits on behalf of parents in Ocean Hill, Park Slope and
Red Hook, in Brooklyn, during the 1968 New York
teachers' strike. He works as volunteer counsel and as an
activist on poverty law and rights for welfare rights
conferences. Born in New York, he now lives in Tucson
with his wife and three sons.